NARCISSISM

A SURVIVAL GUIDE TO TAKE CONTROL OF YOUR LIFE AFTER NARCISSISTIC ABUSE

THIS BOOK INCLUDES:
Healing From Emotional Abuse,

Narcissistic Mothers,

Toxic Relationships,

Narcissist Abuse Recovery

HOPE UTARAM

Copyright © 2020 by *Hope Utaram*
- **All rights reserved** -

The content contained within this book may not be reproduced, duplicated or transmitted without direct written permission from the author or the publisher.
Under no circumstances will any blame or legal responsibility be held against the publisher, or author, for any damages, reparation, or monetary loss due to the information contained within this book. Either directly or indirectly.

Legal Notice:
This book is copyright protected. This book is only for personal use. You cannot amend, distribute, sell, use, quote or paraphrase any part, or the content within this book, without the consent of the author or publisher.

Disclaimer Notice:
Please note the information contained within this document is for educational and entertainment purposes only. All effort has been executed to present accurate, up to date, and reliable, complete information. No warranties of any kind are declared or implied. Readers acknowledge that the author is not engaging in the rendering of legal, financial, medical or professional advice. The content within this book has been derived from various sources. Please consult a licensed professional before attempting any techniques outlined in this book.

By reading this document, the reader agrees that under no circumstances is the author responsible for any losses, direct or indirect, which are incurred as a result of the use of the information contained within this document, including, but not limited to, — errors, omissions, or inaccuracies.

1 Book

Healing From Emotional Abuse........ 1

2 Book

Narcissistic Mothers...................... 134

3 Book

Toxic Relationships...................... 268

4 Book

Narcissist Abuse Recovery............ 416

HEALING FROM EMOTIONAL ABUSE

RECOGNIZE THE HIDDEN NARCISSISTIC RELATIONSHIP. DISCOVER HOW TO RECOVER FROM CHILDHOOD TRAUMA DUE TO EMOTIONAL ABUSE CAUSED BY PERSONALITY DISORDERS AND LIBERATE YOUR SOUL

HOPE UTARAM

Table of Contents

Introduction..3

Chapter 1 How To Get Comfortable With Yourself....11

Chapter 2 Knowing The Root Of Your Suffering.......20

Chapter 3 Relaxing With What Is Without Judgement
....25

Chapter 4 Your Behavior Is A Choice......................40

Chapter 5 Being An Aware Observer Of Your Life....49

Chapter 6 Mindfulness Meditation Practice And Its Purpose..61

Chapter 7 Practice Makes Perfect............................75

Chapter 8 Children In The Narcissistic Relationship
....86

Chapter 9 A Strict Set Of Rules...............................96

Chapter 10 How To Move On From The Narcissist..104

Chapter 11 Living With One, Dealing With One........117

Conclusion...132

Introduction

One of the things that you have to realize is that a narcissist does not see the need to seek help from a therapist because after all, they think that there is nothing wrong with them. Recovery is for those who have been through abuse. If you have been or are in a relationship with a narcissist, it is high time that you left and sought help for a professional. It is this kind of support that you need to rebuild your self-confidence and bounce back your self-esteem.

Trust me; you are better than you have ever thought possible. The narcissist might have managed to puncture your self-confidence and even crushed your self-esteem, but most importantly you are just a victim. You are not unworthy like they want you to believe. Finding a health professional that has a specialty in trauma recovery will help you journey through the healing process to recovery. If you are not able to leave the relationship, a therapist can also help you to learn the best ways in which you can communicate effectively with your abuser so that you can set boundaries that they will respect and hence, protect you so that they will no longer take advantage of you.

Here are some of the steps that you will have to go through to help you journey through healing to recovery.

Step 1: Cut contact

Once you have left the relationship, keep at that! Stop maintaining contact with your abuser. The main reason why you went is that the affair was not working for you. Therefore, there is nothing that will happen that makes things feel better. The best way to recover from abuse is for you to block all forms of communications.

If you have joint custody of the children, the truth is, you may not be able to wipe this person entirely from your life. It is therefore advisable to create a strict custom contact. And can only communicate on matters regarding your children using third-party channels only! Otherwise, ensure that you have set up court orders for all forms of agreements.

Think about the extreme trauma bonding, the gross abuse and the addiction that you had to the narcissist. Sometimes the best way is for you to accept that the only way you can recover from such damage is to pull away and cut your losses once and for all. Think of abstaining as a way of protecting yourself from hurt. In other words, each time you initiate contact with your abuser, you are handing them the ammunition to blow you off.

Remember that you lived with them and so they know what your weak points are and how they can wound you even more profound. It is until we heal that you will stop forcing yourself on the narcissist for love or craving them or even justifying to ourselves to give them a second chance when we completely stop contact that we can begin to heal.

Step 2: Release that trauma so that you begin functioning again

If we are going to heal, we have to be willing to reclaim our power. We have to do the exact opposite of what we used to believe; 'I can fix him/her, I will feel better.' Your power belongs inside you. The moment you take your focus away from your abuser that you will be able to channel that power into rebuilding your self-love and paying closer attention to making yourself whole again.

At first, it might seem like understanding who a narcissist is and what they do is essential. But the real truth is that these things cannot heal your internal trauma. What you need to do is to decide to let go of that horrific experience so that you can be. You will begin to rise, get relief and balance again once you have decided to take your power where it belongs-inside you.

Step 3: Forgive yourself for what you have been through

When the insecure and wounded parts of us are still in pain, we often are pushed into behaving like children who are damaged. We are often looking for people's approval and especially from our abuser, we hand our abuser the power to treat us as they see fit. And that's the time you will realize that you have given them all your resources-money, time and health. The most unfortunate thing is that while doing that, you end up hurting the people that matter the most in your life-your children, siblings, parents, and friends.

Yes, it might be hard to forgive yourself from this, but you can do that if you want to rebuild your life and everything that you lost to your abuser. By working through your healing process, you will soon find resolution and acceptance. You can move away from lacking self-love and respect to living a life full of truth and responsibility for our well-being.

You will realize that, when you forgive yourself, you acknowledge that this was all a learning curve and this is the experience you learned, and hence, you are going to use that to reclaim your life. It is when you release your regrets and self-judgments that you can start setting yourself free to realize greatness in your life irrespective of what stage we are. The point when you will begin to feel hope again, hope that will steer you forward into fulfillment and a life full of purpose.

Step 4: Release everything and heal all your fears of the abuser and all they might do next

Do you know what bait to a narcissist is? Anxiety, pain, and distress. One of the thing that can perpetuate another cycle of abuse no matter how we tell ourselves that we have separated from them. It is indeed true that abusers can be relentless. In most cases, they do not like being losers. But one thing that you have to understand is that they are not that powerful and impactful as you may have thought them to be.

They need you to fear and go through pain so that they can function. Once you have healed your emotional trauma, they fall apart. Therefore, it is crucial that you become grounded and stoic by not feeding into their drama; this way they will soon wither away along with their power and credibility with them.

Step 5: Release the connection to your abuser

So many people have likened their freedom from a narcissist to that of exorcism. When we liberate ourselves from the darkness that filled our beings, we are allowing ourselves to detox and let light and life to come in. If that light has to take over the shade, the darkness has to leave so that there is space for something new to come in. In the same manner, it is essential that you release all the parts that were trapped by your abuser so that you can tap into a more supernatural power, the power of pure creativity.

When you disentangle yourself from the narcissist, it is not just about cutting the cord; it is also about releasing all the belief systems that you might have associated yourself with unconsciously. It is only then that you can break free to being a new person and not a target of a narcissist.

Even though it might be tempting to seek revenge on your abuser, this is something that you have to try hard to avoid. Rage has the power of pulling you back into deeper darkness and a game that your abuser is an expert at in the first place. The best form of revenge is one in which you decide to take back your freedom and render your abuser irrelevant.

And is likely going to crush their ego, and they will be powerless that they cannot even affect you. Often are in despair when it hits that you are a constant reminder of their extinction. It is at this point that this ends and your soul contracts to allow love and healing in so that you can be whole again.

Step 6: Realize your liberation, truth, and freedom

Traditionally, we learn that loving ourselves is a very selfish act. However, when it comes to finding liberation and freedom from the hands of our abusers, it is a very critical step that allows us to take in the truth and let it set us free from captivity. Yes, it is something incredibly difficult to do, but it is a necessary step to achieving liberation.

Often, society has taught us that we are treated by others the same way we treat them. However, this is a false premise because we get treatment according to the way we treat ourselves. In other words, the measure of love that we get from others is equivalent to that we feel about ourselves.

Therefore, when we open up to healing and recovery, we are opening the doors for others to love us in reality and more healthy ways than ever before. It is this act that serves as a template by which we teach our children so that they do not carry around unconscious patterns of abuse that were passed to them by our ancestors. Only starts when we decide to take responsibility for our happiness and freedom. We slowly become the change that we would wish to see so that we can let go of being someone's victim and stop handing other people our power.

In other words, we take back our lives by doing everything necessary to aid our inner healing irrespective of what the narcissist does or does not do, something irrelevant either way.

It is at this point that we can thrive despite what we have been through and what has happened to us.

Chapter 1

How to get comfortable with yourself

Understanding your narcissist

Just like a dark hole, a narcissist is able to get into your life, devour your health emotionally and physically. Most especially, a narcissist is able to take away your sanity and manipulate your sensibilities. The strangest truth about a narcissist is that they are attracted to empaths, yet the two are the extreme opposite of each other. There is this compelling pull that draws these two kinds of people together, which as many believe is the universe's way of maintaining equilibrium. For instance, as a typical empath, you have the intrinsic capability to place yourself in another person's shoes and exert deliberate efforts to help them heal. Whilst doing this for a good cause, you as the empath lack the ability to draw boundaries between helping such people and actually falling into being a victim of their condition through chronic self-sacrifice. On the other hand, the narcissist lives within great traumas and conditions; hence they ideally hide behind an idealized version of themselves. This self-image comes off to you, the empath, as being highly attractive and charming, yet in the real sense, they are highly self-centered and indifferent. When these two extreme characters come together, they form a destructive bond that eventually harms the empath. Both characters collide as they attempt to learn and grow out of their conditions through trial and error. Therefore, it happens that your narcissist is the person who takes advantage of your empathetic nature when your characters collide.

Recognizing the Narcissist

While Narcissistic Personality Disorder is one condition, narcissists come in different forms and kinds. This categorization is based on how the narcissists behave towards others. For one to be known as a narcissist, they have to portray characteristics such as a lack of empathy, a dire need for admiration as well as a magnificent view of themselves.

Also, most of the narcissists display some specific behaviors towards their partners. These include getting rid of people they no longer need or love-bombing their victims. However, narcissists behave differently depending on the severity of the disorder traits within them, and what their external environment has exposed them to. Therapists have for a long time attempted to separate these narcissists into distinct categories and understanding them helps you in owning up to your character traits that attracts narcissists. It would be pointless to be shown how to protect yourself from narcissists without first looking at how different narcissists act within their conscious limits, which will involve hurting you. The more you know them, the more you can consciously act and make decisions concerning your relations with them.

Healthy and Extreme Narcissism

One thing that most people do not know is that there is a continuum from healthy narcissism to extreme narcissism. Whenever we hear of the word narcissism, we associate it with all sorts of negativity. The explanation below changes the narrative and deepens our understanding of the entire phenomenon.

In their assessment of the concept of narcissism, Brummelman et al. (2015) described healthy narcissism (HN) as that which entails the possession of considerable degrees of self-esteem without necessarily being withdrawn from a shared emotional life. Extreme narcissism (EN) was described as that which denies people the ability to have a meaningful relationship because they lack self-esteem. Ideally, healthy narcissism makes one take pride in self-image, beauty and often times the triumph of a tough task. Although this joy in one's beauty and achievement can be momentary, it has a powerful sensation. This narcissism type has been considered helpful in managing one's relationship with others because if you can experience joy in being yourself and the impact you have on the world, then you can easily carry through difficult times. It prevents one from the burnout that most people experience after a series of failures. In the case of a romantic relationship, a healthy narcissist is able to take heartbreaks and disappointments in a reasonable manner. They are able to be reasonable because they feel good about themselves. Usually, healthy narcissism mostly grows as part of child development where children at the young age of 2 begin to feel like the world revolves around them based on the love their parent gives them. As they grow up, such people realize that other people have needs as well, and they continue feeling good about themselves as they accommodate others.

Since extreme narcissism is what this book mostly focuses on, it is important to differentiate between healthy and extreme narcissism. First, as pertains to self-confidence, HN leads to high outward confidence that aligns with reality while EN leads to an unrealistic state of grandiose importance. HN enjoys power and admiration, while EN seeks power at all costs without reasonable reserves. Further, HN has regard for other people's ideas and beliefs and does value them, while EN devalues people without feeling remorseful and has antisocial behaviors. HN has values and workable plans to follow while EN has no particular path and easily changes course due to boredom. HN develops from a considerably stable foundation of love as a child while EN has mostly experienced a traumatizing childhood that conditions them to not be considerate of others.

Extreme narcissists are further put in the following categories based on how they manifest the narcissistic behaviors

Vulnerable Narcissists

Also known as closet, covert, compensatory or fragile, a vulnerable narcissist is one who is shy by nature. Often, they dwell within an inferiority complex that develops from childhood; hence they lack the capacity to trust, love or care for other people. Their emotional state is full of self-unworthiness and hatred. They tend to over-compensate these feelings by looking for other idealized individuals with whom they will feel special about themselves. They use techniques such as guilt-tripping and gas lighting to make their target empath give them sympathy and attention. Their main aim is to reclaim supremacy and command of their lives and to compensate for traumas they have faced before.

Invulnerable Narcissists

Also referred to as the elitist, this is the conventional type of a narcissist, one who is bold and highly un-empathetic. They are the complete opposite to the vulnerable narcissists who suffer from a deep sense of inferiority complex since the invulnerable narcissists tend to believe that they are superior to other people. They seek glorification and pleasure, and they are constantly seeking this kind of attention from people they are in a relationship with. Usually, they can do anything to climb up and dominate another person. They can be described in simple terms as braggers and self-promoters that have a constant dire need to prove they are "superior."

Both extreme types use various narcissistic traits such as manipulating other people to fuel their delusions, unfaithfulness, lack of empathy and criticizing people.

Grandiose

Also referred to as classic or exhibitionist, the grandiose narcissist is a very familiar kind of narcissist, one who considers themselves more influential and important. They capitalize on their achievements and seek admiration from others. They often apply a persona that makes them look appealing and charismatic, and they attract their victims by matching their ambitions and energy with their achievements.

Through their know-it-all attitude, this narcissist is always eager to give their opinions even when it is inappropriate, and the opinions are uninvited. They believe that they are more knowledgeable and skilled than anyone else. They like to be the ones talking as others listen. Also, they are bad listeners because they are always thinking about what they will say next.

It is difficult to hold a meaningful conversation with this narcissist.

Also, they have a bullying attitude which makes them want to build up themselves by humiliating other people. Some may appear more brutal in the way they emphasize their superiority. A bullying grandiose narcissist relies on contempt to prove they are a winner.

Seductive

This is the narcissist who uses the technique of making you feel good about yourself, but with the main goal of making you reciprocate those feelings. They will idealize you to capture your attention and get you having that kind of admiration for them. When you have shown them great admiration, they can manipulate your thinking or give you the cold shoulder.

Vindictive

A vindictive narcissist is one who gets totally irritable once you do not recognize the superiority that they try to assert. They are dangerous to be in a relationship with because they aim at destroying you and blackmailing you using your most precious belongings to prove to you that you are a loser. For instance, one may try to get you fired from work, trash talk you to people who regard you and even turn such people against you.

Malignant (toxic)

The behavior of this narcissist is highly comparable to that of sociopaths. They are never remorseful for their actions and have no regard for moral behavior. They are usually arrogant and have a highly inflated ego. They take pride in outsmarting other people and there is often a lot of chaos around them. If they are not caught by the law, they are a great disturbance to the peace of society. Not only do they seek attention, but they also want all other people to feel mediocre.

Amorous

These are the narcissists who satisfy their worthiness by the number of sexual conquests they have had or how their victims help them elevate their status. Normally, an amorous narcissist puts on a pleasing appearance at first glance and will also use gifts to lure their victim. Once they have met their needs, mostly sexual needs, they quickly dispose of them. These are the ultimate heartbreakers who lack remorse for abandoning people and not putting their needs into consideration.

Subtypes

Besides the above major types of narcissists, there are subsets of narcissists which group them not only by how they manifest their narcissistic behaviors, but which also shows how much they like to draw from a relationship with their victims and how hidden their behaviors are. Learning about them can help you further in identifying them. All the above major types of narcissists can fall in the following categories.

Somatic Versus Cerebral

This describes the feature that the narcissist focuses on gratifying themselves. Both types have to use someone else to make themselves look and feel better. Somatic narcissists focus on their physical appearance and like to feel beautiful above everyone else while cerebral narcissists like to be the informers since they feel like they know it all.

Inverted Narcissists

This refers to the narcissist who is co-dependent and they have to attach themselves to other people for them to feel special. They feel fulfilled especially when they get into a relationship with fellow narcissists and they fear abandonment.

Overt Versus Covert

These subtypes of narcissism differentiate between the nature of the techniques they use to manipulate other people and meet their needs. While both types of narcissists do control others for their advantage, the covert narcissist will mostly use methods that are behind the scenes and they even have a ground for denying their actions. Overt narcissists are more direct, and they pursue their needs without care for being discovered.

Chapter 2

Knowing the root of your suffering

Narcissistic abuse can have long-lasting effects on the target of this abuse. These are effects that the narcissist can sometimes be unconscious of or, at the very least, insensitive to. The narcissist does engage in abusive acts because they have a purpose, such as to satisfy their vanity or to manipulate you. But it is also true that the narcissist may not fully understand the effects that their behavior has because they are so self-obsessed and they are not able to connect with people deeply the way that others can.

The idea that the narcissist may not be fully conscious of the effects of their abuse is not mentioned to justify the actions of the narcissist. This aspect of narcissistic abuse is touched on here to emphasize just how out of touch the narcissist is. The narcissist perceives themselves as being set apart from others, so it is almost as if you are a different form of life than they are. Just as the lioness lacks empathy for the wild beast that she slaughters in the savanna, so does the narcissist lacks empathy for the loved one whose emotions they aim to crush because they are unable to escape their inflated self-concept.

The abuse that the narcissist inflicts on others has been touched on in other areas of this book. Narcissistic abuse can include manipulation, blackmail, gaslighting, and belittling. Much of the abuse is emotional in nature, but some forms of abuse can be physical, mental, or designed to isolate. In this chapter, we will explore how narcissistic abuse impacts relationships. We will see that the emotional abuse of the narcissist can leave the individual feeling disconnected, isolated, weakened, and alone.

Emotional abuse

Emotional abuse is such a powerful tool because it can leave a person weak, vulnerable, and incapable of breaking free without knowing why. Human beings naturally seek emotional connections with other human beings. Although the narcissist is generally unable to form a lasting connection with other people because they do not sincerely value others, they do recognize the value that emotions have in forming a connection, and they are able to use their understanding of emotions and human behavior to their advantage.

For example, in a type of mind control called neuro-linguistic programming or NLP, the practitioner of this art can use cues such as involuntary movements, spoken words, physical proximity, and touch to control the thoughts and perceptions of the person that they are using their tricks on. They can use touching (such as placing a hand on the other person's arm) to induce rapport formation with the other person. They can also use eye contact and subliminal messaging to introduce thoughts in the other person's head.

Although most narcissists have not studied NLP, they also behave in this way. The narcissist knows how to behave to get people to like them and what to say to manipulate them. The emotions of the narcissist may be cut off and inaccessible to their significant other, but they understand emotions well enough to permit them to use the emotions of the other person to their advantage. They know when you are sad; they know when you are happy. They know when you may be feeling confident or when you might be feeling particularly dispirited. The cues that you send the narcissist reveal your emotions to them, and they are tools that permit them to abuse you.

This emotional manipulation can have several impacts on a relationship. It can lead the other person in the relationship to have low self-esteem or experience bouts of emotional whirlwinds, where their emotions are up, down, or uncontrollable. This type of emotional abuse can cause you to feel that your emotional needs are not being met in the relationship, even if the narcissist occasionally says or does things to indicate emotional closeness. This emotional manipulation can also lead you to feel sad, even sadder than you were when you were alone.

Isolation

One of the goals of the words and deeds of the narcissist in a relationship is to isolate the other person. This isolation serves two purposes. One, it places the other person in a situation where they are too weak and emotional to leave the relationship, which gives the narcissist someone to continue to abuse for their vanity. Two, this isolation serves the narcissist's codependency need. They may not value you, but the narcissist still needs you on a certain level. They need the validation that comes from being able to belittle you and abuse you. They need to be in a relationship with someone who agrees to be less than them because it satisfies the inflated self-image that they have created for themselves. Therefore, one of the biggest impacts that narcissistic abuse can have on a relationship is to isolate one of the partners effectively and prevent them from being motivated to leave.

Disconnection

The emotional abuse and isolation of narcissism can leave the target feeling disconnected. Human beings form connections by having meaningful interactions with others. This allows the emotional needs of the individual to be met while the corresponding emotional needs of the other person also are met. This type of emotional bonding lies on a spectrum with empathy. Empathy is a way of being emotionally connected with other people without the need for words.

Because the narcissist is false in their display of emotion, and they use words to deceive and manipulate, the other person in the relationship feels disconnected rather than connected with their partner. They may notice this together with exhaustion or confusion, and this is all related to the inability to form a real connection with a narcissist. Also, the other person in this relationship becomes disconnected from the other important people in their life and society as a whole. This disconnection is perhaps more important because it can discourage the individual from leaving the relationship (and thereby reinforcing the isolation). Working on forming connections with people outside of the relationship with the narcissist is actually an important step in breaking free.

Chapter 3

Relaxing with what is without judgement

Although there is no way to be certain why some people are narcissistic (while some are not), Narcissistic Personality Disorder is often associated with traumatic experiences in early childhood. Trauma and abuse seem to cause some children to get stuck psychologically, failing to progress from the early and more self-centered stages of development.

All infants are naturally narcissistic in the sense that they care only about their own needs and are unaware that other people exist separately from themselves. Experts in child psychology believe that newborns initially perceive themselves as omnipotent and unlimited by anything, despite the fact that they are completely dependent on others for all their needs.

Why would a powerless infant think of herself as limitlessly powerful? The newborn can't tell the difference at first between herself and other people. Whenever she needs something, her parents or other caregivers immediately and unfailingly provide what she needs. To a newborn infant, the caregiver seems like an extension of the self, an instrument of her own will. Sigmund Freud referred to this as "primary narcissism," the natural and healthy narcissism of the newborn baby.

As the infant develops, she slowly discovers that her needs will not always be met instantly. She sometimes has to cry for a while before anyone picks her up or feeds her, but she learns that she can still rely on them to meet her needs consistently. Over time, she comes to realize that her caregivers are separate individuals rather than extensions of herself and that she is not really omnipotent or unlimited. Infantile narcissism develops into an understanding of human relationships based on affection, boundaries, and mutual trust.

Unfortunately, this process doesn't always work out the way it is supposed to. If the infant's needs aren't consistently met, trust, and a sense of healthy boundaries never get the chance to develop. Instead, the powerful self-centeredness of the newborn remains, along with a deep and painful sense of distrust, insecurity, and anxiety.

Healthy Ego

Some psychologists speak in terms of "healthy narcissism" and "destructive narcissism," while others prefer to use the word "narcissism" exclusively for the destructive manifestation of an unhealthy ego. Either way, a healthy sense of self is very different from the toxic and basically false self of the destructive narcissist.

A person with a healthy ego is self-confident, but his self-confidence is consistent with reality and his own place in the world. The narcissist is not just self-confident but grandiose, seeing himself as unique and special compared to other people. He may even believe that normal social rules apply to other people but not to him, or that there should be no reasonable limits on what he can demand from others.

A person with a healthy ego might be comfortable with power and may even enjoy it, but a narcissist sees power as the most important goal in life and will pursue power over others even if it harms them. His ability to empathize with other people is limited or nonexistent, and he relates to other people primarily as objects.

A person with a healthy ego genuinely cares about other people and respects their basic autonomy. A narcissist will express care for others if it seems like the right thing to say at the time but does not respect their autonomy and will take advantage of them without caring how they might be affected.

A person with healthy ego development has a sense of personal values and can follow through with long-term plans. A narcissist has no underlying sense of values and finds it difficult to stay focused on any one thing for long because he gets bored and distracted so easily.

Finally, a person with healthy ego development is usually someone who experienced a balanced combination of support and boundaries in childhood. Most narcissists experienced some combination of childhood damage to their self-esteem along with a lack of appropriate limits or boundaries between self and other.

The narcissist's inner self is basically stunted, trapped in an early stage of development. He wants to hold on to the newborn's illusion of being unlimited and omnipotent but doesn't trust other people to meet his needs unless he can control and manipulate them into doing so. He doesn't really think of other people as separate from himself but sees them as tools for getting his own needs met. Without a healthy sense of self, he can only avoid facing the reality of his situation by controlling others.

The most common cause for this failure to completely develop is neglect and abuse, often at the hands of a narcissistic parent.

Narcissistic Parenting

Narcissistic parents don't treat their children as unique individuals but as extensions of their own self-image. For a narcissist, the child's absolute trust and dependence on the caregiver make them the perfect source of narcissistic supply—that is, until the child begins to develop into an independent person. This is already a difficult task for the child of a narcissistic parent, who may never have experienced the combination of trust and healthy boundaries needed for healthy ego development. Still, most children will begin to develop a sense of self over time despite these barriers.

This is something the narcissist simply cannot allow, so the narcissistic parent interferes with the child's independent development to keep the child dependent on them. Through guilt-tripping, emotional blackmail, undermining, and all the other techniques of control and manipulation, the narcissistic parent prevents the child from ever really growing up.

The narcissistic parent will often pressure the child to get good grades or excel in sports or impress others in some way. Affection and praise depend on high performance and are withheld as a punishment for any mistake. This is because the narcissistic parent sees the child as an expression of his own ideal self, but it can cause the child to see love and affection solely in terms of external validation. Without the experience of being loved for his own sake, the child of narcissistic parents can develop an unhealthy fixation on how other people perceive him.

Narcissistic parents insist on being the center of their children's lives. At the same time, they often belittle and undermine their children, especially for not living up to their own unrealistic expectations. Over time, the child can learn that the only way to get praise and affection from others is to do just what they want at all times without question. They can just as easily learn that the most effective way to deal with others is through guilt-tripping, manipulation, and other head games.

In effect, the narcissistic parent trains the child to perceive the world and human relationships in a dysfunctional way. This doesn't always turn the child into another narcissist, but it is almost always profoundly damaging to the child's self-esteem.

Effects on the Child

Different children react differently to narcissistic parenting, due to differences in individual temperament as well as the presence of other influences in the child's life. For example, the child may be exposed to examples of loving families and healthy relationships outside the home or may have a healthier relationship with one parent than the other. The child may experience emotional support and affection from some other source, leading them to recognize that something is fundamentally wrong with the type of parenting they get from the narcissist.

For whatever reason, many children of narcissistic parents grow up as kind and empathetic people, though they may experience other problems due to their traumatic childhood. However, many children of narcissistic parents do go on to become narcissists as well, creating a cycle that can extend across multiple generations.

In some cases, the child never develops the sense of trust and stable affection most people experience in infancy. Instead, he experiences the world as a place where even the most important caregivers cannot be counted on. The child may grow up to feel empty inside, fearful and insecure in relationships with others, and unable to develop a clear identity of his own.

In an attempt to fill this sense of emptiness and earn love and affection, the child may repress her own feelings and her own needs to concentrate solely on pleasing the narcissistic parent. The child's underlying resentment and anger about the situation are pushed down beneath a pleasing façade, to come out later in other ways.

This façade or mask can become habitual, a "false self" based on what the other person wants to see. The true self underneath is filled with anger and self-hatred, because the child has never been loved for his own sake and believes himself to be unlovable. Over time, he learns to mirror the grandiose and unrealistic self-image of the narcissistic parent, as well as the behaviors of control and manipulation that allow the narcissist to protect and maintain the false self like a suit of armor.

Although narcissistic abuse in childhood is a frequent cause of narcissism, some people may develop into narcissistic adults without necessarily having been abused.

Parenting Styles

According to counselor Diana Baumrind, parenting styles can be divided into three general categories.

Authoritative parents have high expectations for their children, but they also treat them with love and warmth and are generally responsive to their needs. This parenting style is a healthy balance of love and strictness.

Authoritarian parents have high expectations but treat their children without much warmth and are not particularly responsive to their needs. This may seem similar to narcissistic abuse, but Baumrind's parenting typology was intended as a description of normal parenting variations, not abusive extremes. The authoritarian parenting style is demanding and somewhat cold, but not extreme enough to be considered abusive.

Indulgent or permissive parents don't set high expectations for their children. They don't do much to monitor their child's behavior or correct faults instead of giving the child the freedom to develop on his own. Unfortunately, this includes tolerating rude behaviors such as nagging and being selfish, childish traits that can be described as narcissistic. An authoritative or authoritarian parent wouldn't tolerate that kind of behavior, but the permissive parent prefers to ignore it.

Studies have shown the authoritative style to be the most effective style of parenting overall. Children with authoritative parents tend to be more successful and happy in life than children with either authoritarian or permissive parents, who are more likely to suffer from mental health problems and to abuse alcohol and other substances.

Some experts in child psychology have added a fourth parenting style to this list: the "neglectful" style. Neglectful parents are similar to permissive parents in that they fail to set consistent boundaries, but different in that they do not offer the child much warmth or affection. In this version of the list, authoritative and permissive parents are affectionate and warm, but authoritative parents also set standards and boundaries more effectively. Authoritarian and neglectful parents are both relatively cold or distant, but neglectful parents also fail to establish limits or boundaries.

According to a research study by Carrie Henschel in Behavioral Health, the permissive and authoritarian parenting styles were both associated with narcissism in children. Henschel speculated that permissive parents might encourage narcissism by failing to set healthy limits and letting the child get away with demanding and rude behavior. In addition, permissive parents were more likely to praise a child effusively or describe her as "special" regardless of her actual achievements. The combination of being praised as special without really doing anything and not being corrected for mistreating others could be enough to create the grandiose but shallow self-image of the typical narcissist.

Henschel also found that the authoritarian parenting style could produce narcissistic traits in children. Considering the similarity between the high expectations and low warmth of the authoritarian parenting style and the behavior of a narcissistic parent, it makes sense that authoritarian parenting could also tend to encourage narcissism. However, the authoritarian parent's relative coldness is not as extreme and doesn't include the manipulative head games of the narcissistic parent.

Henschel didn't consider the effects of neglectful parenting, but some of the permissive parents in her study might have fallen under that category as well since it was added to the list as a variation on the permissive style. It's easy to see how an emotionally distant parenting style could contribute to narcissism in the child, especially when combined with a lack of boundaries and limits. Children learn how to care for others when their parents care for them, and they learn how to respect boundaries when their parents set limits on acceptable behavior. A child of neglectful parents might not have the opportunity to learn either empathy or respect for boundaries.

Narcissistic Entitlement

Henschel's research into permissive parenting might explain one of the most frustrating aspects of narcissistic behavior—the narcissist's seemingly endless sense of entitlement.

According to narcissistic abuse expert Melanie Tonia Evans, the narcissist feels entitled to get whatever he wants whenever he wants it and perceives any refusal to give him what he wants as a horrible injustice. This can include anything from attention to affection to money to sex—there are no legitimate limits on what he has the right to expect from other people in the eyes of the narcissist. Even though the narcissist treats others as if they have no rights, he expects others to respect his rights at all times.

Evans traces this colossal sense of entitlement to four separate causes, any one of which can produce a narcissist. The first is abuse and neglect, such as the experience of being raised by a narcissistic parent. The second is being raised by overly permissive parents who fail to establish boundaries and never say no. The third is being raised by overly indulgent parents who try too hard to give the child everything he could ever want. The fourth is being raised by parents who put the child on a pedestal, creating an overblown but basically fragile sense of self-worth. The child ends up perceiving herself as being special and better than others, entitled to anything she wants just like Violet Beauregarde in Charlie and the Chocolate Factory.

As Evans pointed out, the act of putting your child on a pedestal like this is also narcissistic, as the child is treated as an extension of the parents' ego. This suggests that parental narcissism may be a factor even when the parent isn't actually abusive. The narcissistic parent uses the child to prop up his own false self and influences the child to see the world in the same way.

Other Factors

Other factors may also contribute to the development of a narcissistic personality. Researchers have found some physical differences between the brains of people diagnosed with narcissistic personality disorder and other people. Narcissistic people seem to have less gray matter in two areas of the brain: the prefrontal cortex and the left anterior insula.

These areas of the brain are associated with the ability to experience empathy for others as well as the ability to regulate emotion. This implies that people with a narcissistic personality disorder may have difficulty keeping their own emotions from spiraling out of control and may also find it hard to empathize with other people's feelings. Quick to feel anger or anxiety and slow to feel empathy, the narcissist may simply be at the mercy of her own emotions.

Of course, it's difficult to say whether these brain differences really cause narcissistic personality disorder or whether they are just one factor among many. For example, having less gray matter in your left anterior insula might not make you narcissistic on its own, but might make you more likely to become narcissistic with the right life experiences. As with many other mental health problems, a narcissistic personality disorder may be caused by a combination of environmental and genetic factors.

Problems Associated with Narcissism

Narcissism tends to go along with other mental health problems and personality disorders. People diagnosed with NPD often suffer from depression. They are also more likely to be diagnosed with Bipolar Disorder, also known as manic depression. The person suffering from Bipolar Disorder will alternate between extremely depressed and manically energetic moods.

People with NPD have high rates of substance abuse issues and are especially likely to abuse cocaine. They have high rates of anorexia and may also have higher rates of other personality disorders, including Borderline, Anti-Social, and Paranoid disorders.

Narcissism is so strongly associated with other mental health issues that counselors usually make a diagnosis of NPD after the patient comes in for some other reason. For example, the narcissist may seek treatment for depression after a breakup caused by his own narcissistic behavior, without any insight into his own role in the breakdown of the relationship. Even though he can tell that something is wrong, he still believes the other person mistreated him rather than the other way around.

Although the narcissist is deeply unhappy and incapable of forming healthy relationships with others, most narcissists are unwilling and unable to see themselves as the problem. Seeking help for narcissism would mean admitting that the narcissist's ideal self is actually fake. Because the narcissist can't bear to do this, he blames everyone else for his problems instead.

The therapist who realizes her patient is narcissistic may make a diagnosis of NPD but will have a hard time making any progress as long as the narcissist continues to cling to the false self. Narcissists in treatment are known for arguing with their therapists, and being stubborn about treatment, impervious to any argument the therapist may present.

Chapter 4

Your behavior is a choice

Just as there are different types of narcissists, there are two distinct types of codependents. These are passive and active codependents, and while both exhibit traits of codependency, they typically present in different manners, typically in regards to their fear of conflict.

Passive codependent

The passive codependent is quite fearful in general. This is the kind of person who is likely to avoid conflict at all costs and will give in to whatever the enabler requests. These are the ones that are typically found in relationships with narcissists or abusive individuals. Because the passive codependents are so afraid of conflict, they are easy to manipulate into obedience.

Further, passive codependent is far more afraid of being alone. They believe they are capable of manipulating and controlling the narcissists in their life, and they attempt to do so, hoping to manage the situation and retain some semblance of control. These attempts are typically quite covert, and they are quickly found to be unproductive, particularly against the narcissist. After several attempts of trying to control the narcissist and learning that there is no use, the passive codependent typically gives up trying and instead decides to reside passively in the relationship. She still meets the needs of the narcissist on demand, feeling that she is only valuable when she does so, and becoming thoroughly addicted to the relationship, but she never does much to stir up trouble. She is terrified of the consequences of attempting to fight back.

Submissive and stoic, she does not emote much. Her emotional needs are discarded altogether for fear of losing the narcissist if she dares try to care for herself or express displeasure. Instead, she seeks to martyr herself to the narcissist and sits back and allows the relationship to slowly consume her.

Active codependent

In contrast, the active codependent is a bit more willing to put herself out there. She will attempt more overtly to manipulate her narcissistic partner, and she does not fear conflict in the same way that the passive codependent does. She does not fear the conflict, nor does she fear the pain she will feel in inciting an argument, so she is far more likely to confront the narcissist if she feels she has to.

Active codependents are more manipulative in general. They are willing to do whatever it takes to keep their partners in line, such as appealing to guilt or threatening self-harm if they do not get their way. They will use emotions to get their partners to obey them, or at least try to, and this can sometimes cause issues when partnered with a narcissist, as the narcissist does not care about the emotions of others.

The active codependent, much like the narcissist, is likely to push for instant intimacy and closeness. The active codependent will tell all sorts of intimate details of her life, thinking that it creates further trust and therefore love. Especially if these details pertain to past abuse meant to instill anger toward the abuser, this is an attempt by the active codependent to manipulate. It also creates a victim narrative that can sometimes ensure that the person the codependent is attempting to manipulate decides to act out of pity, which of course, the codependent sees as love.

The active codependent, because she is so likely to use overt manipulation tactics, is likely to be mistaken for a narcissist at first glance. She manipulates others in an attempt to get them to stay close to her, but unlike the narcissist, she is trying to be needed so she can serve the other person, rather than trying to draw in a person to manipulate into doing anything she wants. She, like the narcissist, is attempting to feed her own ego with other people, but she is doing this the opposite way, in which she takes care of the other person to feel better about herself, whereas the narcissist needs to be catered to in order to feel better about himself.

This is how the codependent and narcissist become the perfect enabling pair for each other. They each provide what the other needs in what is almost a symbiotic relationship. The problem is that this relationship involves two people entirely self-serving. The catch is that they are self-serving in ways that happen to balance each other out.

The active codependent believes that she can control the narcissist in some way, and she will attempt to exert that control through the above manipulation tactics. She may even resort to such tactics as withdrawing attention temporarily and other tactics that the narcissist is likely to employ. The problem here is that the narcissist will not respond kindly to such attempts, and the entire situation is likely to escalate into something far more insidious and dysfunctional than the original relationship was in the first place.

Codependency anorexia

Essentially the last attempt at self-defense, codependency anorexia occurs when the codependent turns off her ability to be harmed emotionally. After a life of living with narcissists, constantly being used to meet narcissists' need for supply, the codependent has a moment of clarity. She realizes that this is her life and that she cannot bear to continue living in that manner.

The codependent realizes, at this moment, that she cannot control that she is attracted to narcissists or other abusers. She sees that every time she has found someone that has seemed perfect, she has been met with abuse not too long after and that she has remained in those abusive relationships for far too long. She realizes that her relationships have involved a revolving door of narcissists and abusers in and out of her life, somehow drawn by her codependency as if it were a beacon advertising her as free to abuse, and she acknowledges that she can no longer put up with the pain any longer.

Rather than continuing to suffer, the codependent decides to instead essentially turn off the emotional side of herself. She shuts off her capacity to feel relationships, withdrawing deeply within herself and essentially swearing off of love and relationships. Rather than risking another abusive or narcissistic relationship, she chooses to instead isolate herself.

Of course, isolating herself comes with its own host of problems. First and foremost is that she never attempts to manage her trauma and baggage she carries with her after what was likely quite a long history of abuse. She does not acknowledge what the problem is and instead dips her head into the sand, refusing to fix the problem. While withdrawing is a sort of coping mechanism, it does nothing to help the codependent with healing.

Further, this only serves to run away from human contact in general. The codependent may be avoiding further narcissistic abuse, but she is also avoiding any sort of meaningful relationships as well. She fails to see that there is real, healthy love out there and instead retreats further away from the romantic world. She removes the option for healthy love entirely. While many people can live without affection or romance in any real form, many people consider doing so something they would never want to do.

The codependent reaches the state of codependency anorexia when she manages to entirely separate her emotional and sexual needs. She decides to withdraw herself from all meaningful human contact. She is intentionally starving herself of love and intimacy in an attempt to protect herself, but along with not healing, she is actually just making her wounds worse. Humans inherently seek out companionship. They crave love and intimacy, and without it, they may begin to suffer very real consequences.

Both mental health and the future ability to create healthy relationships suffer during this state of anorexia, in which the codependent is constantly and consciously avoiding human contact. She sees every point of contact as a possibility for danger, and she frequently does whatever she can to steer clear from even perceived possibilities of danger. For example, if she is out at a holiday party that she was mandated to attend for work, she may attempt to avoid anyone she perceives as someone who may be interested in her. Even the smallest kindnesses would be avoided, as the codependent struggles to identify the difference between love and pity or compassion, and if she feels like she might be at risk of opening herself up to a relationship, she is likely to shrink back behind her barrier she has built up, withdrawing emotionally altogether. She sees being closed off as being safe from harm, and she will retreat to that point at any time she feels vulnerable.

Ultimately, the codependent in the midst of anorexia does not recognize how that deprivation of love and sex can cripple her. She may have avoided hurt, but she has also condemned herself to a lonely life, away from any meaningful connection, and that is not a life that very many people want to pursue. People are hardwired to want to connect with each other, and just because she was hurt before does not mean that she will be hurt again. She can learn to love again if she tries to do so, but she is often too afraid to try.

This can lead to an unhealthy attachment to children or family, as neither of those groups risks relationship harm. Unfortunately, this means that children of codependents who have chosen to starve themselves of love may find themselves enmeshed with their parents, meaning that they are used as support rather than being supported by their parents. This is commonly referred to as emotional incest, in which a parent turns to a child to provide the support that is typically provided by an intimate or romantic partner. The child would be the ear to listen to the parent whenever she was hurting or stressed out, but this only puts the child at risk of becoming codependent as well, as the child learns that his own needs are unimportant when compared to the codependent parent's.

Ultimately, this state of codependent anorexia is harmful to everyone involved. The children of the codependent find their own mental health suffering. The codependent is left behind, lonely, and hurt. There is plenty that the codependent can do in order to ease that pain and begin transitioning back to the world of romance. She can seek therapy. She can be evaluated for mental health issues, such as PTSD after her constant barrage of narcissists and abusers running rampant in her life. She can find support groups meant to show her that she is not alone in her suffering. She can begin opening up to friends and family and slowly expanding her circles. What she should not do, however, is seek out a new relationship before she is ready, which may not be for a very long time. She should, however, remember that love is out there somewhere and that it can be attained without concern for abuse.

Chapter 5

Being an aware observer of your life

Narcissistic abuse is insidious, slowly penetrating every part of your life. The longer you feel trapped in the abuse, the more lost you become, until eventually; you are just floating through life, a mere shell of the beautiful, personable individual you were before entangling yourself with a narcissist. Little by little, the narcissist broke you down, until one day, you no longer recognize yourself in the mirror. While narcissistic abuse is incredibly damaging, it does not have to be permanent, and you can recover from its effects, though you may always bear some of the scars left by the wounds. If you feel as though you might be in a narcissistic relationship loaded with abuse, this chapter will provide you with the telltale signs and put names to the various types of abuse you may have faced. Please remember, no abuse is worth tolerating, and no matter what anyone else has said, no one deserves to be abused. You deserve happiness and healthiness, and you can attain it. If you feel as though you are being abused and you need help immediately, do not hesitate to reach out to other people around you, or to call your emergency services or your local domestic abuse hotline. There is help available to you and you do not have to be trapped any longer than you already have been.

Types of abuse

Narcissistic abuse comes in many different forms, and some of them may surprise you. Many behaviors that you may have seen as controlling or that made you uncomfortable may actually be types of abuse that you have overlooked for too long due to a lack of physical evidence of your abuse. Keep in mind that not every type of abuse has to be physical, and there are many other kinds that can leave far worse scars than a fist can. If you are experiencing any of these, understand that you are well within your rights to leave, and leaving is the healthier option. You are not forced to live in an abusive situation, no matter how afraid of failing to live on your own you may be.

Verbal Abuse

Verbal abuse entails yelling, belittling, or any other type of verbal put-downs. These are said with the intention of tearing you down as opposed to being some sort of negative, but still constructive, criticism, and verbal abuse should not be overlooked just because it does not leave physical marks. This may involve name-calling, insults, telling you how useless you are, criticizing you, attacking you, interrupting you, and any other intentionally harmful use of a voice. Even demands, threats, and sarcasm are forms of verbal abuse. In order to decide if something is a form of verbal abuse, consider the context and whether it was malicious. If contextually, it was said to hurt you, then it is likely verbal abuse. If it was something that put you down but was meant to be of benefit to you, it may not have been.

Manipulation

As discussed in depth, manipulation is one of the narcissist's favorite games. They love to exert control over you, pulling your strings to get their desired results with just the right amount of deniability. Oftentimes, these manipulative tactics are done in a way where it seems harmless to outsiders, but you feel it in your gut that it was hostile or demeaning. Trust your gut reaction.

Emotional Abuse

Emotional abuse involves punishments, threats, intimidation, silent treatment, or other acts that sway your emotions. It is meant to belittle you and keep you in fear. This is intended to trigger the FOG response, keeping you stuck in the loop of fear, obligation, and guilt. It also involves playing with your emotions, such as building you up with love bombing only to suddenly tear that love and affection away in the blink of an eye. Anything that toys with your emotions are a form of emotional abuse.

Physical Abuse

This is perhaps the most obvious of the abuse tactics used by narcissists. Any abuse that physically harms you or keeps you trapped in a form of physical abuse. There may be displays of aggression, such as punching doors or walls, or acts of holding you in place when you want to leave. If the other party's hands are ever on you without your consent, it is physical abuse.

Sexual Abuse

Even in romantic relationships and marriages, sexual abuse is an issue to contend with. Just because you are married or have consented to sexual acts in the past does not mean that your permission is indefinite. Some narcissists will use this in order to keep control over you or to serve their own needs when you are reluctant.

Neglect

Neglect is typically considered in the context of a child with a narcissistic parent, though it could be seen in other contexts too if the narcissist is in a position of providing everything needed to survive but has refused to do so. In the context of children, this can include leaving the child in a dangerous situation or starving.

Financial Abuse

Financial abuse entails withholding all money or the vast majority of the money, and only providing the victim with a small amount, or in some cases, none at all, even if the victim is the one who earned it. This is to keep the victim dependent on the narcissist for everything, enabling easier manipulation in the future. This can be done through threats, theft, or even using your name and private information to take out credit cards in your name and build up debt with them.

Isolation

Isolation involves putting a gap between the victim and anyone that may be a support system for the victim. Your contact with the outside world may be restricted in order to grant the narcissist a more complete control, but also to ensure that the abuse is not discovered.

Signs of Abuse

People who are abused by narcissists often report similar signs and symptoms of the abuse. While not every person will follow this pattern exactly, many people will exhibit some of these symptoms if they have been exposed to systematic and regular narcissistic abuse.

Feeling Detached

Detaching yourself is a form of a defense mechanism called dissociation. In this state, you feel detached from your emotions, and in some cases, your body. It is one of the more defining features of experiencing trauma and is frequently seen in survivors of narcissistic abuse. The mind tries to sequester the traumatic event away in order to try to cope with it, but this can have some serious implications, as you may begin to fragment yourself into multiple pieces just to cope with the abuse you have endured, and you may begin to experience altered levels of consciousness and see effects to your memory.

Walking on Eggshells

Those who have lived through trauma often go out of their ways to avoid anything even remotely associated with the trauma. You may constantly start avoiding people that remind you of your abuser or being careful to avoid saying some of the phrases he used frequently in order to avoid feeling a sense of being triggered. You may begin watching what you do or say around your abuser in hopes of avoiding another bout of abuse, but you likely still are his target. This leaves you feeling anxious most of the time, with that sensation of walking on eggshells as you desperately try to avoid setting your abuser off.

Self-Sacrificing

Through being abused and having none of your needs met for an extended period of time, you have given up on meeting your own wants and needs. Your goals and desires are cast aside in favor of catering to the narcissist, ensuring that you never upset or trigger him in an attempt to avoid further abuse. Ultimately, you are left without ambitions or hobbies, having let your entire self be consumed by the narcissist for his own personal gain.

Health Issues Related to Psychological Distress

Oftentimes, your psychological distress manifests physically. Your weight may have fluctuated drastically, or your body, overwhelmed by stress, has begun to show signs of aging or you find yourself getting sicker than you ever have before. Abuse raises cortisol levels as you stress, which suppresses your immune system. Your sleep is interrupted by trauma, which further raises your stress levels.

Distrustful

After being betrayed so thoroughly by someone you once trusted or loved, you find yourself constantly feeling threatened from all sides. You trust nobody around you and seek to protect yourself by remaining hypervigilant around all others, even when the people around you may have given you no signs that they would harm you.

Self-Harm or Thoughts of Suicide

As depression and anxiety develop in the face of abuse, you may find yourself having thoughts of harming yourself or of committing suicide. You feel as though suicide may be the only real way out of your situation, and find yourself struggling to cope. You get to the point that you feel like death is favorable to living any longer trapped with your abuser. Remember, if you are having these suicidal thoughts, or thoughts of harming yourself, you are having a medical emergency. Please seek help as soon as possible to help yourself stabilize so you can get yourself out of the situation that drove you this far in the first place.

Self-Isolating

While the abuser frequently engages in isolating the victim in order to keep the abuse hidden, the abuse victim also may engage in self-isolation. After feeling shame for suffering through abuse, or feeling as though you have let yourself get into this situation, you may be afraid or embarrassed to let other people know about your situation in fear of having them judge you. Especially in a social climate that seems to favor abusers and blame the victim, you may be afraid of stepping out and asking for help, so you instead turn inward and refuse to see anyone.

Blaming Yourself

It is easy to blame yourself for being stupid enough to get trapped in such a bad relationship in the first place when you find yourself suffering through narcissistic abuse. However, keep in mind that you did not ask to be abused, and you did not deserve it. The narcissist is skilled at manipulating people into seeing what he wants them to see and you fell for it, as did others, and as others will do in the future. This is not a flaw with you; it reflects solely on the narcissist.

Self-Sabotage

Victims of abuse frequently find themselves developing an inner voice that reflects that of their abuser. The victim develops shame related to the situation, and in many cases, self-sabotages due to a perceived sense of worthlessness. Because the abuser has beaten the victim down so much, the victim has come to accept the narcissist's narrative of the world surrounding them.

Living in Fear

Narcissists take offense any time anyone around them is experiencing joy or success, and oftentimes, it is during those periods of success or happiness in which the narcissist escalates, punishing anyone who dares to have something to be happy about. This causes the victim of the narcissistic abuse to develop a fear of success or enjoyment. The fearful disposition also allows for the narcissist to continue to remain the center of attention with less competition.

Protecting the Abuser

Oftentimes, the victim feels some twisted need to protect the abuser from the consequences of such heinous actions. This is a coping mechanism that is meant to help assuage the cognitive dissonance that only someone who has been abused by a person declaring love can understand. The victim may feel as though there is a need to protect the narcissist due to obligation and because the narcissist claims to love the victim. The victim usually takes a share of the blame and says that things are not as bad as they seem due to feeling as though the victim will be unable to survive without the narcissist there to help.

Results of abuse

Ultimately, even after initially escaping abuse, you may notice the long-lasting effects of living with such a toxic monster. Remember, this is not a reflection of you, but of the abuse, you endured, and it will take time and effort for you to work past these hurdles and become the person you deserve to be. The most frequently noticed behavioral habits after having escaped a narcissist's abuse are echoism and some mental health disorders.

Echoism

In the Greek myth of Narcissus and Echo, Echo was cursed. She was only able to repeat what was said to her last, and as she fell in love with Narcissus, she was only able to repeat what he had said. He did not love her back, and ultimately, cursed to repeat his words; she faded away and died, leaving behind only her voice, which would echo anyone who called out around her.

Like the nymph, Echo, those suffering from echoism fail to develop a sense of self or have that sense of self eroded away. Typically the most empathetic and emotionally sensitive people, those who become echoes feel as though they have left behind their identities. They put their needs last, ultimately developing a fear of having needs in the first place. They feel as though having needs and acting upon them is enough to prove that they are selfish, though that is really just a projection tactic the narcissist has used to convince the victim to forsake her own needs for his sake. Echoism is the ultimate sense of people pleasing, and these people suffer, even after leaving the relationship altogether, as the internalized belief that the victim cannot seek to engage in self-care or have any sort of identity away from the narcissist is ingrained.

Mental Health Issues

Those who have suffered from NPD, especially when it was particularly toxic, may find themselves suffering from other mental health issues. The constant strain of trying to satisfy the insatiable narcissist can develop into anxiety and depression, both of which take their tolls on the individual. Constantly having needs gone unmet and receiving criticism if you dare attempt to voice discontent or that you need something can lead to both anxieties at confrontation or a feeling of depression as you come to believe that the situation is hopeless. Through repeated trauma, you may even develop post-traumatic stress disorder, particularly when the abuse suffered from the narcissist is particularly bad.

Ultimately, leaving a narcissistic abuser is the only true way to avoid harm and protect yourself and your mental health. The longer you are in the relationship, the harder it gets to let go as the trauma-bonding makes leaving seem like an impossibility. Despite the abuse, you feel as though life could not happen any other way, and you find yourself stuck. Remember that you do not have to remain in such a relationship, and leaving is always an option.

Chapter 6

Mindfulness meditation practice and its purpose

When you start to recognize the toxic behaviors that narcissists bring into your life, it's natural to feel turned off and want to get some distance from them. When a victim pulls away from a narcissist, but does not firmly resolve to cut off all connections to them, we call this "Going Low-Contact." For many victims, this is the first small step towards revolutionary changes in their social and professional lives.

Still, for a victim of narcissistic abuse, going Low-Contact is a bit like an alcoholic trying to scale back to two or three drinks per week, rather than embracing full abstinence. In some cases, it is truly the best option for the victim--for example, if you share custody of your child with a narcissist, or if you are financially dependent on their continued positive opinion of you. But even in these cases, it is imperative for the victim to maintain strong boundaries, and be vigilant of all their interactions with the narcissist, so as not to allow any subtle or subtextual abusive behaviors to slip through the cracks.

Remember that for the narcissist, all attention is good attention; they may mislead you to feel, for a time, that you have gained the upper hand in the relationship by listening to your complaints about their behavior, even allowing you to yell to express your frustration, or prompting you to "get even" with them. While you might imagine this to be painful or difficult for them, they may, in fact, enjoy being yelled at, because it proves to them that you are still overwhelmed by the emotions they are inspiring in you. It makes them feel powerful. They might want you to feel that you hold power in the relationship for a short time, but this is usually a tactical trick to reel you back in, and lull you into a false sense of security before they exhibit further abusive behaviors. Their goal is to keep you engaged and enthralled, with more of your energy focused on reacting to the narcissist than on feeding your own well-being.

Is it time for a change?

Victims of narcissistic abuse often feel very uncertain about how to move forward, because they are halfway (or more) convinced that they are the problem, and the narcissist has done nothing wrong. The tactics outlined in chapters five and six work cumulatively to train victims to blame themselves for the abuse they suffer through. They have been told that they are melodramatic; that they are overreacting; that they are imagining things; that they are crazy; and that they, the victims, are in fact the ones who possess an overinflated sense of self-importance.

But if you've found yourself here, reading this book, chances are that you know, somewhere deep in your gut, that this relationship isn't good for you. Maybe you've noticed your personality or physical appearance changing the longer you're exposed to this person; perhaps you're experiencing emotional symptoms that you can't easily explain, like depression, anxiety, social fear, or chronic rage. Maybe you've simply realized that you dread spending time with this person, because the relationship only serves them while draining your energy.

Here is a checklist to review whenever you feel worried that a relationship might have become toxic, but you cannot see a clear solution, or trace the source of the problems within it. If you identify strongly with these feelings, that is a pretty strong indicator that something in the relationship needs to change, or at least be examined with a careful eye. Practice listening to your gut, and honoring your feelings. They are not simply an inconvenience, as the narcissists in your life may have taught you to believe; your emotions are powerful tools that can help you avoid danger, and find true happiness.

You don't know which way is up anymore

This is a common effect of frequent gaslighting. In a relationship with a narcissist, victims are often told that their accurate perceptions of reality are delusional. A narcissist might call their victim an ugly name, and then mere minutes later, deny that this ever happened with enough conviction to actually convince the victim that they imagined the entire incident. If you frequently leave contentious conversations with the potential narcissist in your life feeling like you couldn't summarize the discussion to a therapist or other interested party, this may be part of the reason why. It's highly recommended that you start keeping a journal of these discussions and other incidences of inappropriate or abusive treatment; this will help you to recognize and prevent the narcissist's further attempts to gaslight you and avoid accountability. It will also help you to build more trust in your own judgement, and maintain a stronger resolve when the narcissist attempts to hoover you back into their manipulative grasp.

You find yourself in a defensive position over reasonable requests

Narcissists are experts at blame shifting, which means they are great at making their victims feel self-conscious about the realities of their victimhood. Say, for example, that you are best friends with a narcissist who frequently love-bombs and then discards you, showing up without invitation whenever they need your attention, but then standing you up for agreed upon dinner dates. It is perfectly reasonable for a friend in this situation to express dissatisfaction at being stood up, and ask the narcissistic friend to work on improving in this area of the friendship. But a narcissist could easily react by implying that the victim is somehow emotionally weak for not wanting to eat alone, or for needing their validation. They might even go so far as to blame the aggrieved friend for choosing an inconvenient place or time to meet, or having poor communication skills that prevent them from adequately expressing how important it is to them not to be stood up.

This is an attempt to change the subject, or move the goal post, of the argument. If you find it endlessly frustrating to try and keep these sorts of conversations on topic with a certain person in your life, or find that you're having the same argument over and over again without your needs being addressed or the problematic behaviors changing, take note of this fact and proceed with caution. You should never have to apologize or become defensive when asking for a common courtesy from someone who claims to care about you, so long as the request is made in a respectful manner. When you do, you subordinate yourself and set a precedent for others to treat you as a doormat.

You have to explain the basics to an adult, as though they are a child

Do you remember Bill Clinton's impeachment trial, when the whole nation watched the president of the united states--presumably a very well-educated and socially savvy individual--ask to have the word "is" defined and clarified for him? We can't necessarily diagnose the former president as a pathological narcissist, but his behavior in that setting was certainly exemplary of narcissistic argumentation tactics. Narcissists cannot accept blame, express genuine remorse, or handle shame, so they're not above playing dumb or skirting on technicalities in order to avoid facing the consequences of their actions. You may be feeling mentally exhausted if there is a narcissist in your life who routinely puts you in the position to explain the rules of common human decency--for instance, why it's rude to interrupt people, or that it's inappropriate to smile or laugh at someone else's emotional pain--as though the narcissist is a five-year-old who couldn't possibly be expected to know any better. It's important to note that you may also have this experience with people who truly do not know better, such as an individual on the autism spectrum; by contrast, though, a person on the spectrum will likely be able to acknowledge it if these issues have been brought to their attention in the past, even if they have not yet corrected the offensive behaviors, whereas a narcissist will feign complete ignorance.

When you think of them, you feel split in two

Like someone who is head over heels for Dr. Jekyll but terrified of Mr. Hyde, you may feel as though you simultaneously love and hate this person. This is an unfortunate result of the cycle of abuse; for all the negative experiences, there are also extreme highs in the relationship, usually ones that overshadow positive experiences in your healthier, more stable interpersonal connections. You may also feel confused about which side of this person is real: the perfect, blameless, unimpeachable figure that most of the world sees, or the monster who comes out every once in a while to terrorize you and a few other unlucky victims. Finally, you may feel split in two based on your knowledge, from past experience, that dealing with them puts you in a real bind; even when you know you ought to stand up for yourself, or for justice on someone else's behalf, you know you'll be damned if you do and damned if you don't. The narcissist won't listen to reason or tolerate dissent, and even if you are in the right, you're all the more likely to be punished for it.

You feel nervous or anxious about situations that never bothered you before

In a relationship with a narcissist, positive and negative reinforcements are doled out seemingly at random. The only logic that can be applied to the rules in this relationship is that of the narcissist's moment-to-moment desire, so you may be lauded for a certain behavior on one day, and then inexplicably punished for doing the same thing at a later point. This dynamic creates a sense of constant tension in the relationship and anxiety in the victim, who doesn't know what they are doing right or wrong. As such, the victim may develop anxieties around specific triggers--people, places, situations or circumstances--feeling that, although they once were comfortable managing these things, they no longer understand what is expected of them, nor do they know what to expect from the trigger in question. Essentially, the victim learns to associate their negative memories and emotions with the circumstances, rather than with the narcissist who made a normal situation unmanageable for them.

You feel afraid of advocating for yourself

Some people naturally struggle to speak up or be assertive with others, but victims of narcissistic abuse tend to feel a very specific brand of fear in regards to asserting their needs in interpersonal relationships. This is because narcissists treat their lovers, friends, colleagues, and families as inferior beings whose needs are secondary; furthermore, they train these individuals to fear that advocating for themselves is inherently narcissistic and makes them unlovable. Victims don't just feel nervous about speaking up--they are truly frightened that asking for fair and equal treatment will result in a catastrophic loss for them.

Spending too much time with a narcissist can destroy a person's internal barometer for healthy levels of self-esteem, so if you find yourself frequently tolerating intrusions over your personal boundaries and feeling afraid to enforce them, it would be wise to seek out the help of a therapist or counselor. Anyone who is afraid to advocate for themselves might as well have a bullseye painted on their foreheads, as they are extremely likely to fall into imbalanced relationships with even more narcissistic abusers.

You can't remember the last time you said "no"

Narcissists train their victims to be "yes" people. Over time, victims learn that they are only as valuable as their ability to please the narcissist (or their flying monkeys), until they reach a point where they don't just help others because they want to--the urge to please other people becomes imperative, and failure to please others results in deep, haunting shame. In any relationship, whether it is romantic, platonic, familial or professional, you should feel fully welcome to say "yes" to things you want, and to say "no" to anything that makes you uncomfortable. If this isn't the case, you must recognize that there is no room for coercion or manipulation in healthy relationships, and take whatever steps you must in order to protect your right to give or withhold consent at will.

You feel queasy or uncomfortable when receiving positive attention, or compliments, from others

This attitude can emerge in victims who have existed in a state of endless competition with the narcissists in their lives. Victims may have been routinely punished by the narcissist for "stealing the spotlight," or grown accustomed to having any praise directed their way negated or invalidated by the narcissist shortly thereafter. This mindset may become so deeply ingrained in a victim's mind that they are still uneasy about receiving positive attention when the narcissist isn't present, and is unlikely to ever hear about the interaction. It can even impact the victim's ability to sustain eye-contact with other people, or to do anything in conversations besides ask questions and listen. This attitude also discourages victims from pursuit of their own goals; they develop a fear of apparent success, because it might make them a target of the narcissist's envy.

You don't know who you can trust

Narcissists like to sow fear and mistrust between their various sources of narcissistic supply, whether they are harem members or flying monkeys. In fact, it may be more important for these people to suspect each other of ill intent than it is for any of them to bear genuine enthusiasm or affection for the reigning narcissist. This prevents their underlings from joining forces to overthrow or expose the narcissist, and creates an atmosphere in which everyone believes the narcissist sees, hears, and knows everything that happens, even when they are absent. Fear and paranoia work to keep victims silent.

You are questioning your values, or regretting morally sound choices you made in the past

It's important for everyone to develop a strong internal moral compass, and to make sure it's defined by personal values rather than based on other people's feelings. Narcissistic abuse can create complex webs of cognitive dissonance within victims, who will be gaslit and told that their well-intentioned behaviors were actually malicious, their emotions are hollow and faked for the sake of manipulation, and their anger or sadness is invalid.

If you are feeling pressure to regret or correct a past behavior that you know in your gut was the right choice, it's important to examine this feeling and question the motive behind the pressure. As an example, if you intervene on behalf of an underdog who is being bullied, and are later made to feel as though this was a self-serving or self-righteous action, you should question these assertions. If you reverse your moral compass and accept these judgements, who does that serve most? Who does it protect? How might things have played out differently without your intervention? The pressure to alter your moral compass may come from a third party, but by asking these questions, you'll usually find that the narcissist in your life benefits most from your abandonment of strong moral values.

Going low-contact

When you've determined that a certain narcissist has a negative influence on your behavior and emotional landscape, there is no reason to keep trying to fix what's broken between you. By this point, you have likely tried every trick in the book to encourage them to treat you with compassion and mutual respect. From here on out, make an effort not to waste any more of your breath or time on a lost cause.

You may still need to maintain good standing in the narcissist's book; they may have financial, professional, or spiritual power over you, or they may simply be deeply entangled in your social circle. Even so, reducing the amount of energy and effort that you dedicate to maintaining and improving this relationship can free up an enormous amount of time for you to dedicate to healing and personal growth.

It isn't usually necessary to explicitly state your desire to spend less time with this person. You can simply stop reaching out to them, while still offering polite replies when they get in touch with you. You can also make a slow but deliberate effort to remove yourself from shared institutions or groups, so long as you're not doing yourself a disservice with this action, or engaging in this behavior simply to spite them.

It is generally ill-advised to use excuses, if and when the narcissist takes note of your changing behavior. While it might be tempting to answer their question of "what's wrong?" with a gentle rejection, saying "nothing, I've just been busy lately," or "oh, I'm just having some personal issues with my family," these kinds of excuses will eventually come back to bite you in the rear. The narcissist might feel that they are owed more detailed explanations, and start prying into your business; worse, they will expect your behavior to revert to "normal," meaning you'll resume worshipping them and putting up with abuse, once this excuse has run its course.

A far better alternative is to let the narcissist feel like it was their idea to withdraw energy and attention from the relationship. The best way to inspire them to do that is by becoming a dysfunctional source of narcissistic supply, using the "Grey Rock" technique to deflect the narcissist's attention.

Chapter 7

Practice makes perfect

Lot of times you must have heard that true healing happens only when you forgive and forget truly form the bottom of your heart.

You may also be wondering and thinking about the same because almost all faiths talk about forgiveness as a path to healing, but at the same time, the question arises as to how you can forgive the person who caused you so much harm and whether it is possible to forgive someone who has been responsible for your devastation, especially when they do not acknowledge what they have done.

Another question that can haunt you is whether forgiving is justified given that the narcissist is wrong on so many levels and is a dangerous person to not only you but also society in general.

You are not alone in this battle, and it is completely normal to face these questions. Do not beat yourself up for having these questions, and thinking along these lines does not make you a bad Christian at all. You might have also heard things like not forgiving will make you unspiritual.

The first thing to keep in mind is that this is your journey alone. You have every right to decide what to do, when to do it, and how to do it.

But it is good for you to know that forgiveness is a part of the journey. Once you have forgiven the abuser is when you truly have moved on. I struggled with forgiveness for many years until I met Diane. We connected through a support group and I was immediately drawn to her because she always spoke about her abusive partner who she still was not separated from with kindness. I wondered how someone was able to go through such cruel abuse and not only remain in the marriage but manage to keep such a positive attitude. While I do not advice anyone to remain in an abusive relationship, Diane had made her decision to stick with Tom. I couldn't understand it, but I definitely respected her position. She shared how she applied a principle of forward forgiveness, meaning that she had chosen to forgive him for the past, present and also any hurt he would inflict in the future.

This may sound shocking to you, but the truth is, it helped me to put things that had happened to me in perspective. If I was truly going to put the past behind me, I had to confront my hurt and anger, and be able to say. I forgive him forward.

Forgiveness does not mean that you have to let the abuser know that he is off and welcome him back into your life. I certainly did not do that. But like they say, un-forgiveness is like drinking poison and hoping someone else dies.

Complete forgiveness also means forgiving yourself. A lot of times despite all the healing and the steps people take or even you might have taken, you will realize that in your heart, you are not free yet. This is because while you have been able to implement no contact strictly and have established firm boundaries, you have forgotten one most important thing.

The most important thing in your self-healing journey is forgiving yourself. This is because nothing matters—no therapy sessions, no amount of self-care or pampering can do you any good—if you have truly not forgiven yourself.

Why must you forgive yourself?

You must forgive yourself because of the constant blame you have gone through. A lot of times during the journey, you will be blaming yourself for allowing the narcissist to abuse you, for trusting him even after his true colors were revealed, for becoming addicted to him and seeking him out despite all the harm he has caused you. In a toxic relationship such as the one with a narcissist, the person who suffers the most is you. You were the harshest with yourself, and hence, you need to forgive yourself.

When you forgive truly, you are not releasing the burden of the narcissist, but you are releasing the burden you put on yourself. By forgiving yourself, you drop the baggage that you have been carrying around, so suddenly you experience freedom. Once this happens, you will realize that you are no longer haunted by the memories, and even if you recollect something from the past, they will not damage you or cause a breakdown.

Self-love and self-forgiveness are the ultimate narcissist's repellents. They work like nothing else.

Forgiveness will also remove the resentment from within that you have been holding for so long. It will cleanse your mind and body and set you free.

Forgiveness also does not mean that you have to forget everything. It is just not possible that you will completely forget everything that has happened to you. There is no way you can completely erase this chapter out of your life. And erasing your memories is not required as well. What is required is that the memories stop having a negative effect on you.

Despite healing from the trauma and even if you have forgiven the abuser, it does not mean that you must forget. Having a memory of the events will help you spot red flags in the future and help you protect yourself. During the healing process, you will eventually move from paranoia that everyone is an abuser to a normal hum being who does not have trust issues, but it always to remember the lessons that you learned, and the most important is the ability to spot red flags from a distance.

Not forgetting will also help you see how far you have come and take note of the stronger person that you are today. It will also make you a wiser person.

Last but not the least if you have survived all the abuse and have managed to heal it means that there is a protective force within you that is guiding you, and you must be proud of that.

Last but not least the entire journey of healing from a narcissist is a spiritual journey more than anything else. This is due to the fact that a spiritual journey is one where you seek reconciliation and education through enlightenment. It is the only journey which allows you to travel within you and discover your soul and mind to attain higher goals.

This journey is unique to each individual, and no journeys are going to be the same.

Healing from a narcissistic abuse forces you to go on a path of self-discovery to answer questions that arise related to anger, why you let the abuse happen, why you still love your abuser etc.

The culmination of this journey is when you have identified the answers to the questions, accepted your internal flaws, and worked on repairing them. This is the reason the healing is more a spiritual process. It is the moment of self-discovery, which will teach you that you are entitled to love and respect.

This spirituality from the narcissistic abuse comes in waves and not at a single point in time. You slowly start realizing that

- you are appreciating all the self-love and care you are giving yourself and also acknowledge that self-care is essential for leading a fulfilled life;

- it is completely fine to be a little "selfish" at times because only when you are happy, it can you lead a happy life, and this happiness comes from within;

- you are extremely comfortable with the boundaries that you have established and no longer feel guilty for enforcing them;

- you no longer have intrusive thoughts about your narcissistic ex, and his presence also does not bother you;

- you are completely in charge of your mental and physical space and will not allow anyone to intrude into them without your permission;

- you start honoring yourself more and stop putting others needs before your needs (you no longer suffer from a savior complex);

- you completely acknowledge that a narcissist cannot be changed and that it is not your job to fix him;

- you do not break down when problems arrive; rather, you start looking for solutions on your own (this is a huge step in the right direction because this indicates that you trust yourself and your judgment something that you would have struggled with in the initial days after the abuse).

In addition to the above, you also understand and accept that whatever happened to you was not a punishment but rather a divine lesson from God. As weird as it may sound, this is the truth. All this was essential for you to discover your true potential and accept yourself. Over time you will realize that these punishments are lessons that will help you overcome all the false beliefs that you have about yourself.

You will change from being a codependent person who also needed approval and feared rejection of a confident individual who is not dependent on anyone's approval. The narcissist will cease to have any control or power over, and no reaction will become a routine for you, not something that you need to practice carefully.

You will also realize that transformation is the only way to living your best life, and this is the key to leading your life in an emotionally fulfilling manner. This does not mean that you will never face any problems in life again or that life will be a bed of roses. This means that with the transformation that has taken place, you will be able to tackle the problems in a calm and matured manner with all the new strength that you have acquired.

Spiritual healing is the healing of your "inner spirit." It is the process of working on the life force energy within you and getting back this energy that belongs to you.

Another important learning is that from a spiritual perspective there are no victims. During the initial phase of recovery, everything seems so difficult because you consider yourself as a victim.

Considering yourself a victim will not help you grow stronger; it will rather make you weaker. This is because for centuries, society has considered victims to be weak, and victims have always been associated with weakness. You also must have grown up thinking the same. As long as you feel weak, you can never heal and move forward.

But in spirituality, there are no victims. You will come to understand this as your healing journey progresses. You will understand that each of the events that happened to you was just experiences. The abuse was also an experience that you allowed to happen at some level. You start considering the abused person as a teacher and your experience as a learning experience that taught you a lot about yourself.

You learn intuition from this experience and trust early warning signs. It is not that you would not have experienced early warning signs during the initial stages of the relationship, but you consciously decide to ignore them—you push them away and stop giving your intuition the attention that it deserves. Through the healing process, you start learning to trust your intuition again. Once you start trusting your intuition, you are no longer in a dangerous position where you will fall for a predator such as a narcissist.

You were in a dangerous situation when you were a victim. Because when you are a victim, you lack self-worth and hence attract the wrong kind of people into your life. This danger will continue forever, and there may be chances where you will move from an abusive relationship to another, and the cycle will continue.

The secret for this cycle of abuse to stop is healing from inside. The truth is though abuse happens from the outside, your inner soul gets damaged, and hence, the healing must happen inside. When you are fully empowered, you stop acting like a victim because you no longer feel like one. This automatically will prevent you from falling for abusers such as a narcissist in future because you will walk away as soon as you spot the first sign of a narcissist or any other abuser.

Spiritual healing will also help you understand that your past served a purpose in life and taught you whatever you needed to survive the future. Now that the purpose is over, the past left you, and you must be grateful for the lessons that past taught and also grateful to God that you do not have to live that fearful and traumatic life anymore. So how does one attain spiritual healing? I would say it is simply by drawing closer to God and engaging in spiritual activities like prayer, fasting, studying the bible and meditating on God's promises. You might not feel strong enough to pray for long hours and that is not the point. What is most important is that you spend time talking to him, just like he was seating in the room with you and pouring out your heart to him.

Listening to spiritual songs also have a way of calming me personally, so on the days where I felt too overwhelmed to pray, I just played some music on my phone, over and over. The peace that comes from God is like no other, there is no way I would have made it out with my sanity intact without the help of God.

Chapter 8

Children in the narcissistic relationship

Knowing what you have learned about narcissism, you might wonder why a narcissist would have a child in the first place, considering their desire to be taken care of and adored, rather than care for someone and tend to their every need, especially that of a child who needs a great deal of praise and attention.

People have children, whether they are narcissists or not. It doesn't depend on something like that when you and your partner decide to start a family. A narcissist might enjoy having a child or more than one because it creates an immediate relationship with someone in which they will always have power and authority. In the parent-child relationship, in the opinion of the narcissist, the child will always be beneath them because of the nature of their relationship and their difference in age and life experience.

Sadly, and unfortunately, for the child of the narcissist, they will quickly learn that they exist to please and serve the parent, rather than the parent meeting all of the needs of the child first. The child of the narcissist is there to serve as a healthy reflection of their accomplishments, achievements, and overall perfection.

Just as narcissistic abuse can occur in a romantic partnership, it can also occur in the parent-child dynamics. A young child with a narcissistic parent will learn that they must act and behave as the reflection of their parent, including fitting into behavior and/or mold of personality that is dictated by the parent. It can cause a great deal of anxiety in the child starting at a very early age because they are being persuaded to deny their unique personality to be the mirror reflection that the narcissistic parent desperately needs them to be.

Failure to comply with the wishes of the narcissistic parent, for example, if the child wants to create and set their life goals, the parent will display actions of covert and overt punishment, including avoiding, ignoring, denying, and rejecting the child for a while. The parent will see their child's autonomy as a slight against them as if the child was intentionally betraying them.

A narcissistic parent is hard for a child to understand or trust. They are unpredictable and often confusing, rarely consistent in any direction with their attitudes toward their child or partner. The narcissist is impulsive, unpredictable, and capricious. A child wants stability, trust, and an ability to feel safe as they learn to explore the world.

An inability to understand or make sense of the interpersonal "stunts" of the narcissistic parent can lead to the child internalizing feelings of shame, blame, or guilt when they don't live up to the parent's expectations. This can look a lot like what you read in the last section about the symptoms of narcissistic abuse, in which the child will assume that it is their fault that their parent is unhappy and that they should feel bad as a result of it. A narcissistic parent is completely oblivious to the harm and damage they are causing their child. The message the child receives is basically, "you are only worthy of love if you comply with my expectations and wishes of you."

Commonly, all of these issues are reflected as the child of the narcissist grows up and starts attempting to have relationships of their own. It is in adulthood that they begin to process the trauma of what their narcissistic parent caused them as a developing person.

Children of Narcissists as Adults

A distorted child-parent relationship can create a lot of serious emotional and mental issues as you get older and work on having your relationship experiences. Children of narcissists will tend to seek out or gravitate toward challenging or dramatic relationships because it was what was modeled for them as a child. It is what they know love to "look like." Growing up with the belief that you are not essentially good or lovable, causes the issue of only seeking out partnerships that will perpetuate that belief with another partner.

It is rather common for any child, whether they are in a narcissistic child-parent relationship or not, to seek out relationships in their adult life that replay what they learned in childhood. Asking for something else feels foreign and strange. Imagine a fish out of the water like the child of a narcissist receiving unconditional love from a partner, without expecting anything in return.

Children of narcissists will seek out romantic partners who are critical or judgmental, emotionally distant or unavailable, or who will withhold or deny affection and intimacy. Essentially, they will be looking for a partner who feels comfortable and what they know and understand, replaying the dynamics they shared with their narcissistic/codependent parents.

Of course, anyone can heal from such an experience, and sometimes, a child of a narcissist will find that through some therapy and a few healthy partnerships, they can realize, identify, and defy the issues of their childhood experience with their narcissistic parent. Being able to identify the causes of why you may have issues in your adult relationships often stems from identifying what kind of relationship you had with your early life caregivers.

Oftentimes, when said child chooses to heal, grow, and move forward from their previous way of experiencing their relationships, the narcissistic parent will panic and begin to accuse the child of being "brainwashed" or lied to by the therapist/partner/friend/colleague who suggested they get help to heal their issues. For the parent, this means that they are no longer in control of their child and will have to suffer the consequences of that child's growth and preference to heal the wounds they incurred from the parent-child relationship.

A narcissistic parent might then distance themselves, choosing to reject and deny their child, hoping that their form of punishment will cause their offspring to "see the light" and return to their old dynamic. The parent is very telling in their behavior, as the child can now better see that all their parent wants is to serve their emotional needs and has no feeling for what their child has experienced.

Narcissistic parenting can cause a lot of issues in their child or children, and in adulthood, that child may learn the hard way what they were experiencing with their parent. To break it down further, here is a list of how a narcissistic parent can affect their children:

- The child will feel like they can't be heard or seen.

- They won't have their feelings acknowledged, or their reality validated.

- Rather than being seen as a person, they will be treated as the accessory to the parent.

- They won't be valued for who they are, only for what they can do, especially for the parent.

- The child will develop intense self-doubt, rather than learning to trust themselves and their identity.

- They will learn that how they feel it is less important and how they look is more important.

- They will learn that authenticity is not as good as an image and will then learn to be afraid of "being real" with others.

- The child will learn to behave and act secretively as a protection for the family or the parent.

- There will be no healthy encouragement to develop a sense of identity or self.

- They will not feel nurtured and can feel empty of emotions.

- They will learn that it is not good, or dangerous, to trust anyone.

- They will usually feel manipulated or used without understanding the feeling.
- The child will learn to "be there" for the parent, rather than how it should be when the parent is present and available for the child.
- Emotional development is stunted.
- They will feel judgment or criticism instead of unconditional love and acceptance.
- Feelings of not being good enough will develop.
- There will be no role model for creating healthy connections and relationship bonds.
- They will fail to learn healthy boundaries with others.
- They will learn to develop codependency and therefore, will not learn healthy self-care and self-love.
- They will be shown to seek validation from outside of the self instead of learning to validate the self from within.
- They will learn a mixed message of "make me proud" but also "don't do anything better than me."

- Will not learn to compliment the self or celebrate the self during important successes.

- May suffer from depression, addiction, anxiety, or other issues in adulthood to cope with the trauma of childhood.

- Will grow up assuming or believing that they are not lovable, or worthy of love because of the parent denying or rejecting them

- Will grow up with low self-esteem because of the shame in child-parent dynamics

- They will straddle a life of being someone who self-sabotages, overachieves, or fluctuating back and forth

- The child will have to learn the hard way how to reparent themselves once they break free from the parent-child dynamics in adulthood

The effects of being the child of a narcissist are intense, long-lasting, and deeply ingrained into the behaviors, emotions, and even physical qualities and attributes of a person. It can be psychologically and emotionally damaging and can lead to a lifetime of dealing with the programming instilled by the narcissistic parent during their child's formative years.

It can be difficult to tell that someone is a narcissist because of how charming they can be at the moment and how easy it is for them to get slippery as a fish when they are being questioned. They are very cunning, and even some psychologists can miss the red flags when they are being presented with a child's emotional or psychological pain.

Because a narcissist will never claim accountability or responsibility for their actions or behaviors, it then falls upon the child to take the brunt of the blame, guilt, shame, and remorse for anything that goes on. Every situation is different, as every family and every individual are different, but the red flags and hallmarks are the same. Review the above list to see if your child might have some of these symptoms, or if you can identify whether you may have been affected by a narcissistic parent when you were a child.

The opposite of narcissism is empathy. If you are in a situation with a child who is dealing with a narcissistic parent, then the best way to counter the damaging effects of the narcissist's abuse is to parent with empathy, offer compassion and support, and help to create a secure attachment so that the child in question can experience a healthy love bond that they can carry into their adult life.

It is important to remember that narcissism is a spectrum disorder and takes on varying degrees of severity. Whether you are the child of a narcissist, or you are in a relationship with one with whom you are trying to co-parent, it is important to understand this disorder so that you can help your whole family in healing, ending patterns and cycles, and breaking through to having healthier partnerships and bonds of love, for everyone involved.

Whether it is just for the sake of yourself, or perhaps your children as well, depending on the seriousness of the abuse and the effects on your happiness and well-being, letting go and moving on can feel scary, but this book is here to help offer you guidance as you explore and examine your options.

Chapter 9

A strict set of rules

Rules are essential to the continuation of every narcissistic relationship. When leaving a narcissist, you'll likely receive a text or other form of communication along the lines of, "It's funny how you don't think you need to live by the rules. Just saying."

The 'rules' are their rules, and you don't need to live by them. No one has to live by a narcissist's warped set of rules. Narcissists and sociopaths, in general, have a certain set of rules their victims are expected to live by. These rules help to ensure control over their victims, that the dictatorship is kept alive and well.

Narcissistic rules can be enforced through covert or overt tactics, such as lies and manipulation as previously discussed, and through controlling behavior, and physical and mental abuse. The basic premise of all narcissist rules is that every action taken by the victim must appease the narcissist. The victim must think of the narcissist first. Spousal victims must give their narcissistic lover one-sided love, respect, and adoration at all times that will never be reciprocated. Don't expect it to be.

The effectiveness of the narcissist's rule-making and the enforceability of these rules rest in the victim's willingness to submit. All relationships have rules, per se. It's usually expected that a spouse remains faithful, that the couple has an open line of communication and lets each other know their whereabouts if they go somewhere unexpectedly. But, not only do narcissists refuse to abide by these basics, they take the setting of rules to the next level, and it's up to the victim to recognize the unhealthy ones inevitably established.

Controlling the way someone dresses, calling excessively and repeatedly, and putting alerts on cameras and devices informing the spouse of the whereabouts of their significant other at all times is not normal. Enforcing rules that have to do with obeying the narcissist is not normal. An example would be using a tool on their phone to be alerted every time a garage door is opened or setting up alerts on a joint bank account to be notified every time money is withdrawn even minuscule amounts. These things aren't accepted as normal by most individuals. They're non-physical, yet dangerous signs of narcissistic control.

Three additional and equally powerful rules the narcissist constructs early on, and need to be noted by a potential victim, are as follows:

- I can falsely accuse you of doing things you never did, and you are not allowed to make a liar out of me by defending yourself.

- You are not allowed to expose me and reveal the things I really did. You must cover up what I do and say and keep it a secret.

- You are never allowed to confront me. I'm the only one who is allowed to confront anybody.

Simply put, the narcissist expects their victim to suffer in silence. Any retaliation against their general, all-encompassing rule is a threat to the narcissist's false self and, therefore, simply unacceptable. The narcissist expects everything to roll off the back of their victim. Their behavior is 'no big deal' and not to be questioned. You're not allowed to hurt, to get angry, to be frustrated, or to feel pain. You must not only conceal any negative emotions you feel, you must shield your abuser from feeling discontented.

There are consequences for deviating from the rules. It's difficult to describe the wrath of a narcissist's rage if you've deviated from the rules to anyone who has not been through it first-hand, but victims know very well the dire effects.

Stealer of ideas

One should never let a narcissist take over a project that is near and dear to their heart. The narcissist won't only take total control of the project, moving forward in whichever direction they choose, they'll dictate the entire process and upon completion, take full responsibility for its success, even claiming that it was all their idea. This is the same as asking a narcissist to go to couple's therapy. They'll likely refuse should their spouse make the suggestion until the stakes are high and they're about to lose everything, bring it up and blame the victim for not wanting to go—for giving up so easily.

It's unwise to do favors for narcissists, even if it's in one's nature to help others. The narcissist will take full advantage, asking more and more of that person until there is nothing left. When one finally says "no", they'll be called worthless or selfish.

If the narcissist asks someone to take on a project they will ultimately get credit for but is incapable of handling for one reason or another, this is absolutely a red flag. Ensuring its successful completion allows the narcissist to parade the rightful owner's accomplishment as their own as soon as the work is completed.

Lack of empathy

Narcissists are incapable of possessing genuine empathy, even toward their own children. In fact, they don't feel commonplace emotions at all, especially those related to being at fault for causing hurt, such as guilt or remorse. But, as masters of manipulation, they take note of normal human emotions and are able to mirror them for their own benefit. For example, a narcissist witnesses a breakdown takes expert note of the accompanying behavior using their photographic memory, a common trait and files it away to mimic at a time that they deem beneficial. They're experts at analyzing human emotion, memorizing, and mimicking it, at will.

The narcissist mimics these behaviors while in the public eye to prove they're capable of caring for others. They may give generously to charitable organizations, advocate against world hunger or other societal issues and attend meetings, conferences, games, and other social events at their child's school. The one thing all of these efforts have in common is that they're done publicly for attention and for the benefit of the narcissist's reputation.

Narcissists are especially mindful of displaying empathy if they're attempting to attract a new mate. They prey on the vulnerable, often hand-picking unsuspecting abuse victims, promising to be their savior. Narcissists pretend to express empathy for their victims' trauma to solidify their position of power as the victim's 'knight in shining armor'. If they're still married or committed they'll disparage their current spouse or partner rather than attempting to hide it from their new target. They'll paint themselves as a victim and manipulate their new target to gain the empathy they crave.

A narcissist will go to great extremes to create an empathetic façade when attempting to attract a new partner. If the church serves as their hunting grounds of choice, which is common, they may hand-pick the most vulnerable member who is leaning on spirituality and the comfort of the church community to heal. The narcissist's presence in church creates a false persona of a good, moral person for their intended victim. They'll join the same groups as their target to get closer while studying and making note of what makes the victim tick. The narcissist may later use their position in the church to amplify the perception of perfection to others and increase their control the victim.

Narcissists are known to have 'picture' memories. They're highly skilled at taking mental images of their victims in the earliest stages, noting and committing to memory their appearance, clothing style, speech patterns, interests, and idiosyncrasies. This information gives the narcissist the knowledge and ability to make the victim believe they're everything they've ever wanted in a mate. Later the narcissist uses this knowledge to solidify the victim's sense of inadequacy. Once their initial study is complete, the narcissist makes their move.

Before inviting their victim over for the first time, the narcissist may replace their décor with religious art to aid in their deception. They may feign a keen interest in spirituality, publicly declaring their stance on social media. The more likes a narcissist gets the more their ego is fed and the more apt their victim is to accept the false persona. Once the victim is enthralled and the narcissist has complete control, the empathic behavior stops and their true personality is revealed.

If a victim is able to recognize the mirroring tactics and escapes the trap, going completely no contact, they'll start to identify the contortion they dealt with during the relationship. Over time, they'll recall each lie and each demonstration of false empathy, when something evokes a sudden memory of time with their abuser. This sudden recall of trauma at the hands of the narcissist is called Post-Traumatic Stress Disorder (PTSD), which is covered in more detail later in this work.

PTSD generally requires professional treatment by a therapist for proper healing.

Mistreatment of Service Workers

Narcissists have a fervent need for attention and only enter into relationships when they know they'll benefit. Every relational arrangement is based on this premise. Even the briefest of encounters exist solely to serve their purpose. Superficial interactions, such as with a server at a restaurant, are not complicated by a deeper, more intimate connection. Therefore, the narcissism will surface much faster than it does when the narcissist wants to impress a potential mate. It's crucial to pay attention to their actions in these situations.

During the developmental stage of a relationship, it's helpful to note how your partner treats wait staff, flight attendants, grocery store cashiers, and other service employees. More than likely, if they're on the unhealthy narcissism scale, they'll treat these individuals with disrespect, just as they would anyone they deem inferior and decides their sole purpose is to wait on them hand and foot.

Chapter 10

How to move on from the narcissist

Ultimately, once you have escaped and begun to heal from the narcissist, you may be wondering how do you ever fully move on from the narcissist, particularly after he so thoroughly won your heart? It is definitely not an easy task, but if you have made it this far, you can do it. Moving on from the narcissist involves disengaging from the narcissist, practicing mindfulness, and bettering yourself. Through these skills, you will be able to distance yourself from the narcissist further, understand your feelings when you want to go back, and you can find a constructive way to use your feelings toward the narcissist.

With affirmations, you will have a tool in your back pocket to help you remember your value and what you want out of life.

Disengaging from the Narcissist

Disengaging from the narcissist will involve going through various stages, much like grieving. This is your process of letting go of the narcissist and recognizing that the relationship is ruined and needs to be ended permanently. Though easier said than done, disengaging and detaching from the narcissist is crucial to healing. Similar to the stages of grief, you will go through three distinct stages when you are attempting to disengage from the narcissist before finally reaching stage 4: freedom.

Stage 1: Refusing to take the blame

In stage 1, you refuse to allow yourself to be blamed for anything that happened. You tell yourself that you did not deserve what the narcissist did, and even though you may have ended the relationship, it was not you that degraded the relationship to the point that it had to be ended. This stage involves you recognizing that the narcissist will never give you what you deserved in the relationship. The narcissist will never be the partner you wanted him to be, and you recognize that. You acknowledge that the narcissist is flawed beyond your own ability to repair someone and that his destructive nature is not yours to manage, nor is it something that can be forced upon you. The narcissist becomes someone that you may love still, but you recognize the truth in the situation and that the relationship has to end for everyone's sake.

Stage 2: Anger and resentment

At stage 2, you realize that all of the hope you had for the relationship and the narcissist is being replaced. At this stage, you are angry. You see that the narcissist is not the person you wanted, and you begin to resent him. Even if you still have feelings at this stage, you are not likely to act upon them. Your eyes have been opened to the truth, and you refuse to allow the relationship to consume you any longer. At this stage, you no longer care about the manipulation the narcissist has likely been slinging at you to try to get you back. You really recognize that you deserve better than to be treated poorly or with disrespect. You feel the need to stand up for yourself and better yourself. You want to live a life of happiness, not one in which your sole duty is to provide someone else with the happiness you have been deprived of feeling for so long.

Stage 3: Detaching and setting yourself free

When you finally hit stage 3, you are finally detaching. The very sight of the narcissist or the mere mention of his name could be enough to make you feel sick to your stomach, and you realize that the love you had for him once upon a time has faded away. You have instead worked on bettering yourself. If you have been going to a therapist or been interacting with a support group, you are beginning to take their advice more frequently and realize that it works. You are far more concerned with getting what you want and need than worrying about the narcissist. You make your decisions based on what is best for you as opposed to anyone else, and for the first time in a long time, you can practically taste freedom.

Stage 4: Freedom

At this point, you are finally free. You no longer allow the narcissist to have any sway on you and you have likely cut all contact with him. You have completely and utterly separated yourself from the narcissist, and you could never feel better. Your freedom was earned through metaphorical, and quite possibly literal, blood, sweat, and tears, and you plan on enjoying it, no matter what the narcissist has to say about it.

Practicing mindfulness

Mindfulness, at its simplest, is the idea that, when engulfed in chaos and strong emotions, you are able to take a moment to detach from the situation at hand and observe what is happening from a rational perspective. You sort of retreat within yourself to reflect on how you are feeling and why you are feeling the way you are in the hopes of finding answers that can help you better cope with what is bothering you.

This is a particularly useful way to identify any emotional triggers, those things in the outside world that automatically trigger you to feel everything the narcissist has programmed you to feel. There are undoubtedly some left in you after a relationship with a narcissist, but learning them all can take plenty of time and patience. When you want to practice mindfulness, you want to fully understand why you are responding the way you are.

This is a fantastic skill for anyone to have, as mindfulness can aid in controlling emotional outbursts, as well as help lessen stress. It is an incredibly healthy coping mechanism and is absolutely valuable to learn. Mindfulness involves five steps that will allow you to achieve the state of mindfulness. This state is a state of quiet, internal attentiveness. When you are first learning mindfulness, it is best to do so in periods of calmness to master the art before eventually beginning to use it when tensions run high.

Sit down

Step 1 in mindfulness is sitting down or identifying a quiet place in which you can quietly and safely focus on your breathing. Anywhere is acceptable, so long as you can focus and you are comfortable, so maybe try to find a quiet corner in your home, or underneath a tree in your yard. The important part here is that you need to be calm and relaxed wherever you choose.

Choose a time

With the goal in mind, choose how long you are willing to dedicate to your first few attempts at mindfulness. Typically, you are better off starting with a shorter period at first and slowly working your way up to longer ones. Perhaps, for your first time, set a goal of 5 minutes of mindfulness.

Pay attention to your body

Choose a comfortable position and really focus on your body. You want to choose a position in which you feel stable and relaxed, and that will be comfortable for the duration of your mindfulness. Once you have settled in, really start to focus on your body. Attempt to feel every part of yourself, starting at the tips of your toes and slowly working your way up to the top of your head. You should do this slowly as if you were mentally scanning yourself. Pay attention to any areas that are particularly tense and try to relax them.

Breathe

Focus on your breathing. Take one breath in and try to follow the feeling of it all the way into your lungs, holding it there before exhaling, and repeating. Make sure your breaths are deep, cleansing breaths, and really focus on each one.

Keep your mind on track

Any time you feel your mind wandering, quietly put it back on your breathing without judging yourself. Remember how you are supposed to feel compassionate about yourself? This is a good place to start! Particularly, in the beginning, it is easy to get distracted, and that is nothing to be ashamed of. Just regroup and continue.

After completing all the steps, you should feel far more relaxed than when you started. This can be a fantastic tool to use to unwind after a busy or stressful day, or when you feel your temper rising. As you master being able to call yourself to mindfulness when calm, you can begin using it as a coping mechanism when you feel frustrated or stressed out, or any time you start to debate whether returning to the narcissist would really be too bad. Oftentimes, those insecurities are tied to some sort of physical distress, and you should try to let them go as best as you can.

Another trick for mindfulness that some people find works well, particularly when emotions are running high is the 5-4-3-2-1 rule. In this technique, you seek to identify things around you with your various senses, engaging them instead of allowing your negative emotion to consume you, and when you focus on yourself again, you are better able to manage your own reactions in the future.

Sight

First, start by identifying five things around you that you can see. Be as descriptive as possible with yourself if you can be. Perhaps you see a blue ball with a woven texture on the ground, smooth, clear glass on the table next to you, and a sky the color of a clear blue ocean that you dream about vacationing to see. When you have identified five things to yourself, you are ready to move on to your next sense

Touch

Next, focus on your sense of touch. Notice four different things around you that you can feel. Perhaps you feel sand giving way beneath your feet, or a cool breeze caressing your hair. Whatever you feel, try to identify four as specifically as possible. Really feel each one the best you can, and focus on every single detail. Notice how your hair tickles your face when the wind blows it, or how your entire body shifts as the sand does beneath you, compensating for the moving surface.

Hear

You should then focus on your hearing. Listen for three things around you and really take a few moments to hear them. You should pay attention to how they sound, following their melodies and rhythms the best you can. If you hear a bird trilling, focus on how its song rises and falls and how quickly it does.

Smell

Fourth, you will identify two different things around you that you can smell. Do you smell your perfume? What is the scent you have this time? Is it sweet? Musky, do you smell the scents of flowers warming in the sun? Try to identify as many elements of the scent as you can.

Feeling

Lastly, identify one thing within you that you are feeling at that moment. Are you angry? What is that anger doing to your body? Is it speeding your pulse up? Is it making you tense up? If you are sad, do you feel that hollow feeling spreading in your chest? Are your shoulders hunched? Figure out how you are feeling and how it affects your body.

With your mindfulness achieved, you will better be able to deal with whatever emotions your body was reacting to, choosing healthy, rational reactions as opposed to exploding or acting with emotional impulses.

Bettering yourself

As you continue on your journey toward getting over the narcissist, you should put work into yourself. Attempting to better yourself gives you something else entirely to focus on, aside from the narcissist and will keep you busy. You will not have time to worry about the narcissist as much if you pick up a new hobby, such as learning to play the piano. You can even use this hobby to insert into time that you usually spent with the narcissist. For example, if you always spent Friday nights together eating takeout and watching your narcissist's favorite television program that you always secretly hated, you could instead use that weekly allotment of time to work on your new skill. Perhaps you choose this evening time to work on scales or try to learn the new songs your piano teacher has assigned for the week. Maybe instead, you look up video tutorials on how to play all sorts of songs that you listen to that remind you to stay strong.

Ultimately, learning a new skill and bettering yourself can only help you. You will never be worse off if you focus your energy and attention on learning a new skill, but if you use that time to focus on the past, dwell, and mope, you are likely to feel guilty about it later. Overall, it just makes more sense for you to spend that time focusing on things that will better you or can give you some new sense of self-worth to replace the damage the narcissist has done.

Affirmations

One last useful skill to learn when trying to get over the narcissist is learning how to form proper affirmations. An affirmation is a small sentence you use to remind yourself of an objective or goal or to reaffirm your own boundaries. They are usually quite short and are a common part of many different therapies, including cognitive-behavioral therapy, which teaches those who are using it to restructure their thinking. The idea here is to reverse the damage that the narcissist has done to you through all of his cruel words and demeaning comments. You listened to his cruelties for so long that you internalized them, and affirmations seek to do the exact opposite using the same concept. You will repeat your affirmations to yourself so often that you will convince yourself that they are true. Over time, you will begin to believe them, just like you believed the narcissist's disparaging comments. Affirmations have three key parts to them: They must be positive, self-directed, and present tense.

Positive

The reason you want to focus your affirmation on the positive is that it will shift your entire way of thinking. You will feel more positively if you think more positively. This uses the idea that you attract what you think. Think of it this way—in cognitive behavioral therapy; it is recognized that thoughts influence behaviors, which influence feelings, which influence thoughts, and the cycle continues. If you have a positive thought, it will lead to positive behavior, which will create a positive feeling, which will then create more positive thoughts. Positivity breed positivity, and ultimately, that can present itself all over your life. Your positivity will spread throughout your life, starting with that one simple positive affirmation, just as the narcissist's negativity spread through you.

Self-directed

Your affirmation must focus on yourself because ultimately, the only thing in this world you really have complete control over is yourself. When you are talking about yourself, you cannot come up with a way to deny its truth if you are thinking it. By focusing on yourself, you can make it come true. If you say that you will breathe before reacting to tense situations, you have the influence to make that happen. That is the important part here—you make it happen. If your affirmation focused on anyone else, you could not guarantee its validity, nor do you have any control over whether it happens. This makes it difficult to really trust or rely on.

Present tense

The reason for a present tense affirmation is that saying it at the moment prompts it to be true at that moment. If you say that you will do something, it is ambiguous whether that means immediately or sometime in the future. It is easier to sidestep that problem altogether and keep the affirmation present tense.

With these three rules in mind, you are ready to create your affirmations. You take all three aspects and stick them together to create a sentence like:

- I deserve to be treated with respect, dignity, and kindness.
- I am enough the way that I am right now.
- The way I see the world is trustworthy, and I always trust my perceptions of what is happening around me.

Each of these affirmations provides some sort of guidance and prompts you to believe in yourself more. You can create affirmations for virtually any situation that you think would benefit from them, and you should use them whenever you feel they would help. At the very least, make it a point to recite each affirmation to yourself at least ten times a day at the same time every day to make it a habit. For example, you could tell yourself, "I am enough the way that I am right now," every time you sit down in the car to drive to work. Every day, you repeat it several times to yourself, and eventually, that thought becomes just as reflexive and habitual as putting your seatbelt on when you get into your car. This is how you slowly shift your mind from the one poisoned by the narcissist into the healthier one you deserve.

Chapter 11

Living with one, dealing with one

Although it is said that only one percent of the population is considered to have Narcissism, you can encounter Narcissists in many different situations. They are hard to deal with, especially if you are in a personal relationship with them. If the Narcissist is a member of your family or your partner, it is considered one of the toughest situations to deal with. Narcissists often have ulterior motives when talking to someone and sometimes they can even be cruel because they don't really care about the other person's feelings. Let's see what ways a Narcissist can influence your life and tips that you can use.

Dealing with narcissists you live and work with (tips included)

If you are living with Narcissistic parents, there is a fair chance that you will end up as a Narcissist too. Some scientists believe that Narcissism can be passed down through genetics too. Genetic link could be a cause, but more often the reason is the way the child is raised. We already mentioned that Narcissistic parents are not the best at raising children. They usually focus on their own needs and have really high expectations of how the child should perform. The child becomes a reflection of the parent and gives the parent the sought after attention. When we were talking about the consequences of being raised in Narcissistic families, we saw that some of those parents ignore their children, only talking to them when it benefits them in some way. Children live a life full of drama and they learn how to suppress and cut off their emotions. The Narcissistic parent doesn't really understand the feelings that their child is going through, so they just don't pay attention to it, they ignore it, which is why many of these children are ignored and abused. If the child; however, tries to do something that the parent doesn't like, it can end up being a big problem. The parent can belittle and humiliate the child until they agree with the parent. Children raised by Narcissistic parents usually have trouble forming a connection with others because they never formed a proper attitude towards feelings. On the contrary, they shut them down because it wasn't desirable to have emotions that don't meet their parents' needs. They are mimicking the behavior that they saw in their parents because those were their role models. As they were growing up, thinking about others wasn't something that they would even consider. If you think that you were raised by Narcissistic parents, maybe you could talk to a trained professional to help you out. Even if you don't have Narcissistic Personality Disorder yourself, it is good to have somebody to share your worries with.

If you are living with a Narcissistic spouse it can be really hard. First of all, you've spent some time building up a relationship with this person. Then, if the kids came and you even purchased a home, you have basically built up your whole life around them. Many people are charmed by Narcissists without even realizing it because the Narcissist can certainly be persuasive and know how to manipulate the situation to get what they want. Since they are addicted to attention, as long as you give the Narcissist the attention that he wants and he wants to get something from you, the Narcissist is going to be your best friend. The problem starts when he's done needing you or if you start disagreeing with him. If you ever got into a fight with the Narcissist, you probably felt used and demeaned. You later realized that no good agreement came from it and it's because a Narcissist has a way of putting things to his own accordance. You may end up dealing with the Narcissist for a long time, for many years even. They can keep up their charming behavior for a long time and, especially if you are living together, it becomes easy to excuse the Narcissist's occasional destructive behavior as having a bad day at work or believing that you were the one who caused the issue. By the time you realize that you are dealing with a Narcissist, you are already having a long life built around him and it is hard to get away.

If you are living with a Narcissistic friend, it can be especially hard to deal with it. It can be that you've known this person for your whole life and maybe there were some situations that you felt like you should cut that person off because they don't treat you well. And even if you tried to do so, your Narcissistic friend came back, repented, and was even more charming than before. This is a standard Narcissistic technique because that person wants you to give him attention or is terrified by the thought of being alone. That kind of friend will always come back telling you that he's sorry for the way he has acted and, basically, beg you to come back to. If you thought about breaking off a friendship because that person doesn't seem to care about your feelings and you feel like they're using you, you are most likely dealing with a Narcissist. Like any Narcissist, this person is also really good at keeping someone around if they want them. This kind of friend will do and say anything to keep you around to make them feel good, so if you try to break it off with them, they will start behaving awful. While these people can be charming and amazing when you first meet them, they can also be your worst nightmare when they want something. If you feel like you are always being used or you get in big fights whenever you offend your friend, that means that he is a Narcissist and the thing is that during those fights, they can never even take the blame. As long as everything is going according to their plan and wishes, things will go well. But if things start to change and to stray from the Narcissist's plans, that means trouble. If you have this kind of friend, you should consider a way to break off from them. Try limiting the contact. Maybe slowly at first, that can be a small but a good step. You should also consider finding people who will look after you and be there to support you.

If you have a Narcissistic boss or coworker it is can be tricky and it can influence you on multiple levels. If you enjoy the job you do and it happens that you have a Narcissistic boss or coworker, it can be particularly hard to deal with them and you will have to work hard. There are; however, some things that you can do that can make your life easier.

You should try not to take their promises seriously. If your Narcissist boss or coworker wants you to do something for him or her, they are going to sweet-talk you. If you take their talk seriously, you can get disappointed. If you learn how to recognize Narcissists and you realize what they are trying to do, you will understand that as soon as the promise is inconvenient for the Narcissist, they will act like the promise they made never existed You also should never try, and waste your oxygen, telling the Narcissist that he is wrong. From their point of view, they can't be wrong. Never. They believe that they are more superior to others and if you confront them, they will act as an enemy. The best way to deal with them is to just ignore them. Try and ignore their charm too. Like we mentioned several times, Narcissists can be very charming people when they want something. If they can gain something from you, they are going to be your best friend and they will try to use their charm on you. Once the Narcissist gets what he wants, he stops being so friendly and excludes you quickly when he loses interest.

You need to establish who the enablers are. A Narcissist, especially if they are a boss and have gained some power, will surround himself with people who will do anything for him. His endless need for supremacy and desire to manipulate will make him treat other people like puppets for his needs. If you don't want to become one of these people, you will need to establish who the enablers are and to start working with them. This way you will get what you want. For example, if you have a Narcissistic boss and you want a raise, you will ask someone who is close to the Narcissist to help you out with this. This enabler will be even more useful if the Narcissist needs a favor from them.

They say that there aren't many Narcissists in the world; however, as soon as one gets into your life, it can be difficult for you to get rid of them. The Narcissist regularly wants to keep you around so that they can get all the attention they want or they just need you to fulfill another need for them. They will in no way do something for you unless it is going to benefit them in some way. There is never a time when they will do something that will concern you or your well being and they'll never do something for you just because of the fact they are your friend. The truth is that you can use some techniques and strategies to deal with a Narcissist. If nothing else, they will help you deal with them and will make you extra prepared when they come around.

Techniques And Strategies

- You need to determine the type of Narcissist you are dealing with. How you deal with each type is different also. A vulnerable Narcissist, for example, doesn't have the highest self-esteem, but the grandiose Narcissist will push everyone and everything over to get what they want. If you need to make an ally of the Narcissist, the grandiose Narcissist is the best choice, you just need to convince him that the goal benefits him as well.

- You should acknowledge that you are annoyed. It is common that a Narcissist will get under your skin. If you feel frustrated because whenever you start doing something, the Narcissist goes around interrupting you and wanting all the attention, you should admit and acknowledge that frustration. It will help you deal with the Narcissist later.

- You need to appreciate where the behavior comes from. When you understand how Narcissists feel and why they act as they do, it might not help you accept it but it can help you deal with it. If you establish and understand that the Narcissist isn't considering other people's emotions because he is incapable of feeling empathy, it will be easier for you to avoid being caught up with them or influenced by them.

- You should keep your expectations realistic. Narcissists will always have limitations on their emotions. It is important to remember that even if it is fine to enjoy some good qualities that come with a Narcissist. If you learn to accept that their emotions are limited, it will help you to stop asking and expecting something that they can't provide.

- It is especially important that you don't make your self-worth dependent on them! If you do that, it is just going to make you feel bad in the end. People often fall into a trap of trying to make the Narcissist happy. But the Narcissist won't be happy no matter how hard you try. Don't try to confide your deepest secrets and desires to the Narcissist because they won't take it seriously or cherish them and will probably use them against you at some point if they feel like they need to.

- You should try to turn something to their benefit. If you want to learn how to successfully communicate with a Narcissist, you need to understand that you always have to show him how it will benefit him. Talking about your own needs is not going to work with the Narcissist and being demanding or acting angry won't work either. Instead, you should show the Narcissist how you can be helpful to the Narcissist so that they will consider helping you.

To be able to deal with Narcissists requires a lot of patience, learning, and self-management. Since they don't react to situations as most people do, you can't go and use conventional methods to deal with them. While others may be around you or work with you because they feel something about you or because they want to help, the Narcissist is not going to understand how that works. He is going to do things according to his own beliefs which are not based on common behavior.

Dealing with a narcissist you love

When you are in love with a Narcissist, or in a relationship with one, it can be very hard to see what your next steps are going to be. When you deal with the Narcissist at work or if it is your neighbor, you can consider leaving your job, finding a new one, and just stop communication. If you have a friend who has Narcissistic traits, you can just try and find another group of friends. But what to do when the Narcissistic person is someone you've been with for years? Someone who you have kids with and who you love? There are many challenges that people need to go through when they have a relationship with a Narcissist and there are a lot of reasons that they consider too important to break off that relationship.

The hard part is realizing that you are living with a Narcissistic spouse. First of all, you love this person. And what if you have a family and kids with this person? What if you have built a life with them? When you think about it, changing jobs sounds easy. Finding a new group of friends sounds easier too. Still, there are a few techniques and strategies that can help with Narcissistic spouse or partner.

Techniques And Strategies

- You need to be safe, as some Narcissists tend to turn to abuse when they are not able to get what they want, but this is not the case with all

Narcissists. However, if you are dealing with abuse that is a product of Narcissistic behavior, it is time that you finish that relationship.

- You need to give yourself permission to think about yourself and not always be thinking about your partner and putting him first. Narcissists are very good at convincing you to think about them all the time but you need to reconnect with yourself and try to meet your own needs.

- Never forget to remind yourself of your own self-worth! Narcissists always try to belittle you so they can feel superior and have the admiration that they want. You need to find a way to always remind yourself that you are smart, lovable, and deserving; even if your partner might tell you otherwise.

- Learn how to deal with your insecurities. Use all the resources that you can get to help deal with any insecurities that you might have. It doesn't matter if those insecurities were provoked by your Narcissistic partner or if they are something that you are dealing with from before. Your insecurities make you more vulnerable and you need to learn how to overcome them.

- You need to accept that you are not able to change your partner. The main reason for this is that usually, the Narcissist doesn't see a reason to change. He doesn't see a problem because from the way that he sees it - everything is normal. Don't forget that people with Narcissistic Personality Disorder have a twisted image of being normal.

- You also need to accept that that kind of behavior is about the other person. You are not the one to blame and you don't need to feel guilty or try to justify the other person. If you feel like your partner or spouse has Narcissistic traits, you should consider sharing what's going on to a friend or some other person of confidence. You should consider what you see as unacceptable behavior and if your attitude about it has changed since you started to be with your Narcissistic partner. You should also determine if you've been making up excuses for your partner.

- Once you decide what the right boundaries are, tell your partner about it. You shouldn't expect that this kind of initiative will go without consequences. The Narcissistic partner will probably just ignore all your requests and will refuse to follow any boundaries. If you decide to do this, you need to prepare yourself to leave if there isn't anything else that you can do.

If you realize that you are in a relationship with a Narcissist, you need to learn how to accept that you need to end that relationship.

Can a narcissist change?

At this point, the cure for Narcissistic personality disorder doesn't exist. The only way that people with this disorder can get help is through individual, family, or group therapy. However, the most efficient form of therapy for this disorder is Cognitive-Behavioral Psychotherapy (CBT). The reason why CBT is the most successful treatment, is that it helps the Narcissist to understand their negative behaviors and replace their negative beliefs with positive ones.

The Narcissist won't change completely, but he can build more constructive behavior and they can get to the point where they understand the negative effects they cause. Keep in mind that not every Narcissist can change. That is why is important to determine which type of Narcissist are you dealing with, or what type of Narcissist you are. A Narcissist maybe can't change, in terms of science, but he can learn to build more realistic expectations toward others and himself. He can also learn how to relate more positively to other people.

Tips That Can Help You With The Change

- As we already mentioned, keep in mind that different types of Narcissists have a different motivation, thus different ability to change their behavior. Try to determine the type and see who you are really dealing with

- Narcissists don't have an insight into their negative traits; therefore they see themselves as superior that is why it is even harder to make them realize negative aspects of their personality. This is where therapists can help the most. They will make the Narcissist realize the point of view of others.

- This is also associated with the fact that Narcissistic positive self-perception is stronger than others' perceptions and reputation.

- You need to make Narcissists realize that they are Narcissistic since they usually aren't aware of that. In most of the cases, they don't even realize that others don't see them as glorious as they see themselves

- If normal methods don't work, you need to keep in mind that some Narcissists search for help if they feel desperate or anxious. If they face constant failures in their workplace or with their partners, it is likely that they will be willing to go to therapy.

- If a Narcissist is able to acknowledge a weakness, that is also a good sign and he is on the path of recovery, and he will tend to invest more in his personal growth.

- Last but not least, be mindful of the reasons for a Narcissist to change. It is easier to help them if they do it for their own benefit. As you know, Narcissist won't do anything for anyone else, so instead of asking "do it for my sake", consider convincing them that a change of their behavior will benefit them very much.

Conclusion

Thank you for making it through to the end. The next step is to focus on healing and rebuilding your sense of self. Narcissistic abuse can teach victims unhealthy coping mechanisms, such as unwarranted defensiveness, numbing the self to emotional experiences, or self-medicating to dull emotional pain. These legacies of the abuse will need to be confronted, examined, and dismantled in order to free yourself entirely.

If private therapy isn't readily available to you, remember that there are lots of other resources out there designed specifically for abuse victims, adult children of narcissists, and people who have escaped cult-like groups or institutions. Support groups can be immensely healing, whether they are found in physical or virtual spaces. If you're unable to find one in your area, it might make sense to look into starting one up. Narcissistic abuse can lead victims to feel lonely and isolated, even when they are surrounded by love; but internet search data tells us that the problem of narcissistic abuse is indeed widespread. You will never know how many other people understand your experience, and have survived similar forms of abuse, until you reach out to share your story.

No matter who you may turn to in search of validation, never forget to honor yourself in your healing practice. You deserve recognition; you deserve respect; you deserve love. And if others do not offer you these things, you are fully entitled to bestow them upon yourself.

NARCISSISTIC MOTHERS

HOW TO SURVIVE ABUSIVE PARENTAL RELATIONSHIPS CAUSED BY PERSONALITY DISORDERS. RECOVER FROM CHILDHOOD EMOTIONAL CARELESSNESS. A COMPLETE GUIDE TO DISCOVER HOW TO HEAL

HOPE UTARAM

Table of Contents

Introduction..136

Chapter 1 Narcissistic Mothers............................138

Chapter 2 Understanding Narcissism....................150

Chapter 3 Narcissistic Personality Disorder...........168

Chapter 4 Characteristics Of Narcissistic Parents...181

Chapter 5 The Future Of Your Relationship............196

Chapter 6 Narcissistic Mothers And Their Sons.....202

Chapter 7 How To Deal Withnarcissistic Parents....216

Chapter 8 Recovery..223

Chapter 9 Healing From Narcissism....................234

Chapter 10 How Manipulations Influence Your Mindset..243

Chapter 11 Therapy..261

Conclusion..265

Introduction

As a girl that grew up with narcissistic parents, especially my mother, I understand that this is a giant burden to overcome. Understanding what a narcissist is and how they work can help you combat the issues that toxic parents can have on us as adults. As we learn how to cope and work through different strategies, it can truly enable us to become better parents when we have our own children.

In this book, I am going to go over what narcissism is and the traits of narcissistic personality disorder. It can manifest in a variety of ways and there are many signs that you are dealing with a narcissistic parent. In addition, I'm going to discuss the effects that this can have on you as the daughter of a narcissistic mother. We are also going to talk about borderline personality disorders and the consequences that come to you when you are raised by narcissistic parents.

There will also be a discussion on emotional intelligence and how it impacts your relationships. Looking over social skills including what they are and how they can help you deal with toxic people or your toxic parents will also be included. I will give you a good foundation on neurolinguistic programming and how it can help you in positive ways.

On top of all of this, we're also going to discuss Cognitive Behavioral Therapy and how it can be used on a daily basis to help change your thought patterns and the way you deal with people. Lastly, the outlook over how you can protect yourself from abuse whether it is mental or emotional. Knowing how to be a wonderful mother and avoid the narcissistic tendencies that you grew up with is probably one of the most beneficial pieces of this book. On that note, let's get started.

Chapter 1

Narcissistic mothers

Like most mothers, there are many reasons why a narcissistic mother would want to have a child. While they want to love and care for their children, they may also want to have children for all the wrong reasons. They may feel that having children makes them look better in the eyes of other people. Another reason is that it provides them a sense of entitlement. After all, if they are a mother, people should naturally want to help them. Finally, having a child will give them someone who worships the ground they walk on, at least for a few years. However, many narcissistic mothers also wanted to have a child because they always dreamed about it. They feel this is part of their life's mission.

No matter what their reasoning behind their desire to become a mother is, it is important to remember that your mother does love you. You will read a lot of information online that says narcissistic mothers have trouble loving their children. While it looks like this from the outside, the inside of a narcissist is different. The truth is, they love differently because of their narcissism. Until they learn strategies to help control the personality disorder, they will naturally put themselves first. As a child, you should never forget that you are a part of your mother. She cared for you when you were in her womb while you were growing and developing into a soon to be newborn. No matter how the journey has unfolded, there was always love for you in your heart.

No matter how you feel about your mother, one of the biggest steps that you need to take is to recognize that your mother has a diagnosable mental illness. The connections and chemicals in her brain are not the same as they are in your brain. In other words, your mother cannot help that she thinks the way she does. She went through situations in her life which led her to become a narcissist. Of course, knowing this doesn't always make it easier, however it can bring you to a point where you are ready to start forgiving your mother for all the pain and hurt she caused you over the years.

Realizing Narcissistic Personality Disorder is a mental illness is also a big step for someone who suffers from the disorder. Since this book isn't just for children who were raised by a narcissist, but also the person who lives with the disorder, it is important to understand that there is help for everyone. Once you reach the point where you understand that you have a psychological disorder, you can begin to turn your life around. You can start understanding yourself better such as the way you think, why you think this way, and how you can change your method of thinking.

The help that everyone can receive through a therapist is not going to fix everything overnight. It is going to take a lot of time, patience, compassion, and love to overcome the years of damage, pain, and stress that the personality disorder caused. However, the more you work towards creating a better life for yourself, the more you will create a better life for your child. This is something that takes a lot of courage, strength, and is something that you should be proud of.

Signs Of A Narcissistic Mother

There are several signs of a narcissistic mother ("Characteristics of Narcissistic Mothers", n.d.). While I will discuss many of the common characteristics, there is still a lot that will not be mentioned. This is partly because there are dozens of characteristics and partly because everyone is different. While narcissistic mothers will hold some of the same personality traits, there are many other traits which vary from one mother to the next.

Whether you are a mother or child, these signs can be difficult to read. As a mother, you can't imagine you treated your child this way. As a child, it can bring back painful memories. However, in order to overcome the past, you need to recognize the common signs. Not only will this help you further understand Narcissistic Personality Disorder, but it will also help you move toward the future.

She Will Deny Everything

Part of Narcissistic Personality Disorder is placing blame on other people and denying wrongdoing. The biggest reason a narcissist will react this way is because they have a strong need to uphold their best image. Even if people realize they are lying or denying involvement, a narcissist will continue to do whatever necessary to act like they did nothing wrong. As a child, you were often blamed for what your mother did. This is because you were the easiest target to use since you were less likely to argue or speak the truth to avoid receiving her wrath. Furthermore, most children want to protect their parents, just as their parents are supposed to protect them. Even if you didn't receive protection from your mother, you still felt the urge to protect her.

Your Mother Lies to You

Narcissists are known to lie. They do this in order to manipulate or control you to get what they want. They will also lie to themselves. They need to do this in order to make themselves look better in front of other people.

Many narcissists are believed to be compulsive liars, but this isn't necessarily true. Narcissists usually know when they are lying whereas compulsive liars don't always understand they are lying.

It is important to remember that everyone lies at some point in their lives. We also lie for different reasons. While you were often hurt by your mother's lies, it is important to understand this is another part of narcissism. They lie to cover their tracks and avoid looking bad to someone else. They may also lie to try to feel better about themselves. This is especially true for a narcissist who understands their mental disorder and is trying to overcome it.

She Is Manipulative

One of the biggest traits about a narcissist is they are manipulative. A narcissist will use various manipulation tactics in order to gain control of the situation. For example, your mother negatively compares you to one of your siblings, shames or embarrasses you when you don't comply with what she wants or says you are ungrateful and don't care about her.

There are various forms of manipulation ranging from good to bad. A narcissist will rarely use a good form of manipulation such as using manipulation to help someone else hence having an altruistic purpose. For example, when a therapist manipulates you by asking a question in a certain manner, they do so to help you understand yourself better. Negative forms of manipulation are used when someone tries to get you to do something for their own benefit. These are the forms of manipulation your mother will use.

One manipulative tactic is the guilt tripper. There are many examples of guilt trippers. For example, a mother and her son are out discussing whether he should accompany his mother on a shopping trip or go out with his friends. The 13-year-old son tells his mother that he would rather go out with his friends because he can hang out with her at anytime. During the summer, he rarely gets to be with his friends. As he is about to walk out the door, the mother starts using guilt-tripping telling him, "If you really love and care about me, you would spend time with me." Even if the son is starting to understand this is a strategy his mother uses to get her way, he knows that he will feel guilty if he goes with his friends instead of her. He also knows that she will continue to make him feel guilty, even weeks from now about this event. Therefore, he allows his guilt to take over and decides to go shopping with her instead.

If you ever heard your mother use phrases such as "If you knew what I have been through..." or "If you were a good child, you would..." she used guilt-tripping in order to get what she wanted. In reality, she didn't really mean what she said, as manipulators rarely use meaningful tactics to get what they want. She knew this strategy worked on you, so she used it. If you ever stopped listening to her guilt-tripping, then you may have noticed she stopped using it and turned to a different strategy.

Shaming is another form of manipulation which can be used publicly or privately. Today, there are a lot of forms of public shaming thanks to social media. A lot of parents praise other parents who post pictures or videos of their children holding up a sign saying what they did wrong and what their punishment is — this is a form of public shaming. While most of the parents who have done this rarely use this form of discipline, a narcissist will often resort to shaming their child.

Your narcissistic mother might have used the same reasoning to shame you throughout your life or she may have used different reasons. Salem is now 33-years-old and barely talks to her narcissistic mother. She is trying to learn to forgive her mother through therapy but often finds this difficult as she is raising her own two children. As a mother herself, Salem doesn't understand why her mother shamed her so much. This is something Salem could never do to her own daughters. She specifically remembers how her mother would often refer to her as a "bad child" because she was born on a Sunday, which is the day of rest according to God. Salem remembers how her mother would often say, "You already put me through giving birth to you on a Sunday," every time she asked Salem to do something she wouldn't do. She would often use this reason to tell other people how bad her child could be.

Many people refer to public and private shaming as the "Shame Game." Some of the most common reasons narcissistic parents shame their children are to feel superior, weaken self-esteem, gain control, drive someone into self-blaming or self-destruction, manipulate someone into taking responsibility, and isolate them.

The reality about shaming your child is no matter how often you do it, you are emotionally abusing your child. The effects of shaming children in any setting are self-hatred, addiction, self-harm, low to no self-esteem, externalizing or internalizing anger and other negative emotions, fear of intimacy, emotional and physical withdrawal, crippling anxiety, depression, perfectionism, and underachievement.

The self-esteem attack is another form of manipulation. One of the main reasons narcissists use this tactic is to ensure that you believe they are better than you. A narcissist always needs to find a way to keep up their image, whether this is privately or publicly. The most common forms of self-esteem attacks are name-calling, extreme criticism, put-downs, judgments, and labels. Your mother probably said many things to you in order to attack your self-esteem. Some of the most common examples are "Why are you so stupid?" "You will never amount to anything," or "You are worthless." Other types of attacks are not as direct. For example, a narcissistic mother would tell her daughter, "Only girls working the street corner wear those clothes in the daylight."

Another reason that your mother may have attacked your self-esteem was to ensure you wouldn't engage in certain behavior again. For example, if you didn't listen to her, she might have told you that you are "deaf and worthless."

Another form of manipulation is being competitive. Narcissists will turn almost anything into a competition. This can often be a fun game when you are a child, at least until you find yourself losing all the time. One example of this is during the movie Mommie Dearest when the character Joan Crawford, portrayed by Faye Dunnaway, and her young daughter, Christina Crawford, portrayed by Mara Hobel, are swimming in the pool. Joan tells her daughter they should race and she agrees. As the scene unfolds, Joan wins every race against her daughter. Near the end of the scene, Christina gets upset at her mother and tells her that it's not fair she always wins. Joan responds by letting her know she will always win against her because she is bigger and better.

Narcissists will tell their children, "Whoever can do this first, wins!" and always find a way to win. They might even try to be nice by giving you a head start or a warning, but they will still win in the end. If you do end up winning, you will find that your mother becomes irate and might attack your self-esteem in order to gain the upper hand.

The silent treatment is another form of manipulation. This happens when the narcissist withdraws any emotion and forms of communication. For example, a mother who gives her child the silent treatment will ignore them even if they try to ask a question or are in need of something. No matter how often they try to talk to their mother, she will act like she didn't hear them or just walk away.

It's important to note that when she is giving the silent treatment, she is also paying attention to how you are responding. She will pay attention to your facial expressions or gestures as she wants you to feel sadness or fear. She usually wants to see that you are feeling fear of abandonment or rejection. Once you start showing signs of these emotions, she will often start responding to you again. Therefore, one way to end this type of behavior is to disengage and not respond in the way she wants and expects you to respond..

Another type of manipulation is gaslighting or making you feel you're the "crazy one." Before I go any further, I want to say that a narcissist is not "crazy." They have a personality disorder which makes them think a certain way. When a narcissist uses gaslighting as a tactic, they are trying to make you believe they didn't say something, even if you remember them saying it. They will tell you that you said something, which you don't remember saying. They will do this so often that you start to believe they are right and you are wrong. This can make someone feel they are "going crazy."

She Uses Codependency to Control You

There are many children who feel they can never live their own life because their mother is always saying, "I can't live with you so don't leave me." While most parents don't want their children to grow up and leave them, they know it is inevitable and a part of life. They also feel this is a bittersweet moment as they are proud of their children for accomplishing milestones such as going off to college, getting their first full time job, and buying their own home. Narcissists don't feel the same way. They need their children with them, even if they don't act like it, because it's the only way they can ensure control over you. If you leave their home or move away, they can no longer hold control over you.

She Reacts Extremely When Criticized

No matter who you are or how old you are, you are going to receive criticism from someone now and then. As children get older, they will often start criticizing their parents for various reasons. While most parents handle criticism well, parents who are narcissistic will react in an extreme way. For example, they might punish you, yell at you, harshly criticize or shame you.

Chapter 2

----- ❧❧❦❦ -----

Understanding narcissism

To understand narcissism, you need to know what it is in itself. Someone who admires their intelligence or their appearance at an extensive level is someone that is narcissistic. They tend to be extremely selfish and have a sense of entitlement that is not warranted. Narcissists typically have a major lack of empathy and they need people to adore them. They will find this adoration by any means necessary.

It is important to note that simply being arrogant or boastful does not make someone a narcissist. It runs much deeper than that. They want to gain control of those around them and be admired at extreme levels, even when it is unjustified. They will abuse those around them to gain this control. Oftentimes, narcissists don't even realize that they have a problem. This makes treating them and changing their outlook extremely difficult.

Regardless of what age you are dealing with a narcissist can be very difficult. It is absolutely the most difficult when you are a child trying to deal with narcissistic parents. In fact, if you are a young child, it is likely that you won't even know what's going on around you just that you are in a bad situation.

Impacts of a narcissistic parent

The impact that narcissistic parents can have on their children is extreme. It can affect the psychological development of the child. This will play a role in their behaviors. In addition, their attitude, emotions, and sense of ethics may be thrown off. The child of a narcissistic parent will have unrealistic expectations that they are trying to meet. This is almost impossible and can completely change how a child deals with the world.

It is important to understand that pleasing a narcissistic parent is almost impossible. Frequently, as a child, this will lead to them feeling as if they are not seen or heard. Their reality will be totally warped. Children that have narcissistic parents are treated as property rather than a person. Obviously, this is going to have major effects on them as they grow and develop.

With these types of toxic parenting skills, many children that are raised in these types of household are not valued as people. Instead, they are praised or criticized based solely on what they are doing. They don't learn how to understand their feelings, and this can lead to terrible self-doubt. As the child of this situation grows up, this self-doubt will play a major role in all of their relationships.

When you are in a situation where you are rated on how you look or how intelligent you are, it is likely that you won't understand or put importance into how you are feeling. It is a vicious cycle that can, unfortunately, turn the child of a narcissistic parent into a narcissist themselves. Being real is not something that will be taught to the child that is dealing with these types of parents. They will believe that their image is exceptionally more important than their true selves.

Keeping secrets is a big part of the narcissist's ways. In turn, the child will be involved in keeping secrets that will keep their family or parent well protected. They will not be able to find themselves, as they will be totally intertwined with what the narcissistic parent wants. There will not be nurturing and, typically, these children will feel emotionally barren. When a child feels this way, it makes it extremely difficult for them to put their trust into other people. This is due to the fact that they understand that they're being manipulated and used by those that are supposed to love them the most.

As parents, we are supposed to be there for our children, however, it happens the opposite way when a parent is a narcissist. This stunts the development of a child in a variety of different ways. Where they should feel loved and accepted for who they are, they will instead feel as if they're being judged and criticized at every corner. This can lead to some major frustration for the child. They will constantly be seeking approval and love but will likely never be able to find it. Not from their parents, at least.

When you are raised in a home where nothing you ever do is good enough, it is obviously going to impact the rest of your life unless you do some work to correct the damage that has been done. Without a role model for good connections with other people, it is very hard to develop these skills. They won't understand what healthy boundaries in a relationship look like. Oftentimes, children that grow up in these types of situations become exceptionally codependent. They don't understand nor do they learn how to take care of themselves emotionally, physically, or mentally.

The child of narcissistic parents will also continuously seek validation. They won't be looking for it within themselves; they will be looking for it from other people. It gets very confusing for these children as they want to do well and make their parents happy, but they absolutely do not want to do so well that they could be looked at as better than their parent. Narcissistic parents tend to get exceptionally jealous of their children when their children do well at something. This will eventually lead the child to a non-understanding of when they actually deserve credit for their good deeds or achievements in life.

Many children that grow up in a household that has one or even two narcissistic parents will suffer from a variety of different disorders. This can include depression, anxiety, and even post-traumatic stress disorder. Oftentimes, this is seen later in life and it can be extremely difficult for them to overcome. There are ways of overcoming the damage that narcissistic parents do, however, it will take a lot of work.

When you grow up in a household that makes you feel that you are unworthy of love, it is, obviously, going to have some major effect on the person that you become. These children are also frequently humiliated by their parents. This leads to terrible self-esteem issues and a sense of shame even when it is unfounded. Sometimes, the child of a narcissist will become an overachiever as they feel they need to be perfect. Sometimes, it goes the exact opposite way. They will simply believe they can't do anything right, even when it is an area they are excellent at. They will tear themselves down and sabotage any chance of succeeding.

Signs of someone having narcissistic traits

Many people have narcissistic traits; however, this does not mean that they have a narcissistic personality disorder. Someone with this disorder will consistently be worried that someone around them is better than they are or that they will hold a higher status than they do. It's like they are constantly looking over their shoulders to see if somebody is at their heels. They have a hole inside of them that needs to be filled with admiration or a sense of superiority to those around them. They need people to think they are the best looking or the smartest person around.

There are some cornerstone markings of people that have narcissistic personality disorders. As noted, they will have an extreme lack of empathy for those around them. In addition, they seek admiration on a grand scale. Everything they do is bigger and better than everybody else.

Commonly, people that have narcissistic personality disorder will be described as being manipulative, arrogant, extremely demanding, and self-centered. They live in a world of fantasy and they are convinced that, for some reason or another, they should get special treatment from those that are around them.

Typically, these start to be seen during early adulthood. Those that are labeled as having NPD will show evidence of their disorder in multiple facets of their lives. This includes work, relationships, and parenting, just to name a few.

For someone to be labeled as having a narcissistic personality disorder, they must exhibit several different traits that are commonly seen among people that have this mental illness. The characteristics that you should look for are:

- Self-importance on a large scale
- A desire for excessive admiration
- Unfounded sense of entitlement
- Consistent thoughts of heightened success, intelligence, power, looks, or love
- The thought that they are special and are only understood by others that are special
- Consistent exploitation of those around them
- Severe lack of empathy
- Envious of those around them or the belief that they are envied by others
- High levels of arrogance

There are many other traits that help to pinpoint those with narcissistic personality disorders. They usually do not deal with criticism very well at all. This may be shown with bouts of anger or withdrawing from society. It is surprising that people with NPD tend to fail, considering they are typically higher achievers. With their inability to take criticism and fix their flaws, they are frequent failures in situations like work.

Many people find it surprising that those with narcissistic personality disorders are prone to afflictions like drug abuse and other mood or anxiety issues. It is thought that this is due to the fact that narcissists tend to have impulse control issues. They also experience higher levels of shame that encourage other life-disrupting behaviors.

While these traits are for anyone that has a narcissistic personality disorder, this book is here to discuss the narcissistic mother. Some of the character traits of the narcissistic mother may be quite subtle while others will be in your face. Detecting a narcissistic parent can be difficult, however, it can help you survive what they put you through and allow you to lead a more normal life as an adult.

Many of us don't realize what is happening when we are children, and therefore, we must learn to deal with it as adults. Knowing the signs of what growing up with a narcissistic mother can help heal the emotional and mental damage that they have caused. In addition, it can help to ensure that you do not do the same things to your children and that you are able to build healthy relationships with them.

Most narcissistic mothers have some very defining characteristics. They will often shroud negative thoughts about you in terms that are enduring. They pretend that they are thoughtful when realistically, they are being hostile or aggressive. This is a serious form of manipulation. You may have found that your mother criticized you in a way that looked like she was concerned about you. Showing that she only wants what is good for you by tearing you apart is not an example of good parenting.

Narcissistic parents are fantastic with manipulation. They never come out and say that they don't think that you're good enough, but they will not pay adequate attention when you have done something good. You may find that they're always comparing you to one of your siblings. Noting that your sibling did it better or that you need to work harder to be like them.

Oftentimes, they will simply ignore you or say nothing at all when you share your achievements. By comparing you to those around, it will tear you down and make you feel as if you are lacking in the things that make a person good. This is seriously detrimental to oneself worth. You may find that once in a while your mom says congratulations, but the tone of her voice says something completely different. This is a form of training. It will help to keep you afraid and in line making her the superior of the situation every time.

If your mother is a narcissist, she probably also violates personal boundaries all of the time. You will feel as if you are not your own person but simply a piece of her. There will be a lack of common courtesies. This could look like your things being given away right in front of you. This will be done with no reason and you will simply be expected to accept it.

Frequently, narcissistic mothers will do and say things to try and humiliate you. This can be done by talking about you while you're in the room but acting as if you are not there. In addition, you will have no sense of privacy at home. The narcissistic mother will snoop through all of your things. Even keeping a journal will be impossible. Regardless of where you decide to hide it, you can rest assured that she is going to find it. She will want to know any and everything about you so that she can use it against you in the future.

If you live in a family with several children, the narcissistic mother will likely choose one as her favorite. She will also have one that she picks on more than the others. The favorited child will be granted privileges that the other children simply do not get. They will receive adequate care and encouragement instead of being torn apart for everything that they've done. This child can truly do nothing wrong in the eyes of a narcissistic mother. They are rarely at fault even when they're caught red-handed. She will pass the blame on to other children to ensure that the golden child does not have any black marks.

Unfortunately, the child that is favored over the others will likely become a narcissist themselves. They will become so used to winning and never being in the wrong that the sense of entitlement that narcissists have is bread in them as adults. They will not be able to take accountability and they will feel as if they are superior to those around them. The narcissistic mother has built them up to feel this way.

As horrible as it is, a narcissistic mother is never going to take notice of how well you are doing. That is unless she can somehow take credit for your achievements. If she can't, it will simply be ignored or compared to someone who did it better. As always, she has to be the best. If you are the one that will be gaining attention or adoration, it will be simply, shut down. In addition, she will find ways to hurt you over your achievements. This can be simple little digs with words or major punishments for small inadequacies.

If you are finding joy in the things that you are doing, it is likely that the narcissistic mother is going to try to tear that down as well. She truly does not want you to feel happiness. She will always try to bring you down a notch. This can be done in a variety of ways, but every way that it is done is detrimental to child psyche.

You will frequently see that she criticizes you unnecessarily. This is frequently done by comparing you to your other siblings or the people that are frequently around you. Trying to tell her about the bad things that are happening in your life will be impossible. She will commonly take the side of the person that has done you wrong. This is to help her stay in control. It is a simple way of showing you that nothing you say or do is ever going to be right.

Narcissistic mothers are excellent at making you feel or look insane to those around you. Trying to talk to her about the things she is doing will be shut down immediately. She will blame it on things like your imagination or simply tell you that you have no idea what you are saying. There may be denial even when it was an upfront event. She may outright say that didn't happen or state that she doesn't remember it happening. When this continuously happens, it is likely that you will stop confronting her about issues at hand. This is exactly what she wants.

The envy that comes from your mom will be an intense period if she feels that you have better looks than she does, or you have received something of good quality. Her envy will be easily seen. She may simply take it from you or go and get something better for herself. Narcissistic mothers, as awful as it is, oftentimes, will compete with their children in all aspects.

The lies that will be spouted are also numerous. At any given point, you can place bets on the fact that she is likely lying about a situation. Lies are excellent for creating conflict. This is also a good way to gain control. Narcissists are careful with their lies and become extremely good at it. They will spin stories to make themselves right not only to you but all that is around you. She will use words that will allow the lies to go to the wayside if she is specifically caught. There will be no outright acceptance of the fact that she is told a lie, instead, she will use words like "maybe" or "I guess".

As noted, manipulation is one of the favorite choices for a narcissistic parent. This can be done in a variety of ways, but it starts very early in life. You will find that it is to pinpoint their manipulation tactics. This is very unfortunate since manipulation is a major issue with many adults. It is extremely selfish and will be used against you as long as it possibly can be.

Narcissistic mothers tend to be extremely self-absorbed. They are also defensive towards any sort of criticism that may be thrown their way. It can often be shown by an explosion of emotions after being criticized. She will terrorize you for trying to show her that she isn't perfect.

Unfortunately, there is no true cause found for those with narcissistic personality disorders. It develops like other mental health issues. It is likely a complex set of circumstances that leads a person to act this way. Many believe that the environment you are in plays a major role in this disorder. If you grew up in a house with a narcissistic mother, you are more likely to become one yourself. This is especially true if you don't take the time to recognize what is going on around you.

Others believe that it is simply genetic that we inherit these traits and that it is unavoidable without serious work. There are also thoughts that the way our brains are wired could be the link as to why this happens. The way we behave and the way we think definitely play a role in who we are. So, if you are attuned to the traits of a narcissist, it can be easier to develop a narcissistic personality disorder

We commonly see this disorder cropping up in teenagers and those that are entering into adulthood. We may see signs of it in children, however, these typically don't manifest into anything more once the child develops socially and emotionally. This is, unless, the child is growing up around other narcissists and learns that the behaviors of their parents are acceptable.

There are a variety of signs that you may be dealing with a narcissistic mother. Through their behaviors and their parenting style, it can be easy to pinpoint. Once you have the ability to see these things about your mother, it can make it easier to cope with. It can provide you with an understanding of what is going on and help you combat the effects of it. Obviously, common knowledge is power and when you are dealing with a narcissist, it can help ensure that you do not become the same.

One major sign that you are dealing with a narcissistic parent is that they try to live through their child. For the most part, parents wish that their children are going to succeed. The narcissistic mother, however, will have a set of expectations that will benefit their own desires rather than those of their children. They will want their kids to accommodate their personal desires while putting their own on the back burner.

If you find that your mom is frequently threatened by your successes, it is also a sign that they have narcissistic tendencies. Their own self-esteem will be impacted negatively when you do well. When this happens, it is likely that they're going to tear their child down. This will allow them to stay the superior person in the relationship. This can be seen with massive judgment on the child, comparison to others that did it better, rejection of accomplishments, and simply nitpicking.

Another sign that your mother may be a narcissist is a huge self-image. They may be extremely conceited about who they are. Frequently, they do not treat those around them very well nor do they treat them as you would other human beings. They simply see people as ways to achieve personal gain. They will even go to the extent of destroying those around them if it means that they will get what they desire.

The narcissistic mother will try to ensure that everyone around them understands how unique and special they truly are. This is typically misguided and unrealistic. It may be that they believe they are the most beautiful, smartest, or own the best things and they want everyone to know it. They need the attention that will help to boost their ego. They have an attitude that says, "look at me and what I can do".

Manipulation is a major component in the narcissistic mother's arsenal. They are excellent at using the guilt trip to their advantage. Blaming you or shaming you for what has happened is also extremely common. These types of manipulation can be difficult to wrap your mind around. Other ways that they will try and manipulate you is by using comparison. Asking you questions like, "Why aren't you as good of a student as your sibling?" is one prime example. It is common for them to offer love as a reward rather than something that you deserve. They also, conversely, threaten to take away love as a form of punishment.

Narcissistic parents frequently have strict expectations for their children. They focus on the small details and if there is any misstep, they make a huge deal out of it. This can truly impact a child's way of thinking in self-esteem. These parents are also very touchy. They can be set off very easily and tend to become irritated at the drop of a hat. This is all due to the fact that they want total control over their child. They will not react in a typical fashion, instead, they will blow up at the smallest of things.

Possessiveness and jealousy are also pretty good signs that you are dealing with a narcissistic mother. Due to the fact that they want total control over a child's life, they may become jealous at milestones of maturity or independence within their child. This shows them that there is separation and they do not handle it very well at all. They may make you feel guilty for doing well and moving on in life. They want to know that you are always there for them and that you are wrapped around their finger.

These are all a good look at the characteristics and actions of a narcissistic parent. However, you should be aware that there are many other symptoms or signs that you are dealing with a narcissist. Keeping yourself protected and understanding how your parent is treating you is not always easy. When you know what to look for, it can become easier. This will help to ensure that you lead a healthy and prosperous life as an adult and that you get out from underneath the thumb of your narcissistic mother.

Chapter 3

----- ❧✦❦✦❧ -----

Narcissistic personality disorder

Most experts in the field of psychiatry believe that Narcissistic Personality Disorder (NPD) cannot be cured. This means that people diagnosed with it will have the symptoms of the disorder all their lives and will have to continually work hard to deal with the behavioral difficulties caused by the disorder.

Although people diagnosed with NPD might experience relief of symptoms and might learn valuable coping strategies, they will still have some signs of the disorder for the rest of their lives. Also, most psychiatrists don't believe that medication works well to control any personality disorder, especially NPD.

Narcissism is a kind of belief a person has about themselves, that they are unique and more important than others around them. With this belief, they often act in particular ways and will do things to boost their image in the eyes of others.

The belief in their superiority over others is so deeply ingrained in narcissists that they experience many difficulties when dealing with other people as they will often treat everyone else as less important.

Narcissistic Personality Disorder (NPD), therefore, is the term that connotes a type of mental disorder wherein the individual affected has an exaggerated sense of self-importance.

Individuals affected with NPD have a deep need for reverence from others, though they lack empathy for others. Individuals affected with NPD do not present themselves for psychological treatment because they do not see that there is an issue with their conduct, even though they are aware that people around them constantly find them very difficult to deal with.

The criteria officially used for diagnosing Narcissistic Personality Disorder are described in the Diagnostic and Statistical Manual, Version Five (DSM-V). The DSM-V is the book mental health experts use to diagnose mental illnesses.

It is pertinent to note that some people might display signs of narcissistic tendencies but do not have full-blown NPD.

A few criteria for diagnosing NPD as described in the DSM-V are:

A. Antagonism, characterized by Grandiosity, and

B. Attention seeking.

The criteria described in the DSM-V can be explained through the actions of the particular individual suffering from NPD. An individual who is affected by NPD will only think of themselves. Their actions will reveal that they think only about themselves and seek to put down individuals around them.

For instance, an individual suffering from NPD may misrepresent their contribution to a work project while deprecating the commitment of a co-worker to the project. The individual might even steal the ideas of others and take credit for the ideas and actions of others. An individual suffering from NPD must be at the center of the universe at all times.

To be diagnosed with full-blown NPD means that a person must exhibit this attention-seeking behavior both over time and in many different circumstances. They must have exhibited it as a young adult, and they must have grown older without much change in their behavior. They exhibit attention-seeking with their family, at work, and in the community. This personality trait seems stable, no matter who they are with and what they are doing.

A person suffering from NPD cannot have their behaviors explained based upon how old they are. For example, many teenagers act like they are the center of the universe and may exaggerate their actions, but this can be explained as a normal stage in their psychological growth, which they will eventually outgrow. However, a person with NPD will never abandon their teenage behaviors. So for an adult, some acts are not considered normal. This is one of the reasons why personality disorders such as NPD are not diagnosed until a person is an adult.

Someone with NPD will seek attention and have a false sense of self no matter what their state of sobriety is. For instance, a person who behaves like a narcissist while drunk, but is a loving and healthy person while sober, would not be diagnosed with NPD because their behaviors are as a result of the alcohol in their system. Someone with NPD will act like a narcissist no matter what their state is.

Taken as a whole, when someone has NPD, they believe that they are the center of the universe and everything revolves around them and as such, they bear no regard for the feelings of people around them, along with the fact that they will not be empathetic with other people.

People suffering from NPD will do whatever they can to be the center of attention and show others how significant they are to the world. They will continue to show these traits throughout their whole lives. Usually, these traits start to show in their lives during adolescence, and they will carry these traits into adulthood.

It is estimated that up to 6.2% of the general population suffer narcissistic personality disorder and that men are more than twice as likely to be diagnosed as women.

How Narcissistic Personality Disorder Develops

As with any other mental illness or personality disorder, there are different explanations for NPD. The causes of NPD could show up independently or exist along with one another in someone's life; this will then encourage the development of NPD.

The first puzzle piece in the development of NPD is genetics. If a family member had NPD, it is quite likely that children and some other relatives might also develop the disorder. This is because of psychobiology; the idea that the brain and human behaviors are connected. If the brain is genetically wired in one way because of the genes a person has inherited from parents and grandparents, then a person is likely to inherit the genes that caused for the wiring to occur in such a way to create NPD. People who have a genetic predisposition are more likely to suffer from NPD than those without it.

The other trigger for NPD is parenting issues. If a person lives with a parent or in a family situation where they are overly pampered, treated continuously as unique, or given everything they ever ask for without any idea that there are limits, they are more likely to develop NPD. Children need boundaries and discipline, and without them, they will grow up with an unrealistic view of both themselves and how the world works.

They incorporate the belief that they are special and perfect into their worldview.

On the other hand, people who grew up with parents who were especially harsh and never valued anything the child did can also develop NPD. The child develops a defense mechanism to offset the negative and constant criticism that they receive. Think of it like a pendulum swinging the other way. If the parent is overly harsh to the child, the child will start to overcompensate by believing that they are entitled to everything, that they are special, and that they deserve the world, just to combat the negativity that surrounds them every single day. This is generally thought to happen because the child may be overcompensating to try to prove their worth to their parent. They want to earn the parent's love and approval.

No matter which type of parent the person with NPD had, the parental behaviors began while the child was young, generally before the age of three.

A third factor that may be relevant to the development of NPD is society's ideas of who and what is important. For example, the idea that the most powerful, rich, and successful are more important than "ordinary people" has become an ingrained belief thanks to mass media's preoccupation with these types of people. In watching reality TV, people who are self-centered, selfish, and rude to others are idealized, whereas people who are caring and compassionate are often marginalized or completely ignored. Second, people receive more approval from outside influence when they are smarter, more prosperous, or have a higher status. This could cause people to work for this higher status so they can receive the same type of recognition. Last, there is a weakening of the community in our society. Children are not often brought up to believe they are part of something bigger than themselves, which leads to kids having more difficulty identifying with others. A grandiose self-image replaces their ability to empathize.

Usually, however, there is a mixture of both genetic factors and environmental factors, both personal and societal, at work with the development of any personality disorder. If a parent or other close family member has the personality disorder, the child will likely grow up both with a genetic link to get it and in an unstable home environment where the traits are more likely to develop. Because many of the traits have been shown to exist since childhood, it is easy to see why the disorder becomes so challenging to treat.

However, that doesn't mean there are not treatments or options for a person suffering from NPD or their families.

You will, undoubtedly, have heard of the term 'Ego'. It is naturally assumed that everyone has one; although some people's egos are much larger than others. Ego is an idea of your self-worth; in many people, this is a fragile item; easily affected by others and their opinions and views.

Your ego will be built upon your own beliefs and experiences throughout life; if you have always met with success, you are likely to have a bigger ego and be more confident. Likewise, those who often meet with failure will tend to have a diminished ego and be less confident in their abilities. Everything you undertake in life will help to build or diminish this ego; it is a moving, almost living thing, and this is an essential, healthy part of life.

Egoism is an extension of this principle; it believes that all actions and goals should relate to yourself; everything that you do should benefit you and help you to reach your own goals. Moving a stage past this and you become someone with NPD; when the achievement of your goals and the benefit of your actions focuses entirely on you. This should be regardless of the effect on those around you. Egoism is often disguised as kindness and generosity; giving someone else a gift without a reward can seem selfless; in fact, it is often a tool used by someone with NPD to manipulate and gain the support of others; the gift can later be mentioned to ensure a favor is provided when needed. A true egotist will not consider the thoughts of others; their interests lie only in what is good for them.

An ego which centers on your own needs above all others is essential for the creation of NPD. What is perhaps the most interesting thing about this is that it is agreed that someone is born without any ego. At the moment you are born, you do not have any preconceived ideas about the world, yourself, or even any knowledge. All these things are built upon from the moment you are born. Your first instincts will be to reach out and explore the world around you; in a baby, this is done through the senses; sight, touch, smell; hearing, and taste. At this point your ego is simply a reflection of what others think and do; if they praise you and smile at you then you will feel good about yourself, if they do not, you will feel bad about yourself. From this simple beginning, your ego will grow and will be fed by the images and experiences around you. From this standpoint, an egotist or someone likely to have a narcissistic personality is a product of society. Of course, this is a very simplistic approach as there are many other factors which will influence the development of NPD; the exact cause is not known but could be linked to your genes.

The definition of egoism is that the self-belief created by your ego is essential to ensuring you make the correct moral decisions and, therefore, behave by accepted moral standards.

Of course, these standards also extend to assist in understanding the development of NPD; egoism accepts that anyone should put themselves first and this self-belief should motivate all conscious actions; this means that self-interest is an acceptable conclusion to any action, which is exactly what someone with NPD does!

Selfishness is also a trait of someone with NPD; their desires are placed above all others. They see themselves as more important and worthy of success than anyone else, and this becomes a justification for being selfish. Almost everyone has been selfish at some point or the other in their life; it could be hanging onto a vital person because they need them rather than it being the best thing for the person or the relationship. Alternatively, it could be something more straightforward, like taking the last chocolate!

However, the traits of selfishness are sometimes essential in parts of life. Business leaders, in particular, need to put the interests of their company first to succeed. This can even be seen to be essential for preserving the jobs and welfare of their employees. However, putting the company's needs first will also ensure that their own needs are being given priority. The very traits which are essential for business success can start someone on the course to a narcissistic personality even if they do not develop NPD.

The economic acceptance of selfishness as an essential trait if the business shows the complications which arise when trying to establish the parameters and definition of someone suffering from NPD; in many walks of life their behavior will be akin with an extremely successful person. By this logic, selfishness is a desirable and even essential trait for those who wish to succeed.

To be genuinely selfish you need to be devoid of empathy or consideration for other people's feelings; this is, perhaps, the critical point at which someone will change from being considered socially 'normal' and having a personality disorder. Anyone who has NPD will be unable to establish empathy with those around them; this inevitably leads to the ability and desire to manipulate those around you as you lose the ability to respect their feelings or needs. This type of behavior is associated with those suffering from NPD as well as psychopaths.

It must be understood that, as with all personality traits, it is essential to have an awareness of self and to look out for your interests. Being selfish is necessary at times to ensure you stick to your principles, values, or simply to complete a job close to your heart. The crucial difference is understanding the effect this may have on others and choosing to do it anyway, despite the emotional and physical consequences. If you are never selfish, you will never stand up for anything you believe in and will be likely to spend your life following the herd, possibly never achieving your full potential.

It has been suggested that selfishness in adults can be created through a difficult childhood. Any child who has little or no praise or even acknowledgment of their existence is likely to retreat into their world. Some of these children will become recluses and socially inept for life; others will build their fantasy worlds to retreat into and escape the harshness of their life. These fantasy worlds will often revolve around having the control, power, and admiration that they are not receiving as a child. These worlds can be carried into adulthood, and a narcissistic personality will develop as the desire to be appreciated will eclipse all other feelings. Again, this development will be in conjunction with other influences and your genes.

Selfishness is a trait of someone with NPD; however, you can be selfish without having NPD. Aside from the healthy form of selfishness which has already been discussed; most people find themselves being selfish because of the demands and stresses of their own lives; it is not a fundamental desire to hurt others but rather a reaction to your environment. Selfish people tend to come across as selfish, while people with NPD are charming and will appear to fit in well, while being very accommodating. This is because they are manipulating and controlling people around them to obtain their own selfish needs. The difference in personality is both easy to spot and an essential part of the difference between someone who has NPD and someone who does not. After all, someone who truly has NPD will be very concerned with looking good to others; this will ensure they get the help they need to achieve their goals. They will appear trustworthy and unselfish when, in fact, they are the exact opposite; the problem is their charm and charisma will hide their true personality and motivation from you.

Chapter 4

Characteristics of narcissistic parents

Mothers are the foundation for their children's attachment to the world. We all tend to learn from our mothers based on the mode she shields and protect us from harm, nurture us, and cares for us. The potential of a mother to meet our basic needs, validate our pain, tune to our emotions, and provide us with a healthy attachment has a significant impact towards our emotional regulation, attachment styles, and our development. However, this is not the same case for those brought up by a narcissistic mother. One of the major sign about narcissist mother is that they taught you to believe that you are an imbalanced and a crazy one; subjecting to endless doubts about yourself and any feelings that you have about them. The other sign is the constant guilt that never goes away. You realize that maybe something is wrong with your mother but you feel ashamed to even think that way and beat yourself instead. The following are the most common characteristics of a narcissistic mother:

- Everything she does is deniable. She presents selfish manipulations as gifts. She is hostile and aggressive but she presents her actions as acts of thoughtfulness. She fulfills her cruelties with loving terms and she always gives excuses and explanations. For her, all she wants is the best for you, to help you. She will never admit that she thinks you are inadequate but instead, when you tell her you have done something wrong, she counters you with something that was done better by your sibling or just respond with silence. However, she will eventually do something cruel to you to teach you a lesson and ensure you don't get above yourself. She accurately separate cause (the joy in your achievements) from effect (denying you to attend the awards ceremony) in a manner that someone who doesn't live in the abuse will never understand.

She uses comparison as her major putdowns. She keeps talking about how someone else did something wonderful on the same thing you did and the contrast is aimed up to you. She ensures that you are no good without even saying a word and spoil your pleasure by congratulating you in an unhappy, envious, and angry voice making you feel useless. She is completely deniable. Even though it is always possible to confront someone by observing their facial expressions, the way they look at you and their tone of voice, the case for a narcissistic mother is different. She makes sure you fully understand the punishment that will follow immediately if you object any of her opinions which makes you afraid, feeling that you are always wrong, but you can't point out why.

Since her abusiveness is long term and you are always her daughter, you will always find it hard to explain to other people why she is bad. She is always very careful about how she engages her abuses and she is always very secretive. She always makes the right timing for her abusive actions to ensure that no one will hear or notice her abusive behaviors. However, to the public, she emerges as completely different and she will always handle you with concern, love, and understanding. As a result, narcissists usually reports that no one ever believes in them. In other cases, therapists end up siding with the narcissist mother leaving the child isolated and helpless.

• She violates your boundaries. You constantly feel like you are an extension of her. She always gives out your property without even asking, sometimes even in front of you and when you complain, she will confront you that it was never even yours. She expresses opinions that were meant to be yours and commit your time without even consulting you. She discusses you while present as if you are not there. She doesn't respect your privacy; she storms into your bedroom or bathroom with or without your consent. She keeps asking nosy questions, snoops into your conversations, diary, letters, and email. She is always digging into your feelings, especially if they are negative and can be used against you. She is always against your wishes without feeling embarrassment or thought. Every attempt at your past autonomy is strongly resisted while normal rites of passage such as dating, wearing makeup, and learning to shave are allowed after strongly insisting and if you try to resist, you are heavily punished. For example, she can say that "since you have grown enough to date, you can as well start paying for your own clothes." If you try asking for age-appropriate rights, control over your own life, grooming or even clothing, then you are considered arrogant and she ridicules your independence.

• A narcissistic mother also has a favorite. She selects one child, or even more, to be her golden child and the other one, or even more, to be her scapegoat. She offers her golden child with all the privileges as long as he/she follows her instructions and does what she wants. She has expectations that the golden child should be respected by everyone in the family while the scapegoat role is to care for the mom. The golden child will never do something wrong unless it's against her mother's will. However, the scapegoat is always at fault which creates divisions among the children where some consider the mom being wonderful and wise while the rest finds her being hateful. The narcissistic mother fosters the division by lying with blatantly unfair behavior. The golden child takes an active role to defend her mother and perpetuate the abuse indirectly by finding reasons to blame the scapegoat in place of the mother. The golden child aids the narcissist mother with her abuses towards the scapegoat ensuring that she doesn't do it just by herself.

- A narcissistic mother also undermines. She can only acknowledge the accomplishments of her children if she is capable of taking credit for them. However, if they don't benefit her, she diminishes or ignores all the accomplishments or success. Whenever you are at the stage and she can't get a chance to be the center of attention, she responds negatively by trying to prevent the occasion altogether; she misses the event, she leaves the occasion early, she acts as if it is not a big deal, or even leave a negative comment that someone else did better than you even did. She even creates unnecessary fights to undermine you and makes you feel unpleasant just when you are about to make a major move. She will often withdraw her efforts and attention whenever you have opportunities she doesn't like and refuse to do even the very little things to support you. She acts nasty towards things you find joyful and those that are connected to your success which makes you feel useless even if she does not directly say it. She always makes sure that regardless of the efforts you are putting towards your success, she takes you down to peg for it.

- She always denigrates, criticizes, and demeans: A narcissistic mother makes sure that you are aware of all the little things. She thinks less of you as compared to what she does to other people or your siblings in general. If in any case, you complain about mistreatment by someone else, she immediately takes the other person's position to attack you even if she knows nothing about the other person. She never acknowledges your complaints or about those people's justices. All she cares is to make you feel that you are never right. Often, she will say some generalized barbs that are often hard to rebut. For example, "No one could ever put up with the things you do," "you are always a trouble maker," "you are very hard to live with," "you never finish anything you start," "you are difficult to love," "you are always difficult." However, she always complains about herself in a sidelong way. You will hear her complain that everyone is so selfish, no one cares, loves, or do anything for her while you are the only person in the room. This is a combination of criticism and deniability.

Additionally, she will always compliment something they did with someone else; something you participated too, showing you that she didn't like it about you. She will always try to show you how her relationship with other people is wonderful in a way that will make you realize that it is not the same between you two. In this case, the silent message she is trying to communicate is that you don't really matter to her. She ignores discounts and minimizes your opinions and experiences. She meets your insights with accusations, denials, and condescension. For example, while studying, she will ironically say, "I think you read too much." Additionally, she will brush off on whatever you say even on those fields you are acknowledged as an expert. She confronts you with smirks and abused sounding or some exaggerated exclamations and ensures she doesn't listen or do whatever you say.

- She ensures you look crazy. If in any case, you try to encounter her about something she has done, she insults you telling you that you have a vivid imagination. This is common across all sorts of narcissists to invalidate your experience over your abuse. She also abuses you that she can't understand what you are talking about. She pretends to forget about very memorable events denying like it never happened, and when you remind her, she does not admit of any possibility that she might have forgotten. This tactic is referred to as "gaslighting," and entails a very aggressive and exceptionally infuriating behavior that is common across all sorts of narcissists. She undermines your perceptions of reality which kills your confidence in your reasoning power, your memory, and intuition which makes you a complete victim to her. Moreover, narcissistic mothers are always gaslight. You will hear them telling you that you are unstable to listen to some certain things. They refer to you as over-reactive, completely unreasonable, hysterical, always imagining, or oversensitive.

Once she has constructed these false fantasies of your emotional pathologies, she will share them with others showing them how helpless and a victim she is with you around her. She always claims to be innocent and states that she completely doesn't understand why you are so angry with her. In fact, you end up being the one who hurt her and thinks that you need psychotherapy. She claims how much she loves and care about you and would do anything to see you happy but she doesn't understand how. According to her, all you do is pushing her when all she wanted was to help you. She complains that she has sacrificed her responsibilities for your empathy and concludes that something is really wrong about you. She uses this as a weapon to undermine your credibility with her listeners by clearly elaborating how perfect she plays her role as a mother.

• A narcissist mother is also envious. Whenever you get something right, she gets envious and angry which only disappears if she loves whatever it is that makes you successful. If not, she will make attempts to spoil it for you, take it from you or get the same but better for herself. She always makes sure that she is on the right track to get what other people have. Narcissistic mothers envy goes way far to even competing sexually with their daughters or daughters-in-law. They are actively forbidding them to groom themselves or even wear make-up while also criticizing their looks. The envy can also extend to relationships where the narcissist mother interferes with their children's marriage and the upbringing of their grandchildren.

- A narcissist mother lies in numerous ways to coun. Whenever she is talking about something that has some emotional significance to her, it's fair to say that she is lying. It is the only tactic she uses to create a conflict in relationships and between those people she lives with. She lies about her feelings, what they have done, and what other people have said about them. She lies about the relationship between you two, your situation, or even your behavior to make sure that your credibility is always undermined. However, she is always cautious about how and when she lies. To the outsiders, she does so in a deliberate and thoughtful manner that can be covered if confronted. She changes whatever you said to take a negative meaning by putting some dishonest interpretations about what you did. When she engages in something bad, she uses preventive lying and speaks before you say anything. When you finally speak, she confronts you with phrases like, "I already knew it." Since she is always very careful with her lies, you might never realize it.

When she is lying to you, she does so blatantly. She will pretend not to remember the bad things she has done. She lies openly even if what she did was so recent or it's something impossible to forget. When you give in with the lie and tries to make her remember about the issue, then she refers to you as having a "vivid imagination." She will confront you with questions like, "why do you hold onto grudges?" Your conversions are always full of brush offs where she makes you feel useless. She doesn't respect you and at the end of the conversation, she makes it not sound good. Your conversations are only based on one rule; you will never win. She only acknowledges she is wrong on very rare occasions and when she does, she admits deniably. For example, she uses phrases like "might have," "she guesses," "maybe" she has done something wrong. She always trims the wrong action to make it sound good. She uses the phrases out of guilt because she knows very well what she did.

• She wants to be the center of attention all the time: Children are the source for adoration and attention for narcissistic mothers. More often, you find yourself doing some chores in the most appropriate time just because she sees you there. You find that something you didn't have to do that day or that week you have to do it on her demand. She creates outdated occasions just to be at the center of attention such as the memorial of someone who died a long time ago. She opts to be the entertainer so that she can be the life of her own party and will make attempts to distract or spoil when someone else drags the attention especially if it's the moment of her scapegoat child. She always invites herself during moments when she is not welcome. When either of you pay a visit, she requires you to spend the time with her and entertaining her is endless. When you happen to do something without involving her, deprived her attention, or refused to wait for her on something, she ends up being raged, manipulated, or even pouted.

Furthermore, older narcissistic mothers use aging natural limitations like doing things that will make them ill as an advantage. For example, if she is deprived of some foods by the doctor, she will intentionally take them to get ill and hence, drag the attention. When they fall ill, they use all the means they can get to you and demand immediate attention and hence, attendance. She expects you to weep over her pain, pat her hand, rush to her side, and listen sympathetically to her endless pain and how awful it is. This doesn't make you any better though; she subjects you to difficult conditions that could have otherwise been avoided. However, if you fail to give her the attention and the audience she is manipulating, she makes you look bad to everyone and she might even seek legal culpability.

• She is ever manipulating your emotions with the aim of feeding on your pain. The extremely bizarre and sick behavior is common among almost all sorts of narcissistic mothers that their children always refer to them as emotional vampires. Sadism is one of the strategies used to feed these emotions to the children. The narcissistic mother is actively needling you about the things you are sensitive to, she keeps saying or doing things just to wound you, she engages herself in a tormenting teasing manner but shortly, you would see a smile over her lips. For example, she takes you to a 3D horrifying movie and later insults you about your childish cry, and then she would smile delightedly over your hurtful face. In many cases, you would hear the laughter in her voice as she says distressing and stressing things to you. You would then hear her gloating over how she teased you and comfortably share with other people on how it's fun to tease you which are like recruiting them to share in her amusement. She seems to enjoy her cruelties and does not have any second thought about disguising that. She makes it clear that your pain is part of her fun. More often, she comes up with offending topics and probes you about them while closely watching at your reaction.

Additionally, this mode of emotional vampirism entails both a demand that the audience suffers while seeking attention as well. Narcissistic mothers always act as a martyr who takes the form of self-pitying and wrenching. She keeps wailing and sobbing that everyone is so selfish and no one loves her and that she doesn't want to live; she wants to die. She cares less on how her manipulation affects other people which is one of the major behaviors of narcissistic people. She is capable of creating dramas in the midst of other people's tragedies showing how she is suffering.

- She is willful and selfish. A narcissistic mom will always ensure that she wins best of everything. She follows and believes in her own ways and will pursue it manipulatively and ruthlessly even if it will cost her some extra efforts or going past the normal behavior. She makes enormous efforts to win something you denied her even if you were right about her not having it or she demanded it in an unreasonable and selfish way. If you are having a party and notify her to bring her friends, she will make sure that her friends will come even if she had not planned about that. She will lie that you are the one who invited them for you to carry the burden of either giving in or making the decision to embarrass them at your doorsteps. If, for instance, she wants to come over to your house and you refuse, she chooses to call your spouse and ends up being granted the permission. However, she will not notify you and will appear as a surprise which will be a total embarrassment to you.

Moreover, since most narcissist mothers are self-centered and selfish, one of the major characteristic common with all of them is that they are bad gift-givers. They will get market things or hand-me-downs for themselves as presents for you. For example, they can give you their old bicycle as a gift and buy a new one for themselves. They believe that new things do not suit you and argue that you are a quid pro quo. However, if you surprise her with something she likes, then she will probably buy you something of your choice but she will ensure that you realize how it pains her to give you anything. As a result, she might buy you an item and get an identical item for themselves or they can choose to take you shopping, buy you a gift, and at the same time, buy something better for herself to make her feel better.

- She regularly shames her children. Narcissistic mothers always use shaming as a weapon to ensure that their children will never develop constant self-esteem or identity to make sure that they will never become independent enough to live without her approval or validation. She publicly shames her children for not achieving much personally, professionally, socially, or even academically. She shames them with regard to their preferences, personality, dressing manner, lifestyle, friends, partner, and career choices. When her children act with any sense of agency, she shames the following fear that she will lose power and control. As a consequence, she instills a sense of being not good enough regardless of their achievements.

- Narcissistic mothers are marginalized. It is weird thinking that some narcissistic mothers are threatened by their children's success, promise, and potential and confronts them negatively by challenging their self-esteem. A narcissistic mother feels threatened and as a result, she makes some effort to put down their child so that they would remain superior. Some of the examples of a marginalized narcissistic mother include rejecting the success and accomplishments of their children, unfair comparison with peers, unreasonable criticism and judgments, and nit-picking. For instance, a narcissistic mother would confront her offspring with phrases like, "you will never be good enough."

Chapter 5

----- ❧❦❧ -----

The future of your relationship

The future of what your relationship will look like with your mother is ultimately going to depend on you and what you think will be the best for your situation. With that being said, I strongly advise taking a lengthy break from talking to your mom while you heal yourself from her abuse and then ease yourself back into any sort of relationship you might share if this is the path you choose. Attempting to heal from your mom's abuse while keeping yourself trapped in the cycle by maintaining a fairly close relationship, or at least a consistent relationship, during the healing cycle can disrupt your results. You might find yourself constantly getting dragged back in despite how much effort you put into healing, which can leave you feeling extremely poorly about yourself.

With narcissistic mothers there are generally three ways that the relationship can go: you can break away entirely, you can have a small relationship, or you can have a consistent relationship with strong boundaries. What you choose will depend on your chosen coping methods and the level of relationship that you can personally handle without feeling impacted by her abuse. This means that after your break you should slowly build your relationship back up and not exceed what feels right for you, to ensure you do not get sucked into old behaviors that could lead to a complete relapse in your relationship.

What to Do If Your Relationship Must End Completely

The idea that your relationship with your mother might need to end completely can be incredibly painful, especially if you have spent a large portion of your life hoping it would get better. Until this point in your life, you may have been under the influence of the belief that you could somehow contort yourself to make things better and that this would lead to your mom like you more and your relationship is fixed. Unfortunately, this is not real and there is no true hope of your relationship ever being the one that you want it to be, as hard as that is to admit. Believe me, it took me a long time and many relapses in my relationship with my mother to realize that she was never going to be the nurturing, supportive, loving mother that I wanted and needed.

If you find yourself in a position where your relationship must end completely, it might be since your mother's abuse is extreme, possibly on the brink of violent, or causing severe toxicity and trauma in your life. Your mother may be abusive to the point where you cannot have even one conversation with her without her creating a web of abuse, which leads to you feeling like you need to end the relationship completely. In this case, what you need to do is completely cut all ties and keep those ties cut. If you find yourself in a situation where the severity of the narcissism is so advanced that you must cut ties, you must remember why the situation got this advanced. When you find yourself wanting to relapse into a relationship with your mother, you must remember the reason why you no longer have a relationship with her in the first place. If you go back and forth in relationships that are this damaging it can be even more damaging as you begin to experience the trauma from your mother, as well as the trauma from yourself each time you "allow" yourself to get sucked in. This can become a huge point of guilt, and it can make healing even harder, so it is strongly advised that if you make this decision you stick to it.

What to Do If You Need to Minimize Your Relationship

In some situations, you may not need to, or maybe you can't, completely end your relationship with your mother. In this case, it is ideal that you minimize your relationship with her. Minimizing your relationship can look however you want it to look, but ultimately it requires you to avoid seeing or talking to your mother consistently. You might find yourself only talking to her when it's the holidays and you are together at a family gathering, or possibly up to once or twice a month. The frequency of this relationship ultimately depends on you and what you genuinely feel that you can handle with your mother.

This is the area where I fall with my mother. The rest of my family is quite close and I want to make sure that I maintain a relationship with them, which inevitably means that I need to be around my mother from time to time. Aside from these visits, however, I do not contact my mother because it does not feel right for me to do so. I feel stronger when I experience life on my own than I do when I attempt to celebrate with or confide in my mother only to be met with emotional unavailability and abuse. For that reason, this is my best coping method. Even with the minimal amounts of time we see and talk to each other, it still takes immense strength for me to stand strong in my coping methods and refrain from getting sucked into my mother's drama and abuse.

What to Do If You Need to Stay Consistent in Your Relationship

Some daughters will continue to have a fairly consistent relationship with their mother, even after they heal from narcissism. This is often very uncommon, however, as it can be extremely challenging to remain truly removed from the dysfunction when you are still regularly being exposed to your mother and all of her symptoms. The daughters who do find themselves capable of consistently communicating with their mothers and maintaining high-frequency relationships require massive amounts of strength to be able to uphold their boundaries and stay strong. It is incredibly challenging to break the dynamic between the mother and daughter in this scenario because the mother already has it so ingrained in her, and it is all the daughter has known since birth. In these relationships, the mother often knows exactly what to say to push the buttons of her daughter to force her back into the abuse cycle.

Due to the complexity of narcissism and the tact and calculated abuse they dish out, it is important to realize that the likelihood of you being able to maintain a consistent relationship with your mother and heal from her abuse is highly unlikely. If you do attempt to retain this type of relationship, there is a good chance that you are doing so because of her grooming and conditioning to force you to believe that it is required and that you are somehow a bad person if you don't. It may even be due to her smearing you and abusing you if you do try to stand up for yourself and get away from the abuse.

Make sure that if you are going to try this that you strongly consider why you are doing it and that if you must, you constantly work on increasing your strength and boundaries and upholding them in your relationship. You can never let your guard down here, or your mother will see the opportunity and attempt to take advantage of it. No matter how far you may get with protecting yourself, your mother will always be attempting to abuse you throughout your entire life. She will likely even go so far as to use compliance as a way to show you that the relationship can be "all better" to reel you in, just to start the dynamic all over again. You must always be cautious and in control of this relationship, no matter what. For that reason, it is likely going to be far too draining for you to uphold and it is not a good idea to aim for this type of relationship.

Chapter 6

Narcissistic mothers and their sons

A relationship that a man has with his mother is as complicated just as a relationship with a daughter and her mother.

I think that what will happen is as we move forward more and more men are going to have to face what is really at the root of some of the things that they're struggling with. A narcissistic mom is someone who is not capable of attuning herself to her children, so her children are like things she owns; her property and they owe her.

A first specific area of the relationship between the male child and the narcissistic mother is her behavior with all people who have a relationship with his son.

The overt narcissistic mother is aggressive, abrasive, and intolerant. For her everybody else is an asshole, everybody else is stupid especially other women. So, it's a little bit easier to see that this person is narcissistic, but you could have narcissistic moms where it's not so easy to spot.

A covert narcissist mother can come off like she actually really cares about her son and you might not be able to witness or understand that there is a dependency that's being fostered.

In both situations (overt and covert) narcissistic mothers are using their sons for a source of supply.

There is an investment happening, there is an unconscious desire to consume the son and to create a dependency which is to always have a source of supply. So that the son never has the ability to go out and become a separate individual from her.

Narcissistic mother's agenda is to make sure that she's number one, to ensure that this young man never goes out and leaves her. So other women are considered a threat, she'll consider his friends a threat and she'll find something wrong with every person that her son brings in the house. She'll have a problem with his friends' mothers or his friends' fathers, she'll have a problem with every teacher his son has.

Another big trouble is the relationship with her husband and father of her son. Often a narcissistic mom has married a very co-dependent man. She puts him down in front of the children and makes fun of him sexually. Lots of men have witnessed how their narcissistic mothers have battered their fathers in front of them, maybe not in front of neighbors and other family members but behind closed doors definitely.

This is the kind of chaos that happens when you have a narcissistic mother and a father who is co-dependent and has been emasculated and constantly beaten down.

If you're the son of this couple, you probably have no idea how to go up against this type of a personality. You are being abandoned emotionally by this man who has just run out of steam. He goes to work, comes home to be criticized and has to sleep on the couch.

Nothing he does is ever good enough. There's always something to complain about and so you've been abandoned by this man who should be teaching you how to stand up for yourself and not be abused, but that's not happening.

On the flip side of the coin, this is your father whom your mom is putting down and you don't realize that what she's doing is really conditioning you to be afraid, to be like him.

She's trying to make sure that you feel dependent upon her and obligated to her and you have the feeling of disappointment. She's trying to find a way to make sure that you don't do to her what your dad has done to her, which is abandon her, because that's the way she sees it.

Mom needs to know that her son has put her in the center of his life. Therefore, the son of a narcissistic mother is terrified, living in a state of survival. There's also the loss of the self and this is a problem in terms of emotional development.

The young boy is not permitted to feel free enough to explore his environment without fear and so there's a lot of insecurity in the young boy who has a narcissistic mom and that carries over to adolescence when this young man wants to bring home a date.

The mom will find a problem with the date and will actually gaslight the date creating a lot of problems. The son will get the message that the mom is not happy that he brought the girl home. Statements like "That girl only wants you for your money", "That girl's gonna go out and get pregnant by you", or "You're gonna have to support her and some kid for the rest of your life" will be floated around. You could be 12 and that's the kind of crap that your mother will be telling you, so you're getting the message.

It also happens that the narcissistic mothers would always play sick the minute her son wants to go out to play baseball or tell her he has a girlfriend. Mommy would get sick and the boy would have to abandon and prove to his mother that she is number one in his life and this just gets repeated over and over.

There's a lot of fear of disappointing mom. You feel obligated to put her needs first and when you're focusing on trying to please mom, you're losing yourself. When this becomes an issue for you, you don't have the ability to connect to it, so you feel like you have low self-esteem and lack an identity.

Now when you're around other people you feel insecure, you have anxiety, but it's absolutely not your fault.

As you get older, get married and have children, your narcissistic mother will be a problem because she wants to make sure that you understand that she comes first and she wants to make sure that the women in your life and even your children know that mom comes first before everything.

Narcissistic mom will see the women in your life as competitors. Your wife will definitely feel like there's a mistress in the room and even though you are not sleeping with your mom, this energy will be a part of your life.

You will be conflicted if you're not aware that mom is a narcissist and that she's trying to control you and she wants to take center stage and she doesn't really care about any chaos she's creating in your life.

Then if you're not aware of that, you might be confused and might push your wife back because you have all these conflicts and you've been groomed since you're a little boy to worry about mommy.

You might also have tremendous fear about cutting your wife off, which is what your mom wants to do. When that happens, she has gained control over a very pretty primitive fear, which is the fear of being abandoned by the person who created you. That's like death to a new born.

You might not realize that your mother is intrusive, that she talks bad about your wife, that she has no compassion or empathy for you, nor does she have compassion or empathy for your wife. You might not recognize that mom talks bad about everybody. You might not recognize that mom has a difficult time maintaining friendships.

You might not realize that mom has to prove superior to everybody, that mom might have a drinking problem, a shopping problem, gambling problem, or that there might be some underlying addiction that you're not aware of.

And because she has primed you to fear being able to set a boundary, you as the son of a narcissistic mom may have marital problems or relationship problems with females who are feeling this heat from mom.

This tug-of-war in the mind of the son of the narcissistic mothers could be serious. They love their mother who has conditioned them to be afraid too much to let them go. Also, they are struggling with addiction or low self-esteem, or that situation where you feel like an alien in your own skin.

If you are a son of narcissistic mother, you may have tremendous cognitive dissonance. You might love and hate her at the same time. You might have tremendous rage when it comes to women because you're so angry at your mom, but you might not understand where it's coming from...and that rage is valid. This doesn't mean you abuse women or blame your girlfriend, or daughter or the cashier you know at the corner store.

What it means is that as a son of a narcissistic mother, you recognize that you have been abused. It means that you recognize that you have not been permitted to grow, develop and attune yourself to what is right. You have not been permitted to be who you are. You have had your emotions screwed with.

You have been manipulated and toyed with for this woman's agenda and the anger and the rage that you feel is valid and that's why it's important to work this out.

In psychotherapy, it's important to work this out with somebody who gets it right. It's very important that if you're going into therapy you find somebody who is well versed in narcissism, especially when it comes to be the child of a narcissist. This person should be able to allow you to express your anger and rage and to get it all out. You can work it out so that you can be more logical and rational about how you feel so that you can make decisions regarding your future.

It's not your fault if you've experienced co-dependency. Lots of men who have narcissistic mothers find themselves co-dependent. They tend to be the type of men that women walk all over, are afraid of making women angry, attract women who lie and take advantage of them.

There is also another take on this: some of these men end up with high narcissistic traits themselves. Where in some situations, mom has put her son on a pedestal and mom seems very sweet and very coddling and very nurturing and all of that, but there's almost an emotional incest that can happen and mom isn't as overt as another narcissistic mom. She's kind of passive-aggressive in her comments about women. She's passive-aggressive about being left alone but the message is "don't ever leave me, I have to come first". So, she might say things like "that girl's not good enough for you" or "she should treat you better".

But then, what happens could be like a mother-son tag-team and if you're not aware of the enmeshment and the dependency upon mom's approval and need for validation and the way she's manipulating the situation, you make sure that she's the goddess of your life forever.

If you're not aware of what's happening, if you don't know that's dysfunctional and that you have not cut the cord to mom, then when you attract a woman into your life there will be a competition and it will be you and your mother against this woman.

If you are the son of a narcissistic mother, there are so many ways this can play out. If you have an overt narcissistic mother it might be easier for you to see it and you might be able to recognize that your mother turned you against every woman you ever brought in the house and she talked bad about everybody: every man, every woman, every child.

She just infused you with the idea that the world is a scary place because she wants you to be the number one in your life to be and be sure that she always has this source of her narcissistic supply.

A healthy mother knows that it's her job to prepare her child for when she is no longer here on planet Earth. Narcissistic mothers don't care, they feel entitled to exploit you emotionally, they will guilt trip you and make you feel like you're not making the right decisions, they will create great guilt inside of you, great shame inside of you.

It will be difficult for you to make a decision without your mother, so as an adolescent she will beat you down and insinuate that you're not doing anything right. That's the overt narcissistic mother that is easier to see. If you want to do things on your own, she will find ways to gaslight you, she will find ways to insinuate that it is a stupid idea, and she will find ways to clip your wings.

As you grow up and attract females, you will have to find something wrong with every female. If you get married, your mom will be a constant source of pain for you and your wife, she will resent your children, she will resent your wife, and she will resent you.

When you tell her that something wonderful happened, she'll find a way to downgrade it. Her agenda is to get you to worry about her, if you give her any idea that she is being replaced there's going to be an issue. It is important if you're the son of a narcissistic mother, you may feel very conflicted and may have anger and rage if you are not aware of what's going on.

There are adult children of narcissistic mothers who become people-pleasers and doormats for women and they actually will attract women who are abusive towards them, because they won't know how to set boundaries. And it's just a repeat, it's like they marry their mom.

And then there are men who take on narcissistic traits, so they feel conflict with their mother. They felt controlled by their mothers, so their agenda is no woman's going to control me, no girlfriend or wife is going to control me because they're a little bit more aware of how they feel about their mother. They might even hate their mother.

They still might want a relationship with a woman and a sexual relationship even, but they might struggle with conflict because their mother was such a tyrant. There are so many ways this programming can manifest in your life, so it's important that we understand that what happened to us in our childhood because it affects us as adults.

You must understand what has happened to you as a result and you must understand the tremendous consequences that having a narcissistic mother has had.

You have been told that life is scary when it comes to getting married there's always a chance that you could get divorced and there's always a chance that you could be abandoned by a woman.

There is always a chance for abandonment issues to manifest. That's really something we need to heal from especially if we have narcissistic mothers because that fear might cause us to be emotionally avoidant and unavailable. It might cause us to be highly narcissistic because we're afraid of being abandoned.

It's so important that all of us recognize how having narcissistic parents affect us as adults and we have to heal this gaping wound inside of our hearts that has been created by this narcissistic parent.

We have a need to be vulnerable, but we're frightened, we're afraid of being engulfed and enmeshed with. We have a need to trust people, but we don't trust people. We have a need to be loved but we don't love ourselves.

This is what happens as adults and so if you are the son of a narcissistic mother, there is help. The most important thing that you can do is researching and understanding the consequences of what has happened to you.

Understand that if you've had a dad who has been beaten down by a narcissistic mother and haven't seen a man assert boundaries and as a result you don't know how to reserve boundaries with a female or with other people, it is not your fault.

It's not your fault if you have a mom who puts you on a pedestal and now, you're starting to realize that she created a dependency on you so that you would never leave her and no one, no other woman would ever replace her.

When you're starting to become aware of that, you might start to feel angry, and that's normal because your childhood was robbed from you. Your innocence and ability to feel vulnerable was robbed from you.

So, your anger is valid, but that doesn't mean now you go kick the dog or take it out on other innocent females. It means you do your work. It means you figure it out with a wonderful psychotherapist.

You might need to talk to specialists and psychotherapists that are skilled in the area of narcissistic abuse and childhood trauma and those that you feel can attune themselves to you. You have to really think about all of that before you go into therapy.

It's very important that if you're going to deal with the psychotherapist, you deal with somebody who when you interview them you feel like they have the ability to attune themselves to you because what's happened to you is that you have had your feelings completely invalidated and have been marginalized.

You have a great conflict inside of you. You have a need as a man to feel seen right. You have a need as a man to be able to express how you feel truly; feel about your mother in a safe place without being judged.

Your friends could say you shouldn't feel that way about your mother or you could have a therapist saying like you have to forgive your mother. But with the right therapist you can actually learn to set boundaries with other people and know that whether you are in a relationship with someone or not you are enough, that you have your identity, that you have a right to be happy, a right to attune yourself to your innate gifts, and you have a right to joy.

So, there is hope that those of you, those sons with narcissistic mothers, you feel heard. It's not your fault, you were raised by a narcissistic mother and the good news is you can heal. The good news is that you can reclaim your right of a healthy and happy life.

You can learn to love yourself and have healthier relationships with other women, you can attract different types of females. You absolutely must know there is hope for you.

Chapter 7

How to deal withnarcissistic parents

The real trouble of narcissistic parents is that they aren't just selectively narcissistic. A lot of people will rib on their parents for being embarrassing at family get-togethers or for being naggy or needy. However, narcissistic parents far exceed the acceptable realm of embarrassing and annoying parenting to the point of being massively damaging to their child's emotional development. Narcissistic parents make one of the gravest of all parenting mistakes: caring more about themselves than their children.

One of the biggest questions you ask yourself when you've been raised by narcissists and you become sick of their mental games is how you can deal with them now that you're of age. There are a few different scenarios that we're going to look at, but they all are relatively conducive to the idea of moving past the neglectful and hurtful grasp of the narcissistic mother and/or father.

We're going to start tackling this by remembering something we've addressed several times in this book: the absolute necessity of admitting to yourself that your parents are not perfect. One of the hardest parts of moving on from abuse, in general, is to admit that there was a problem in the situation and that, unfortunately, you were not above the horrible and disgusting odds of the universe. It can happen to anyone and, sadly, it can happen to you.

I'm going to propose something absolutely unthinkable to you. Perhaps you don't need to maintain contact with your parents. In the last century, especially in the last half-century, societal attitudes toward parental relationships have changed a little bit. For one, there has started to be a lot more awareness about mental, emotional, and physical abuse. These things which normally went unquestioned or were just seen as a harsh reality of life that wasn't really talked about would eventually start to be seen as major negative forces. There is no longer a societal tolerance for violent or abusive undertones within the family structure.

On top of this, people have also started to see dropping one's parents as a realistic option in response to abusive situations. However, some cultures frown at this notion as most still place an emphasis on maintaining family ties above all else and ultimately holding an extreme reverence for your parents, whether or not they truly deserve it.

Fortunately, though, reality doesn't necessarily contend with this idea, and the notion of dropping contact with abusive parents has started to be seen as a more viable option in today's climate. While it still will get you some weird looks, each generation is increasingly accepting affected people's choice of cutting ties with their abusive or narcissistic parents.

So, in essence, the first thing that you should do to deal with narcissistic parents is to limit the effect that they can have on you as much as they can. Really, this is the best thing to do in general, so much of this chapter will focus on this aspect. The thing is that narcissism ultimately comes down to how one person expresses control over another and how they force the person to validate their image of themselves and their incredibly fragile ego. Therefore, it's not uncommon for narcissistic parents to maintain whatever means they have to express control over you. For this reason, it's important that you get to severing these as quickly as possible.

If it hasn't happened already, you should first and foremost set up a plan. If you're still living with your narcissistic parents, then set up a plan discreetly so that you can move out. There are likely options available to you. For example, if you're currently attending college, you can likely live on campus and have the college subsidize it to one extent or another, or it may even be worth taking out loans for the quality of life improvement that it will bring to you.

The next thing you have to consider is what you currently and actively depend on them for if anything. Are they your lifeline in one way or another? Are they currently handling things like your phone bill or your car insurance payment? If so, you need to incorporate these things into your plan. Estimate your personal costs for doing these on your own and incorporate them into the overall cost of living into the rent prices you're estimating.

The sad truth is that if these sorts of things exist, your parents will hold them over your head if you try to move out. They will threaten to cut them off anyway, so you might as well have a plan for when they do exactly that. If you've already moved out, or you're away for college, and they're still trying to hold some sort of unnecessary control over your life - an example might be refusing to allow you to date in college, or else they'll turn off your phone or quit paying your car payments or refuse to help you with your loan payments - then you need to still assert these things in your plan.

One obvious thing that you're going to need to do is to get a job if you don't already have one. Unfortunately, narcissistic parents often won't allow their children to get jobs because it provides them with a sense of independence and makes them less reliant upon the narcissistic parent. Therefore, you may need to couchsurf with friends until you have enough to get off your feet. If this happens, just recognize that you very well may end up being without a phone or driving without insurance for a month or two, so try to allot for these. Avoid driving if you won't have insurance and plan around the local public transit systems if there is one or try to arrange rides to and from your responsibilities from friends and coworkers.

Really, what you're essentially trying to do is to limit whatever hold that they might have over you so that they no longer have anything to hold over your head. This can be the most difficult part of this whole process, but the reality is that if you're dealing with narcissistic parents, there is very little chance that they will ever come around to realizing that they act in a narcissistic manner. In fact, the chances are pretty good that they're never going to even have the self-awareness to do so. This presents you with a very unfortunate ultimatum that you never really asked for: either you can try to limit the overall amount of interaction that you have with your parents and completely mitigate contact with them - which is the path that's conducive to becoming someday fully healed - or you must continue contact with them and risk always having that narcissistic and toxic presence in your life.

In the end, it's unfortunate, but if you really want to be afforded the opportunity to grow as a person and to start to repair some of the trauma that's occurred over the course of being raised by narcissists, you're going to most likely have to cut them off or severely limit the contact that you have with them.

The sad truth is that they are simply unable to maintain healthy relationships because they have no desire to. No amount of wishing on your end will fix this problem. Moreover, no amount of work on your end or attempts to get them to review how they act or argue them into considering why they are the way that they are is not going to go well for you. The best case is that they manipulate you into thinking that they're going to change and then experience a slow return to form as if nothing ever happened in the first place.

Well, that's not true. The best case, if your parents are narcissists, is that they'll have the ability to look inward at what happens and what causes it within themselves. If they genuinely can empathize with you and are willing to put you over themselves, then there may be some sort of headway made. You cannot, however, rely on this possibility.

Once you've taken account of all of the things that you rely on your parents for, if anything, and have a clear-cut plan along with a backup plan, you can finally start to carve out some sort of forward motion. You need to start acting on your plan and moving towards mitigating contact with your parents or cutting them off completely.

In the beginning stages of this process, they will invariably try to guilt you about what you're doing. For example, they'll say things like "Someday I'll be dead, and you'll wish you hadn't done this" or similarly manipulative things to make you feel bad about cutting them off. They may even send you hateful, threatening, or outright toxic text messages, emails, voicemails, or messages on social media. They may try to worsen your position with any family members that they're in contact with by slandering you and making things up about you.

The most important thing is that, firstly, you take the time to mentally prepare for any of the backlashes that you expect of them and that you take steps to mitigate it before it ever even has the chance to happen. Cutting off a parent or parents is one of the most difficult choices one will ever have to make, but if you want the opportunity to move forward with your life and truly start to deal with the trauma they've inflicted upon you, it may be the only proper way to deal with your narcissistic parents.

Chapter 8

Recovery

You might be wondering why most of this book is about the damage rather than the very important part of the recovery. Going back and understanding what happened is a large and very important part of the recovery. Understanding how and why you experienced your existence the way you did, and the dynamics of narcissistic manipulations, is the beginning of the healing process.

You have to take this journey for yourself, no matter how painful it might be at times. You have to find out where your behaviour patterns came from. Instead of experiencing emotions in an infantile state you'd be able to calm the child you were and take a hold of your reactions and emotions as a grown person.

This journey takes time and effort, but it's worth it. Narcissists are very unlikely to change because they are unable to see how much is wrong with them, but you can change.

Steps to recovery

NO CONTACT

In my case, no contact was an easy choice. But if you are a young person there are other things to consider.

Going away physically is not enough and you have to be well enough to make it on your own. There was a time I was not able to get away because of depression and mental breakdowns.

If you are not in a state to cope on your own you need to recover sufficiently first. It is not impossible. Do not rush into anything. For you there are techniques you can you use to minimise the damage of living with a narcissist.

It might be even more beneficial if you can get the narcissists out of you head even when they are next to you. Remember, it is your decency, your guilt, your good nature that feeds them. If you figure out how they manipulate you, you can prevent it and even manipulate them until you can find a healthier and happier way to be.

Learn about those techniques – for example, the 'observe, do not absorb,' and the 'grey stone' technique.

Learn as much as you can about the disorder. Do not directly challenge the narcissistic parent with what you've learned. It's pointless, and it's dangerous at this stage. Resist the urge, though you might experience strong feelings of anger and hurt.

Remember your target is to get better. Recovery should be your goal, not taking the narcissist down.

Once you know more by using the 'observe, do not absorb' technique, you can see through the manipulation and remain unaffected. Start understanding the reasons they behave the way they do and why you react to them the way you do.

'Grey stone' is about not feeding the narcissist with your emotions. Do not provoke them, though they will try to get the best out of you as you get better.

Do what one should do to get away from any abuser when exhausted and mentally unfit – make a realistic plan of escape, or you might make matters worse. In the meantime, keep on learning about narcissism and about techniques to improve your mental health. Do not try to explain to the flying monkeys what the narcissists are. It is your first goal to help yourself, and once you are healthy you can help others.

If you are an adult child of a narcissist

If you are an adult child of a narcissist, then there is no question: go no contact. Do not try to explain anything to them, just get out. You have your own life, cut any contact and stay away from your dysfunctional family of origin. Nothing is worth the mental destruction they cause. They will end up worse off, and you have everything to gain.

The point I am trying to make is that if you are unable to relax when you are with your family of origin, if you feel miserable because of them, then you don't have to stay. You've been conditioned not to believe your feelings. But if you feel bad when you are with certain people, they are not good for you. If you can avoid it, do not force yourself to be near them out of any false sense of duty or fear.

I cannot repeat it enough: do not explain yourself to the narcissistic parent. There is no point of getting into any verbal arguments. They flourish in it, and you will suffer. Don't fight them directly. They will play the victim, and they are expert manipulators able to feed on any attention, as long as they are in some way still involved in your life.

As long as they have an access they will feed on your emotions. If you have to talk to them, stay distant and do not give them information about yourself. Just say you do not wish to have any contact with them, and that's that.

A win against a narcissist is living a good life.

You have to learn to stick with your truth whether others believe you or not. Covert narcissists are not obvious to most people. Start the healing process and work on a new way of thinking and feeling about yourself.

You are going to meet other narcissists, do not let them in your life. And if you do, you have to employ the 'grey stone' and the 'observe but do not absorb' techniques, and try to get rid of them.

Most importantly, forgive yourself for any mistakes you have made in the past. You survived, and you were under attack ever since you were born. It takes someone with ability, sense, and intuition. Embrace who you are, even when you feel fragile and exhausted.

Forgiveness is often used in a religious sense – forgive those who have wronged you. This is not what I mean. Victims of narcissistic abuse tend to punish themselves for being stupid and not figuring out sooner what the narcissistic game was. This is just a repeat of a bad pattern of thinking. It was never your fault, but forgiving is about letting go and moving on. Embrace and respect yourself.

Do not believe narcissists will change

Once you get away, the narcissistic parent will try to get you back with all sorts of pretences. Don't fall for it, not again. Your toxic family has roles, and everything they do is to push you back into the Scapegoat role. Do not give them any information about yourself and do not try to explain anything.

Other things to know about no contact

As I mentioned before, physically getting away from the narcissists will not heal you alone. No matter how far you go, their poison is inside you. It is just the first step, then you have to go through a healing process. If you come from a narcissistic family you have to rethink the entire value system instilled in you and stop feeling inferior.

And as you break free from the narcissistic illusion and your dysfunctional family, you will experience a lot of hatred coming at you from the narcissistic parent and their flying monkeys. And you will be unfairly judged by people not close enough to know what the real story is. You have to get through it and learn to stay with your truth.

Yes, I know how deep the childhood desire to please is. But think about it: If you are liked by a narcissist, you have to worry. If they hate you, it's because you are doing well and you are no longer playing their sick games.

The same is true of the flying monkeys: they are not worth your time. Move on. Even from close relatives - it is not your job to save them from the narcissist. First of all you have to save yourself.

You have to accept that not all people are good, and not all mothers are good. Most are, and mothers are very important, and this is why the few unlucky ones have to deal with a world of pain.

Beginning the healing process

There are things to keep in mind and things to avoid.

Going back to the earliest memories and reviewing them is a good place to start. It's where your brain will not want to go to at first, but it is a necessary part of the process.

Once you start understanding the damage the childhood abuse did, you are going to feel an overwhelming anger. Be angry, but do not act on it. You will not be in a state to make sound decisions about what to do. Remember, your anger will subside with time.

Do not be afraid to feel your emotions, as long as they don't control you. Be honest and try to verbalise what you feel, because you've been made to ignore your senses and your needs. When you experience overwhelming feelings, put your hand on your chest and say aloud how you feel. This works for anger, and for any other strong emotion. Just saying what you feel reduces it by half.

You have to go through a grieving process, grieving the loss of time and the loss of the hope that you will ever have good, supportive parents. Go through the stages without holding back, till you are ready to let go.

Don't break no contact. Learn techniques to improve your daily life and to combat stress and Complex PTSD.

Love yourself unconditionally, because you are going to make the old mistakes a few more times. It's easy to fall into the old pattern of behaviour when you are stressed and tired. Be very kind and patient with yourself when you do, try to calm the little child inside. Your reactions to your mistakes will make the real difference in time.

As a rule, do not try to explain to people who have never experienced narcissistic abuse. They have to experience it, or be very fine-tuned emotionally, to understand your pain. Other empaths, or people with similar experiences, will understand, and finding a community online to share with is the best thing you can do.

Someone who has never been a victim and is reading this might say that the narcissists are as much victims as the people they destroy, because they had some sort of abnormal childhood. They are entitled to their opinion, but not to telling you how to handle your situation.

If you are a victim of a narcissistic parent, for you and me, there are different rules. Do not ever feel sorry for a narcissist. We have our own disorder, and it makes us a prey for predatory types and users. We are who they are after, because the narcissists cannot take from a normal person as much as they can from us.

How to handle the inner critic

The inner critic is the criticising voice inside your head shaped by the attitude of the narcissistic parent. Once you understand how damaging it is you can change it by catching it as it tries to put you down and consciously changing the message to a positive and caring one.

Be patient. The inner voice was formed in your juvenile years and came with the narcissistic inbuilt position of control. It is formed with the toxic shame to work against you for the benefit of the parent.

To get into the habit and develop a positive inner voice, you have to practice saying positive things to yourself. Develop a mantra that works for you and repeat it when you get stressed.

Try to learn to love all those flaws you used to punish yourself for, love your body as it is. It will take time, but once you manage to shift your mindset you will experience enormous relief and a sense of freedom.

Emotional flashbacks

You might have never heard of emotional flashbacks, but as a child of a narcissist you are more than likely to have experienced them.

Those are flashbacks of shaming and humiliating moments of your past. They can pop up in your head at any time and make your mind re-experience them. From embarrassing moments at school, to traffic mishaps, to social blunders. All those times you failed to perform are coming back in a flash, and that does nothing but feed the toxic shame.

It is something the old part of the brain does, and it's looking for danger. This is why it keeps on replaying those moments you found so distressing again and again.

When you have an emotional flashback, the muscles contract, the breathing becomes shallow, the heart beats faster, and it feels like a sharp burn in the mind and makes you flinch and retreat both mentally and physically.

Some memories are stored in a childlike state, as they were experienced. Others trigger the state of toxic shame that is imbedded in the people-pleaser's mind. Being humiliated is registered as danger in your mind, because it was in the narcissistic family.

Dealing with emotional flashbacks

To combat their effect, learn to recognise emotional flashbacks and acknowledge that you are having a flashback.

Then take a deep breath and bring yourself to the present. Say 'I am having a flashback' aloud if you need to. Put your hand on your chest. Remember you are safe and well now, and that you have a choice how to feel. Those flashbacks are useless and harmful, and they are the result of dysfunction and self-hatred.

Relax your body and be very compassionate to yourself. Consciously examine where it came from, and try to point to the underlying issues triggering the wave of toxic shame.

Without the toxic shame, the flashbacks are just human experiences, and everybody has experiences like that. You are not supposed to be perfect or better than everyone to matter, this was the poison of the narcissistic abuser who shamed you out of your mind. Be compassionate and very nice to yourself.

Eventually, you will move your reaction to the frontal lobe, rethink the danger and react with reason rather than with emotion and fear.

Chapter 9

Healing from narcissism

The effect of emotional and physical neglect from a narcissistic mother can be disastrous if you don't find a way out.

Before you even try to recover from the wounds, you need first to notice that you have a wound to heal and that the wound was caused by the abuse from your mother.

Here are signs that you have a wound to heal:

1. You Can't Overcome Perfectionism

You have the need to do more and more than is healthy and appropriate, or necessary. This means you have the drive to be perfect all the time, even in situations when you just need to be average. This is usually a strategy to cope and survive and is aimed at making you survive and get the reaction you yearn for.

The perfectionist attitude s all about the skills that you have gleaned from your parents, that if you aren't perfect, you won't serve in the family.

The bad thing is that many people teach their children that good parenting is all about pushing their kids to be excellent in all they do.

2. You Can't Say No

You are terrified at the aspect of saying no, even when you know that you don't have the capacity to do something. You know that if you negate what the parent wants, you will be faced with a lot of ridicule and shame. The parents will even go ahead and abandon them just because they have let them down.

3. You Set The Bar Too High for any Task

Accomplishments need to be measurable and easy to handle. If you find yourself achieving something but you feel like you want to take it a notch higher, then you need to get some help.

4. You Feel Like Your Mother

If you say some words and you remember what your mother said some time back, and then you are just like her, you need to get out of the loop. When you grow up in a narcissist abusive relationship with your mother, the behaviors usually rub off you, and you will find yourself behaving like her all the time.

5. You Reject Challenges

If someone has the guts to challenge you, you always make clear that you don't want it or the people don't respect you at all. You start disliking them and rejecting their advances excessively. This means you don't tolerate any competition from anyone.

The emotional journey to healing

Before you can take up the healing process, you will go through various stages of grief that will dictate how things work out for you. Here are the stages.

- Acceptance

You have first to accept that your parent was a narcissist. You have to look back and then know that the parent had limited love and empathy to offer you, and this is why you became the person you are today. This means you realize that there is a problem that needs to be handled before you can heal.

- Denial

Here, you deny that the mother you loved so much wasn't capable of the love that you needed. Remember that as a child, you yearn for the love to survive, which means that if you deny this, then you can start looking at things in a totally different way.

- Bargaining

You have to realize that you have been bargaining with the narcissist mother the whole of your life, both internally and externally. You have been hoping and wishing that the mother could change for the better, but it hasn't worked the way you wanted. You have tried so many things over the years to get back their approval and love with no avail.

- Anger

Once you realize that you have been hurting for so long, you will become angry and upset. You now realize that your emotional needs weren't met by the person you trusted the most and that if things had gone the other way round, you would have been a better person.

You will feel angry at your mother for taking you through a hard time, and you will be angry at yourself for allowing your mother to take advantage of your young mind.

- Depression

This is the point when you feel intense sadness because you have realized that this isn't the kind of parent you wanted, yet you had nothing to do with it. You get resigned to the fact that your mother will never be as loving as you expect her to be. You let go of any expectations you have had for years and then grieve the loss of the vision.

When you go through these stages, you will realize that you bounce from one stage to the other, and if you find that you aren't accepting the fact, you need to go back and try the stage again. This is the only proper way to grieve. Don't go to the recovery stage until you have gone through these stages, and you have accepted that your parent had a limitation. To make it work better, try and journal the feelings you experience. Talk to your loved ones and take care of yourself throughout the whole process.

The solutions to healing

Let us look at the various solutions you need to follow so that you heal your body and mind from narcissistic abuse from a mother.

1. Develop Self Compassion

It might be a huge challenge for some people to develop self-compassion. This is because it might trigger some emotional memories for the people that have been exposed to abuse where compassion was used as a setup for the attack. This can also prove difficult if you grew up in an emotionally neglectful home or never received any compassion.

Developing compassion is a huge deal because, in many homes, compassion might be lacking in some areas. The kid might grow up knowing that compassion isn't something that needs to be part of their lives.

To develop compassion, try to be patient so that you can have that kindheartedness toward yourself. Try to understand what you will say to someone else in a similar circumstance, or what the actions of a friend have helped you in the past.

2. Remove Your Inner shame

Your inner child is always hoping that it will become smart, talented, and helpful, but you don't have to will to hack it. You will keep on trying to win the approval of the parent, which in turn makes you self-criticize yourself.

Because of the constant talks about failure in your circles, you will have an inner child that is hurt and confused. It will keep on critiquing anything you say or do.

Eliminate the shame by trying to be vulnerable to the people around you. As you begin to create connections and develop bonds with the people close to you, you will open up, and things will be better.

3. Learn to Trust Yourself

Try to learn to trust your decisions, opinions, and other aspects that make you a human being. Start treating yourself well because the people that are close to you will not treat you the way you want to be treated. Since you have been in an abusive relationship with a mother, you might end up missing out on the role if proper nurturing.

When you learn to trust yourself, you will be able to trust others as well. You will be able to talk to people the right way and develop the right kind of relationship with them.

Stop rejecting yourself and seek to repair the damage that a parent caused.

4.   Take Care of Yourself

The parent with NPD has made sure you only focus on them and ignore what you can do to yourself. This means you will be conditioned to focus on the external part and then avoid looking deep into yourself. At the end of it all, you will find that you neglect your emotional and physical needs, which in turn leads to failure.

Start the journey towards self-care. Have that inner peace that will make you change your life for the better. Have a list of happy things that you want to do each day to change your outlook towards life.

5.   Educate Yourself

Once you realize that your mother was suffering from NPD, try and learn about the condition so that you know what you are dealing with.

Image: learn about the topic

Knowledge is power, and when you have good information from chat forums, blogs, and books, you will be able to handle the process much better. With the right kind of support, you will understand what you have gone through and what you need to do to heal.

6. Know Your Past Role

You need to understand what kind of role you played in your mother's fantasy. Were you the golden child or were you the scapegoat? All you need to understand is that you have been part of a plot that was orchestrated by your mother, and you need to find a way out as soon as possible.

Once you know your role, you need to work with the other siblings to create a unified front against her. When all of the family members understand what is going on, and they come up with the right strategy, they will be able to handle the situation much better compared to going at it alone.

If you don't trust your other siblings or you aren't united, you will have to find a way to shut down the other members and protect yourself in the process of recovery.

7. Have Boundaries

Narcissist mothers don't recognize any boundaries that you set for them. They see you and the rest of the family as an extension of them to control and manipulate them. Whether you were the scapegoat or the golden child, you need to come up with boundaries and assert them.

Come up with healthy boundaries and make sure they are respected by the mother and other family members.

8. Stop Blaming Yourself

If you have been the scapegoat, you always tend to blame yourself when something goes wrong. You should stop feeling guilty for the things that are beyond your control. Instead, try and find a way to stop blaming yourself and assert your authority.

Chapter 10

How manipulations influence your mindset

Manipulation is one of the main tactics a narcissistic mother will use to control and influence their daughter's mindset. Whether their daughter is an adult or a child growing up, mothers apply various tactics aimed at asserting their control and authority on their daughters.

Here, we discuss various harmful manipulation tactics, what the mother aims at achieving, and how you can identify and overcome them as a daughter.

Tactics narcissist mothers use to manipulate their daughters and overpower them

Children who were brought up by narcissistic parents have gone through a lifetime of abuse. A narcissistic mother lacks empathy and exploits her daughter for her agenda. In most cases, this mother refuses to undergo treatment to move from her destructive behavior.

They expose their children to psychological mistreatment as they bully, manipulate, coerce, control, and terrorize them. The children of narcissistic parents are so traumatized, and they are placed at risk of suicide, depression, anxiety, low self-esteem, substance abuse, and attachment disorders.

Should a daughter of a narcissist mother stay in contact with her mother, even as a grown-up, she would continue to experience the same abuse and manipulation in her adulthood. However, as an adult, you can break away. You can seek treatment, reduce contact with your mother, and seek alternative coping methods.

A narcissistic mother uses different manipulation tactics to control and influence the mindset of her daughter. Here, we discuss the different tactics a narcissistic mother will use on her daughter and tips on coping mechanisms and safe-care for the daughter.

Emotional blackmail

A narcissistic mother has mastered the art of demanding from her daughter in the form of a request. Should the daughter say no or request for time to think through it, the mother puts pressure on her and threatens ugly consequences. If the daughter stands her ground and refuses, she will punish her daughter through silent treatment, sulking, withholding important things, sabotage, and, in some cases, violence.

For instance: Your narcissistic mother may call to tell you that she is coming over for a visit, but because you know her abusive ways and your schedule doesn't allow for visiting, you decline her request. Instead of respecting your wishes, your mother will begin talking about how she took care of you, how you are ungrateful, how she sacrificed a lot to see you where you are, but, now, you have no time for her. At this point, she doesn't care what your reasons are but will disconnect the phone and decide not to talk to you for weeks.

How to cope: You must know you are within your rights to say no and protect your boundaries. You have a right to protect yourself from your narcissistic mother's abusive ways and your family members, as well. Don't give in to her manipulations; allow her to sulk or go silent, and when she is ready, she will reach out. Do not, at any time, allow yourself to discuss your decision, and if she leaves manipulative messages, ignore them until she realizes on her own that she needs to respect your space.

Guilt-tripping

Many narcissistic parents use fear, obligation, and guilt to manipulate their children. This is also what a narcissistic mother will use on her daughter. She invokes guilt in you so that you do whatever she is asking for her good, disregarding your personal needs.

For instance: Your narcissistic mother constantly reminds you that you are getting older but without a husband child. She reminds you constantly that you have an obligation to give her grandchildren. If you dare tell her marriage is not your priority as long as you are happy, she is likely to lash out at you, condemning you for wanting her to die without grandchildren. She tells you that if you cared about her, you would have children. She tells you that all her life, she sacrificed to see you have a family, but you refuse to give her grandchildren. She tells you that it is a shame and a disgrace that you are not married at your age and, worse, you have no children.

How to cope: With this kind of talk, you are likely to feel guilty. Be aware of these feelings and discard them. Evaluate yourself and ask yourself if you have anything to feel guilty and ashamed of. Remember, you have not inflicted any pain or harm to them. You are free to live your life as you please, as long as you are not hurting another person. You have a right to your choices. They may not please your mother, but they are your choices, and you must own them. Live your life on your terms.

Shaming

A narcissistic, toxic mother uses shame to manipulate her daughter. She would demean and belittle her privately and in public. She knows your weakness and uses it to bring you down. This is a very effective manipulation tool. Using the flaws of her daughter to shame her heightens her daughter's insecurities, and for her to cope, she agrees to do whatever the mother asks so that she is not reminded of her flaws.

For Instance: You are having a family gathering, and in the middle of having fun and interacting with other members, your mother picks on you to discuss your weight issues. You may be successful, but that is not enough. She shames you in front of everyone on how you don't know how to take care of yourself, and you will end up dying because of your weight. You know you are overweight, and you have struggled with this for long, but she doesn't care how you feel. She says you are bringing shame to her by looking like a balloon and not being a good role model to your kids.

How to cope: When your mother begins to shame you this way, acknowledge the emotional pain it brings you. If you feel you are becoming powerless under her attack, try your best to remove yourself from that situation and get your power back. Under no circumstances, should you let her shaming tactics work on you. Let her know she cannot shame you anymore, and tell her that if she continues, then you have no reason to see each other again. Remind her you are proud of yourself, and you have nothing to be ashamed of.

Comparison and triangulation

A narcissistic mother likes to compare her daughter with the daughters of other people to keep diminishing them. She wants her daughter to fight for her approval and attention constantly by making her feel she is not good enough. She wants her daughter to form the mentality that others are better than her.

For instance: Your mother calls you to tell you that your neighbor's daughter just made partner in her law firm, and she is getting married. She then adds a remark, asking what are you doing with your life and when are you going to make her proud.

How to cope: Do not allow her petty comparisons stress you. Remember that you are running your race at your speed and doing what makes you happy. Know that she is trying to undermine you. Change the subject or cut short the conversation. Tell her you do not appreciate her comparison and that you are happy for what your neighbor has achieved. Do not allow yourself to get into an argument with her because it will just frustrate you.

Gaslighting

This is one of the most common manipulating tactics mothers use against their daughters, as mentioned earlier. With this tactic, a toxic mother distorts reality and denies any form of abuse if you call her out. With this, she will make you feel you are the narcissistic one for even thinking it.

For Instance: Your mother calls to leave an abusive message for you and even more missed calls. This is because you were unable to do something for her. She decides to keep punishing you for it, and when you confront her regarding it, she downplays it, saying that you are making a big deal out of nothing. She would say she only made one call, and her message was not abusive. She makes you feel like you are the crazy one, and you imagined all that.

How to Cope: If your mother used this tactic often when you were a child, chances are, you suffer from self-doubt. Do not give in to this manipulation; instead, notice when your narcissistic mother's false claims don't match with reality. When you suspect a situation to be abusive, note it down, and seek help with a therapist to identify the problem. Go back and evaluate other gaslighting incidences with your mother, and see them for what they are and not what she tells you they are. Do not cover it up to cope.

Third-party reinforcements

When a narcissistic mother notices her daughter is gaining independence and cannot easily be manipulated, she takes her manipulation further by looking for reinforcement. She will convince a friend that you have a problem and confront you in her presence. When the friend supports your mother, you begin to doubt yourself, and guilt begins to build up. In the end, you end up doing what she wanted despite your own needs.

For instance: When you start working, your mother may ask you for money. If you tell her you don't have any, she might say how she had nothing when you were growing up. She would even ask her friend if she remembers how she had to do three jobs and go without sleep so that her daughter can be happy. With her friend's reinforcement, you begin to ask yourself if you are unfair to her.

How to cope: Be alert on all the tactics your mother will use. If you know you genuinely did not have extra to give her, do not allow her to manipulate you this way. You can only give money if you have extra and out of a willing heart, not out of manipulations. Keep in mind that it was her obligation to provide for you as a child, and she cannot use that to manipulate you.

Becoming a victim

A narcissistic mother will always want to play the victim, even though she is manipulating you. You may tell your mother that you feel she doesn't understand you or empathize with your feelings. Instead of listening, she will turn it around and blame you by saying she has done everything to make you feel appreciated, but you can't get enough. She'll tell you that she goes out of her way to listen and advise you, but you do not listen.

For instance: You try to tell her that you do not appreciate how she uses your flaws to shame you, both in private and in public. Instead of her hearing that, she turns it around to say she has been trying to get you to see how you can improve yourself, but you complain instead. She may say all she wants is your happiness, and no matter what she does, you seem not to see that she means well.

How to cope: Always remember your feelings are valid. See the manipulation for what it is. Shaming a person is not helping. If she wants help, she can ask you how she needs it and walks you through what she is going through, but when she criticizes you and shames you, refuse to be manipulated. Be aware when you start thinking that you had hurt her when it was you who was hurt. See the manipulation for what it is, and refuse to be pushed further.

With these signs, it is easier for you to identify and understand the various ways your narcissistic mother will manipulate you, and you can resist the manipulation. Taking to a therapist is also a good way to cope with the effects of manipulation. Do not keep quiet on the manipulation. When you notice it, call it out and avoid getting intimidated in any way. Always remember, you are the victim, and if you are feeling it, then there is something there.

Why is your mother narcissistic?

Your mother is a narcissist, not because she was born as one but because she was conditioned to become one. Children of narcissistic parents often grow up to be narcissists themselves if they do not realize it and break the cycle. Your mother may have been raised by narcissistic parents and knew that as a way of life.

Narcissism, according to psychologists, is a result of childhood experiences. An adult went through developmental states as a toddler, and their experiences shape who they are now, how they relate to their children, and how they see the world. Toddlers who suffer neglect or overindulgence from their parents will grow up with this same perception of life.

When a child is indulged in everything as a toddler, they grow up without knowing and respecting boundaries and end up being narcissists. Because of their upbringing, they grow up believing the world revolves around them. The same signs found in narcissistic mother could be the same signs her parents showed her.

Here, we discuss why your mother has certain traits and how she developed them into narcissistic behaviors.

- Why does your mother feel superior and entitled?

Superiority complex and entitlement is a major trait in narcissistic mothers. This trait is developed from childhood. There are a few factors that may have contributed to your mother having these traits. If your mother was raised by parents who were overindulging her and giving her everything she wanted, chances are, she developed the feeling that she was entitled to have everything, regardless of the cost. Her parents probably made her feel she was more important than anyone else, so she developed the same attitude. However, it is also possible that your mother was neglected as a child and to compensate for that, she demands attention and wants everyone to realize she is superior. Her aim is not to be ignored, and she has the power to do that to her children because the same was done to her.

- Why does your mother need validation and attention?

If your mother was raised by parents who constantly demeaned her and told her she was not good enough, she would grow up believing she is incapable of doing anything right or achieving anything. In everything that she does, she will want to be validated that she did well because her confidence is fragile and suffers from low self-esteem from her upbringing.

On the other hand, if she was neglected and denied attention as she was growing up, she lives with the constant fear of being rejected and abandoned. She will manipulate her daughter into getting the attention she missed growing up because she feels she deserves it. She will do things, not out of the goodness of her heart, but to be praised and for people to see that she is important.

- Why is your mother a perfectionist?

Growing up being told that she was good for nothing, and being compared to others can adversely affect a child. She grows up believing to receive love; she must be perfect. This demand put on her at an early age is detrimental and results in her never finding satisfaction in anything. She will constantly complain, and as a result, she will also expect the same from her daughter, so she will fault in everything that she does.

- Why is your mother so controlling?

The need to control is a narcissistic behavior common among narcissist mothers. This is derived from their need for perfection according to their standards. It feels logical for them to be in control because of their sense of entitlement. When they were growing up, their mothers ran their lives, so why not do the same to their daughters? They like being in control because it makes them feel important and needed. To them, being in control affirms their authority. In their minds, they believe a mother knows best because their mother told them the same thing.

- Why can't your mother accept responsibility?

A narcissist like being in control, but they never take responsibility for their actions. If something goes wrong, they will apportion blame and claim it is your fault because according to them, you never followed instructions. According to her, her methods are perfect, and nothing goes wrong when she is in control.

If she was raised by a mother who always found fault in her, she will, by extension, find fault in others but never in herself. If they are found on the wrong side of the law; she is not to blame but the police officer. In most cases, she finds power in blaming those who are loyal and close to her emotionally to maintain the façade of perfectionism and control. It is easier for them to blame those close to them because they know you are not likely to leave her, but she has no hold on other people.

- Why can't your mother respect boundaries?

A narcissist is selfish and has an inflated sense of self. She knows where the boundaries are, but she ignores them. To her daughter, she feels you are a continuation of herself, so everything about you belongs to her, too.

It is possible that when she was growing up, her mother invaded her privacy and made friendships with her friends. A narcissistic mother will want to socialize with your friends because she wants everything that you have. It is possible that she was never taught boundaries while growing up, and in the same case, she does not respect boundaries with anyone, let alone her daughter. Should you point it out, she will find ways to manipulate you to accepting her invasion.

- Why can't your mother empathize with your situation?

A narcissist is naturally self-absorbed. No one empathized with her growing up, so she doesn't understand why other people's feelings should concern her. A narcissistic mother doesn't apologize, feel remorse, or feel any guilt.

As she grew up, she knew how to suppress her feelings and realize they were a burden as a child, and she expects the same in her daughter. In contrast, she understands anger, rejection, and threats because she experienced them as well. A narcissist doesn't understand sarcasm. She perceives it as agreeing with what she is saying. She does not understand how to relate to another person's feelings because she was taught how to suppress them, and a show of feelings was a show of weakness.

- Why doesn't your mother understand the logic except her emotions?

Using logic to explain to a narcissist how their behavior affects or hurts you is a waste of time. She may say that she understands, but truthfully, she doesn't. She is only aware of her own emotions and feelings. If a mother had narcissistic parents, she only knew how to be manipulated emotionally but not how to discuss things using logic.

- Why does your mother have a splitting personality?

This is a common trait among narcissists. They can be extremely good or bad in character and also in how they view relationships. They don't accept responsibility for anything bad but are quick to take credit for all the good things.

A narcissistic mother was raised under similar circumstances. She believed the child was to blame for every bad thing, but if the child did well, it was because of her. They think of situations as either good or bad. She is unable to remember any positive things in a person, only the mistakes a person makes.

- Why is your mother so afraid?

Most narcissists have buried fears. They grew up being demeaned, ridiculed, and rejected. Their life revolves around the fear of these things. A mother will want to control her daughter all the time to remain relevant. She is afraid of the daughter being independent because it will mean the daughter can leave them. To her, a daughter being independent is not a good thing because it means abandonment and rejection.

If a mother was rejected and neglected as a toddler, she would always be afraid of being left. She wants to control everything and the lives of her children so that they don't leave her.

On the other hand, a narcissist is afraid of true intimacy. They are afraid that others will discover her weaknesses and imperfections that she knows she has but hides from others. They are afraid to be judged and criticized because it means they are imperfect.

- Why is your mother anxious?

Anxiety is a condition present among most narcissists. Your mother is always afraid something wrong is about to happen. She is likely to accuse her daughter of mental illness or being selfish if she doesn't follow her wishes. She grew up being told if she did not do something, something bad was going to happen. She expects negative consequences for every action and is always looking for ways to divert it.

- Why is your mother ashamed of you?

A narcissistic mother harbors shame. She doesn't feel guilty because she believes she is perfect and always right but shames you at any given opportunity. The truth is she is also ashamed. She feels there is something wrong with her and cover it up.

She shames you to apportion blame for what she feels deep inside of her.

- Why can't my mother be vulnerable?

A narcissistic mother is unable to understand feelings. She lacks empathy and needs to protect herself from hurt constantly. Because of her upbringing, she is unable to view the world from the perspective of another person. Your mother is unable to be vulnerable because she is blind emotionally and feels lonely but covers it up. Instead of showing vulnerability, she will jump from one relationship to the next. She desperately desires for someone to see and understand her pain, but she fears to be seen weak. To hide, they are unable to relate to the feelings of others.

- Why can't my mother be able to communicate well and cope with others?

Communication requires thoughtfulness, and cooperation with others requires a real understanding of other people's feelings. If a person cannot empathize, it is impossible to communicate effectively, as well as be part of a team or cope with others.

A narcissistic mother can completely alter how their daughter thinks and perceives things. Through manipulations, a mother can control her daughter so that she will never be independent. Knowing the different tactics a mother would use to manipulate and control you gives you the power to overcome and strive to establish a healthy relationship with her and with others.

Maybe you have always wondered why your mother behaves the way she does. Understanding where the narcissistic traits originate and understanding how they affect her may be the beginning of healing. It is important to understand the narcissistic personality disorder, not to condemn her but to help her overcome her ways, deal with her insecurities, and develop better relationships.

Chapter 11

Therapy

In this final chapter, we're going to get into all the reasons you should go for therapy. There's nothing but benefits when it comes to therapy, especially as a survivor of a narcissistic mother. Let's begin!

Why Therapy Is Awesome for You

You should see a mental health professional because they are in the best position to help you deal with the pain and trauma from your past relationship with your narcissistic mother. A therapist can also help you come up with the perfect coping mechanisms for you, which will be of immense help when you feel the blues coming on.

A therapist will provide a safe space for you to just let it all out. You can talk freely about how you feel without feeling like you're being judged. Even better, the therapist will help you work out the messy, mixed bag of emotions that have you terribly out of sorts.

Dealing with Depression

Depression is no joke, and as the child of a narcissistic mother, you are unfortunately prone to it. Depression is not sadness. It's more. It's like a dark cloud hovering over you. Everyone sees the sun, but all you see is darkness. You can't sleep right, you don't eat right, you're bogged down by guilt, and shame, and you're wondering if you should even be breathing right now.

Sound familiar? Do not worry. Just see a therapist. The therapist can provide you with the best treatment modality for you, help you heal, and grow past your past. They'll also help you to come up with better ways of reacting to things as they come up, as well as better ways to think about all you have been through with your mother.

Dealing with Anxiety

If there's one thing that children of narcissistic parents are not strangers to, it's anxiety. When you engage the services of a certified psychotherapist, they can help you find your center again, by figuring out exactly what situations trigger your anxiety, and then coming up with ways to handle it. They will help you understand why you feel the way you do, and help you move past the anxiety to a tranquil life.

Dealing with Obsessive Thoughts

You might find it's a battle in your mind when you try to drown out the negative stuff your narcissistic mother has programmed you to believe. You might struggle hard with quieting her voice in your head. Besides this, thoughts about going back to her, among other things can simply refuse to go away. It can be so persistent that you even begin to have dreams about it.

A psychotherapist is your best bet for dealing with these irrationally compulsive thoughts you have. They'll be able to help you dig into the root causes of these thoughts, so you can finally break their hold on you once and for all. In addition to that, your therapist can help you out with better feeling thoughts you can use instead, as well as techniques to quiet your mind and be at ease with yourself.

Helping You with Your Relationships

Because of the harm your narcissistic mother has done you, you might find you're having trouble with your relationships and friendships, either on account of her smear campaigns, or on account of you sabotaging yourself by seeking out relationships and friendships just like the one you had with good old mom. A therapist will help you learn to find and build healthier ones, and show you how to keep them thriving.

Helping You with Your Career

If you find yourself flailing in your career because of your mother, or you're not even sure which career decisions to make because you doubt yourself, there's no one better than a therapist to help you out.

You Deserve to Be Supported

Don't think you don't deserve the attention and support of a therapist. You deserve to have a life that is rich, unhampered by your past with your mother. You deserve to live your life to the fullest. You deserve to be healed. So, please see a therapist. Get the help you deserve, now.

Conclusion

Congratulations on getting to the end of this eBook. This book has been specifically written for you, as a daughter dealing with a narcissistic mother, and as a parent, trying to understand themselves. You may have been struggling emotionally for many years with your relationship with your mother. You felt that something has been wrong, and you need to find a solution. Your life has been a series of painful memories and episodes, and you want to make it right.

After reading this book, it is time to take control of your life. You have lived under the control and manipulation of your mother; you are probably doing it to your daughter, and all your relationships are affected. It is time to end the cycle of narcissism in your family. With the information you have received by reading this book, you can now identify how you relate to your mother or daughter or even your grandchild. It may also help you understand how you relate to other people. This knowledge is going to help you seek help to stop the pain from affecting your lives and forge healthier relationships, moving on.

The book has also given insights to understand that if your mother manipulated and controlled you, she did not always do it intentionally but was suffering from a narcissistic personality disorder. When you know the root cause of the behavior, together, you can seek treatment as a family and forgive one another.

This book also helps mothers check on their behaviors to control how they behave. It is possible that you have been displaying narcissistic tendencies toward your children but never realized it. Through the knowledge in this book, you can easily identify and work on any narcissistic behavior before it escalates and damages your child.

Embrace the lessons outlined here, strive to heal, and look forward to fulfilling healthy relationship with your mother, daughter, children, and partner.

Well, my friend, we've come a long way. I believe we've covered a whole lot on narcissistic mothers, and by this point, you should now know without a shadow of a doubt that you were right to pick this book up. It is my sincere hope that I've been able to open your eyes so that you can see your narcissistic mother for who she really is.

Now you know what she is, and you know what to do to free yourself of her clutches, heal, and move on with your life. However, knowing is only half the battle. Are you ready to act?

Are you afraid? If you are afraid, it is understandable. It's also all the more reason you need to pull the trigger without thinking.

Speaking for myself, all the magical, wonderful relationships and experiences I have had in my life happened as soon as I cut off my narcissistic family. You read that right. Family. Seven kids, two parents. That's a whole other book right there. The point is I do know for a fact that there's nothing like the freedom and relief you feel, once you have worked through all the yucky emotions.

There are times when you might want to go back to her. I get it. But for once in your life, you have got to put you first. Not just for your sake, but for the sake of the kids you'll have, or the partner you'll spend your life with, or the good people who will come to meet in life. It would be awesome if you put yourself at the top of this list - for once.

You can heal. Are you ready to? Then seek professional help, and do what needs to be done. All survivors of narcissistic parenting will be rooting for you. You've got this. I hope that one day soon, you will be sharing your own story of freedom, and because of your story, other daughters and sons who are suffering because of their narcissistic parents will have the courage to walk away and claim their lives back.

TOXIC RELATIONSHIPS

Understanding all types of toxicity will help you to find freedom.

Learn to set guidelines with parents and people.

You will learn to live a much more mentally healthy lifestyle

HOPE UTARAM

Table of Contents

Introduction..273

Chapter 1 Comfortable with not knowing.......................287

Chapter 2 Causes of toxic/Negative behavior.................298

Chapter 3 Setting boundaries...302

Chapter 4 Moving on..311

Chapter 5 Acceptance..317

Chapter 6 The roots of suffering.....................................324

Chapter 7 Free at last...331

Chapter 8 The toxic termination process (TTP)..............351

Chapter 9 Exercises to try..368

Chapter 10 Public and private images of narcissists......380

Chapter 11 A narcissistic mother's daughter..................387

Chapter 12 Beating the narcissists at their own game....394

Chapter 13 Statistics on narcissistic personality disorder
....405

Conclusion..416

Introduction

You will learn how to know about toxic relationships. How to know if your relationship is toxic. What to do about toxic parents and family.

Learning which of your friends and acquaintances are toxic and how to deal with them. If you have tried everything you know to do and still nothing happens, then it is okay to walk away.

Toxic relationships

Most of us have encountered a toxic person at one time in our life. These people are the ones that never fail to make you feel horrible about yourself. They do or say something that is serious about you. You might be in the best mood you've been in for a long time, and that one person says a sarcastic remark. It gives you a dirty look. They might have accused you of doing something to them or someone else that you would never do.

They have a knack of ruining your mood, your life, and your day. If you so much as challenge the way they think, they will blame you and everything immediately becomes your fault.

You soon realize that once you have spent time with them, you will feel lousy. You are emotionally drained. You feel sick. You might sometimes experience being physically sick.

That's how people become known as toxic. A simple definition of toxic is poisonous. That makes these people poisonous to you. Now take it a step further. A simple definition of poison is any substance that results in injury to an organism or can destroy life. So, by these two definitions, toxic relationships could end your life because they can be extremely poisonous to you.

Toxic relationships are dangerous. They are depressing, irritating, obnoxious, and annoying. They could get your fired. They could ruin your reputation. They can bring down your spirits. They will chip away at your self-esteem. They will destroy any relationship you try to have. You will throw you into a deep depression. They will make you sick. You might start having panic or anxiety attacks, and your life will become miserable.

You are probably wondering how you can recognize these toxic individuals. Honestly, they are easy to spot. They will make you feel so bad just by being near them. You might have met someone and immediately knew they were toxic. You could sense their toxicity. Toxic relationships can be any size, shape, color, or age. Some toxic relationships might be hard to see at first, but with time, their true self is revealed.

We all have those toxic relationships that have dusted up with their poison. At times, we've been drenched. Difficult people are usually drawn to reasonable people. Some of us have had at least one person who has us bending like barbed wire trying to please them. Guess what, we never ever get there.

The damage they can do goes back to the way they sugar coat all responses to make you think you are the one who's wrong. They will make you question your tendency to misinterpret, oversensitivity, and over-reacting. If you are constantly hurt or changing your behavior when you are around them, then you are not at fault, they are.

Learning their harmful behavior is the first thing you need to do to make them stop hurting you. You can't change what they are doing, but you can change how you react to it. You can show them that they aren't getting away with hurting you anymore.

There are lots of things these toxic relationships try to do to manipulate situations and people to help them. Knowing the different types of person can help you from falling under their influence.

Here is a list of the various types of toxic relationships and descriptions of their characteristics.

The Psychopath: This person has absolutely no conscience, compassion, sympathy, or empathy. They don't feel remorse or guilt. They never learn from their mistakes and delight in seeing others suffer. They are very charismatic and charming. They can cast a spell over you before you know it. You will be drawn to them and their lies before you realize who and what they are. They will appear to be good, but in all reality, they are pure evil. Every one of these people has two different personalities. One is nice. The other is evil. They can do massive amounts of damage everywhere they go, even possibly killing of others. These people are very abusive to their children and wives.

The Pathological Liar: This person will lie about everything. Lying is normal life for them. If they get caught in a lie, they will just tell a different one to cover up. They are capable of looking you right in your eyes and tell you a bold face lie without even blinking. They will walk away smug knowing you believed them.

They will lie to you before they apologize. There is no use in trying to argue with them. They will twist their stories. They will change what happened and retell it so that they start to believe their nonsense.

Don't think you are wrong just because you apologize. To move forward, you don't have to apologize. Just go on without them. You don't have to surrender to them. You don't have to keep arguing either. There just isn't any point. Most people would rather be right than be happy. There are better things to do than argue.

The Emotional Wreck: Everything is high drama with this person. They are constantly upset about something. Their thinking is way too extreme to think about life correctly. They blow everything way out of proportion. They are usually an emotional basket case. Their life is just one crisis after another. If they don't have a crisis at the moment, they will invent one. They talk about it constantly and won't ever be interested in yours, just theirs.

These people will be nice one day, and the next day you will wonder what you did to upset them. There's usually not anything that caused the change in their attitude. You just automatically know that something is off. They could be cranky, cold, sad, or prickly if you ask them what's wrong. Their answer will usually be nothing. They will have a bit of an attitude with their answer to let you know that there is something wrong. This position could be shown by a raised eyebrow, a heavy sigh, or giving you the cold shoulder. If this happens, you could find yourself doing whatever you can to make them happy. You might even find yourself making excuses for their behavior. Now can you see why this works to their advantage?

You need to stop pleasing them. These people figured out that decent people will go to any length to keep these people happy. If you are doing everything in your power to make these people happy, then it is time to stop. Walk away. You can come back if the mood shifts. You aren't responsible for everyone's feelings. If you have done something unintentionally, then ask them about it. Talk to them about it. If you need to apologize, then by all means do. You should never have to guess what you have.

They will make up reasons as to why your news isn't good news. If you get a promotion, they will laugh at the amount of money you will be making. If you save money to go on vacation to the beach, they will make a snide comment about how hot it will be. It doesn't matter what you have accomplished in your life; they will find a way to make it sound less than it is. Do not let them bring you down to their level. You do not need to get their approval, or anyone's approval, ever.

The Joker: These will be the loudest people in the room. The make silly and crude jokes about others. They think they are funny. But in all reality, they are pathetic people. No one likes their sense of humor. They tell off-color jokes, at everyone's expense. They do this to take the attention off of them and their failures. This gives them the confidence they lack.

Mr. Negative: These are the most unpleasant people to have around you. They will find fault with everything and everyone. They have no joy. You might find yourself in a good mood, and they will do whatever necessary to bring you down. They always complain about everything and everyone. They have tremendous feelings of insecurity, jealousy, and hate.

Instead of owning their feelings, they will act like them are yours. This is called projection. They are projecting their feelings onto you. Someone that is angry but won't admit they are angry might blame you for being mad at them. It could be a subtle question asking why you are angry with them.

You will soon find yourself being on the defense and going around in circles. Know what emotions are yours and theirs. If you find you are defending yourself from their accusations, they are projecting their anger onto you. You do not have to defend, justify, or explain yourself. You do not have to deal with accusations. Just remember this.

The Moocher: This person is always asking to borrow anything and everything you have including cash. They will have memory loss when it comes time to pay back the loan. They will never make up for the favor.

Debbie Downer: This person is always in a bad mood. Debbie Downer will go to great lengths to stay in their bad mood. They will broadcast to anyone that will listen to them. This is all they will talk about. Every single negative thing that has ever happened to them. They will talk about what is happening to them and what could occur in the future. If you try to cheer them up or give them positive feedback, all they will have to say to you is "I agree, but..."

If you are trying to fix something that is important to you, Debbie Downers will bring up details from six months ago. They bring irrelevant information to the conversation that will confuse you and again make things look like it's your fault. You will find yourself defending yourself once again instead of dealing with what needs to be addressed. It always ends up being about what you have done.

The Slanderer: This is the most toxic. They will destroy lives and reputations with their lies. They constantly talk about everyone behind their backs, and this includes you.

We all mess up now and then, but the slanderer will let you know that you have. The judge you and dig at your self-esteem to make you think you are less just because you've made a mistake. You are allowed to be human and mess up now and then. If you haven't done anything to them personally, they have no reason to judge.

The Blackmailer: This person works hard to gain your trust and learn all your weaknesses and secrets then they will exploit you if you ever cross them. They are jealous of you but will pretend to be your friend. During all this time, they are making their plans of how to bring you down. They will appear to be trustworthy, but they are just the opposite. They will hold your mistakes over your head and threaten to tell your secrets to everyone if you don't do what they want. These people are very dangerous.

The Arguer: These people like causing fights. If there is a group discussing a certain topic and everyone agrees, this person will be the devil's advocate to get an argument started. They then sit back, smile, and enjoy the show. They will always ask a hateful question that will get a fight started. They are waiting for the moment to state an opposing view and reveal their agenda. When you get upset and try to defend yourself, they state that you are just too sensitive.

The Bully: This person gets an exhilaration out of threatening and intimidating others. They typically bully a person in front of a lot of individuals. They strut around knowing they are the center of attention. The look they get when they are bullying is very scary. You never know how far they are going to take the bullying or if the person being bullied is going to get hurt.

The Manipulator: These people always have a hidden agenda, and it's called control. They will think ahead and plan how they will manipulate someone to get their outcome. They will also confuse the situation at hand. Their malicious manipulations are evil and cunning.

You will hear you never or you always from these people. You cannot defend against this kind of manipulation. These people will draw on that one time you did something wrong. Do not get sucked into this argument. There is no way to win. And you don't need to.

They will always find a way to make you choose between them and what you need to do. You will always feel like you have to do for them. These people wait until you have a prior commitment and then they pounce. The problem is that no matter what you do for them enough is never enough. They are going to make it seem like it is always a matter of life and death, but chances are it won't be.

If you start to feel that you are the only contributing factor to your relationship, you are right. These people will send out a vibe telling you that you owe them something. They also find a way to take a thing from you that will hurt you. Then say to you to point blank that it is for your benefit. This is very common in relationships or workplaces where there is no balance of power. Like telling them, you left all the filing for them because they need the experience. Or inviting people for a dinner party and then expect your best friend to do all the cooking because they are a chef. You don't have to do anything for anybody. If it doesn't feel like it's happening for good, it isn't.

The Runaway: These people after having an argument with others, decide they are not going to pick up the phone to talk about it. They refuse to answer emails or texts. You will find yourself replaying the argument over in your head. You will start to second guess your relationship. You wonder what you did to upset them. You will even start to wonder if they are dead, alive, or ignoring you. This can all feel the same. People who truly care don't let you feel like rubbish without trying to sort it out. It doesn't mean it will get sorted out, but you will at least be trying. This is a sign of their commitment to the relationship when they leave you guessing for a long time.

The Mocker: These people might sound sincere, but their tone says much, much more. Asking someone what they did today can mean so many different things just by the way it was stated. It might say that you thought the person didn't do anything again today. It could convey that you thought their day was better than yours. If you ask them about the tone, they will get defensive and make the comment of it was just a simple question. When in all reality, it wasn't.

You may just be trying to get an issue resolved or clarify something, and in the blink of an eye, the conversation has taken a turn for the worse. It has moved from the matter to the way you are talking about it. It doesn't matter it was intentional or not. You will soon find you have to defend your words, gestures, tone and even the way your stomach moves as you breathe. I know that doesn't make sense. It doesn't need to make sense, but it does to them. Meanwhile, your need is gone to the big pile of unfinished conversation that grows bigger every single day.

Knowing how a toxic person usually will react to you make your radar sharper, and you will be able to spot them easier. If you know how to spot a toxic person, you might keep yourself from being sucked into their world. You won't have to tie yourself in knots to please them.

There are some people that no matter what you do, you can't please them. You will find that some people just aren't a good match for you and most of the times that has nothing to do with you. Don't be afraid to say no to crazy. Be confident in who you are, your quirks, your faults, and what makes you shine. You do not need anybody's approval. If someone is working overtime to manipulate you, then it is because they need you. You do no need them.

If these individuals are your families as your children, spouse, sister, brother, father, or mother, then it will be serious to you.

Do you remember what Jesus had to say about these people? He told his disciples to pick a town and preach the gospel. If the town chose to accept the disciples, everything was good. If the town decided to refuse the disciples and Jesus' teachings he told the disciples just to go on and don't worry about what the town had to say. Jesus told them to go where people would listen to them and take his teachings to heart. They did not need to jump through hoops to get people to listen.

This goes for the toxic relationships in your life. You are who you are. Your real friends will not treat you badly. You can just be yourself when you are around them. You don't need to pretend to be anyone else. You can do what you want and say what you want without fear of being manipulated, put down, or criticized. You can do this because they are not poisoned to you.

The main point is you absolutely cannot associate with the people who are trying to destroy you. They are destroying your happiness, peace, joy, and well-being without even using a weapon.

The best thing to do for these toxic relationships is to pray for them. Ask God to remove all the wickedness from the hearts and remove the crust from their eyes. Pray that they will be born again so their old ways can get replaced with a spirit of kindness and love. You cannot change them yourself. They are run by a darkness that belongs to the Devil. If they choose to follow Christ, the will see you as a friend. If they don't decide to follow Christ, they will see you an enemy. The Devil's goal is to destroy, steal, and kill. That is the same thing toxic relationships are doing to you. You and you alone can stop it.

Chapter 1

Comfortable with not knowing

Narcissists crave admiration and praise. You'll often see them fluttering about social gatherings with a smile plastered across their face, and with more than enough friendly chit-chat to go around. They're exceptionally talented at winning the hearts of acquaintances and friends with their charm and amiable demeanor, and they often take the spotlight at most parties and get-togethers.

With that, you might say that it's a bit of a challenge to find the narcissist, especially because many of us wouldn't think ill of someone who seems so well-adjusted in public spaces. In fact, there are times when those charming people we come across are really just friendly and charismatic, which doesn't necessarily indicate narcissism. So how can you figure out who the vampires are?

Keep these definitive markers in mind:

They're initially likable

If you're meeting a person for the first time and you're worried they might turn out to be a narcissist, it's important to consider their likeability. At first glance, a narcissist can be incredibly friendly and fun to be with, offering great insight and wonderfully spontaneous conversation.

This is a common trait they all manifest because narcissists thrive on admiration and praise. They want to be noticed for their good qualities, so they'll put their best foot forward whenever meeting new people. Whether or not they get to maintain a relationship with you doesn't really matter – what they want is to make sure that everyone they come into contact with feels the same way about them – and that is that they're really friendly and likable.

Giving every new friend and acquaintance the same face creates a consistent image across all their contacts. Everyone they've ever talked to or dealt with has the same thing to say about them. So that must mean it's true, right?

If you've met someone who's just all rainbows and butterflies, does that confirm that they're a narcissist? Not really. There are some really well-rounded and well-adjusted people who are just naturally kind, friendly, and interesting, without any strings attached. What this simply means is that if you do meet someone who seems exceptionally likable, just keep your guard up and watch out for other possible signs.

Conversations always circle back to them

Narcissists might seem like great conversationalists, especially if you're not necessarily guarded against them. But if you've got a heightened sense of narcissism in others, one thing you might notice is that all those great conversations somehow always manage to circle back to them.

You could start out talking about your cancer-ridden mother, and then suddenly find that you're talking about the narcissist's holiday getaway from last year. You could try to segue to your summer vacation plans, but you'll soon realize you're once again talking about their new kitchen remodeling project.

Oh yes, a narcissist can keep the conversation going because they like talking. But what you need to know is that they're mostly interested in talking about themselves. So as that conversation just keeps on going, you might realize that you've come to learn almost their entire history and all the great achievements and experiences they've had, with little room to interject with stories you want to share.

They'll overshare about others

As you continue to talk to these narcissists, you'll notice that they know quite a lot about other people, and they won't be afraid to name drop. So even if you just met a few days ago and you're not too close to each other yet, you'll hear them dropping gossip about common people in your circle.

For someone who's not necessarily on the lookout for narcissists, all the juicy secrets could be reason enough to keep coming back and become even closer friends. After all, this is a likable, seemingly reliable person. So, they seem like a great source for this kind of information.

But, be wary. Often, narcissists get this information by talking directly with the people they gossip about, the same way they talk to you. Their friendly outward nature allows them to tap into the trust and comfort of others, so lots of people often feel safe sharing their secrets with these pretenders.

Whether or not your new friend is a narcissist, it's important that you guard your secrets since you can never tell who's willing to drop sensitive information that you share in confidence. With narcissists, the atmosphere of trust that they create can make it exceptionally easy to lay down even the most private details of your life. They can use this information later to degrade your image to common friends, and thus heighten their own 'polished' appearance.

Issues with envy

A common recurring theme that narcissists tend to talk about is envy. It's brought up in one of two ways: that there are people who are jealous of them, or that they're jealous of other people. When they express jealousy, however, it might not be as overt. This ties in with their tendency to talk about people behind their backs.

When a narcissist feels 'threatened' by someone else's assets – whether their career, good looks, financial status, or achievements – they'll likely try to water down that person's image and make them 'look bad.' In effect, they take out their competition, and win the crown as the most 'successful' or 'admirable' person in the lives of their friends and family.

For instance, Cristina who feels threatened by her sister Isabel's accomplishments might talk negatively about her behind her back. She might tell their cousins or common friends that Isabel is struggling through a problematic marriage, and that her children are defiant and destructively disobedient.

Most of the time, these 'half-truths' are simply inflated and made out to be much worse than they actually are. For example, the marital problems might be nothing more than the typical husband-wife banter that Cristina accidentally overhead during one of her visits. The 'defiant children' might have been a one-time occurrence when Isabel's eldest arrived home a little later than had been agreed.

Despite being partially untrue, she will continue to share this information with the common friends and family members they have in order to give the idea that Isabel's life isn't all that perfect. This deflects the praise she would have received, and thus makes Cristina look far more balanced and pleasant in comparison.

In a lot of ways, narcissists also tend to feel that others are particularly jealous of them. That's why they'll commonly use the statement "... because they're jealous of me," when trying to justify the actions of other people.

For instance, in the example above, Isabel might fire back at Cristina for spreading rumors about her personal life, to which Cristina might reply, "You're only acting this way because you're jealous of me. I don't have to deal with the same problems you do."

Incessant need to be right

We all know when to step down and back off, especially if we're wrong. If you happen to stumble upon a narcissist, though, they might insist on being right even when they're explicitly mistaken. It doesn't matter if the topic of debate is unimportant or trivial, these people will refuse to accept defeat in all of its forms.

Narcissists will showcase aggression when trying to prove a point and will muscle you into agreeing to what they say to avoid being made to look 'wrong.' Even with all the facts laid out in front of them, they will continue to hold their ground. If all else fails, they might end the conversation with a cold, "Whatever you say. What I know is that this is the truth."

Revels in being elite

Narcissists fancy themselves to be better than most, and that gives them the status of an elite. They'll strive to rub elbows with the high, the mighty, the rich, and the famous in order to be considered one of those folks. That's why they often end up in leadership roles because they're assertive, aggressive, and incredibly confident in themselves.

In a lot of ways, it does them good because they often have fulfilling careers and high paying jobs. On the downside, they might have stepped on a few people to get there, without feeling sorry for the damage they dealt.

During conversation, narcissists might keep drawing attention to certain status symbols that exude their elite status. New cars, a new home, children in prestigious, private schools, close ties with successful people, and just about anything else that might make you think, "Wow, this guy is minted!"

A fault-free existence

Have you ever tried to blame a narcissist for a problem or a bad outcome? Consider yourself lucky for making it out alive. These people refuse to accept the blame for anything, because, well, 'they're always right.'

As a result, you'll notice that most bad things that happen in their lives are always pinned on others around them. They're quick to blame even the closest family and friends for all the things that go wrong but will throw a fit and fight anyone who tries to do the same to them.

Even when their narcissistic ways put their relationships in hot water, they'll choose to simply toss that person out of their lives in order to avoid having to claim defeat. That's just how they roll.

People are dispensable

Doesn't matter who you are – friend, family, husband, children. Everyone is dispensable to a narcissist. These people have no problem cutting ties and throwing people away if that means they get to stand their ground and maintain their image.

In some families, a narcissistic parent might completely cut out a child if he or she refuses to follow their parent's desires. 'Disobedient' children that make the parent 'look bad' are liabilities to their image and threaten to destroy the narcissist's exterior shell of perfection.

So, to prevent family and friends from branding the narcissist as an ineffective parent, she will likely cut off the child and perhaps make up a story to wash her hands and put the blame on her estranged kid.

This is common in families with narcissistic parents because they see their children as 'extensions' of themselves. That said, they demand that their children act a certain way in order to maintain their clean, wholesome, and admirable image. Anyone who steps out of line threatens that and is thus unworthy of being part of the family of 'elites.'

A need to control

Since they're 'right about everything,' isn't it only appropriate for them to take the reins on almost every situation around them, whether or not it's actually their place to call the shots? In the example of Jocelyn and Angela, this is a narcissistic quality that's made easy to perceive.

Narcissists need to control everything around them because they feel that they're better equipped to handle any and every situation. They'll call in a plumber just to take the tools and get the job done themselves. They'll dictate the directions from the backseat because the driver is just a little too dense for their liking. They'll take on any chore or task even if they don't want to just to prove that they can.

In families, a narcissistic parent will control anything that their child does or is, from the way they dress, to their academic performance, to the way they should interact with others around them. Narcissists will put severe limitations on freedom in the guise of protection, just because they feel unsettled when their child isn't within view for them to control.

Friendships with narcissists might also feel quite odd. For starters, a narcissist might control your feelings about certain people, especially if those individuals are the ones they don't like. They'll control how you feel, and they'll gaslight you to make you feel doubtful of things that you initially believed.

The narcissist effect

Over time, you'll start to question your friend as the reality of their personality might start to show through the cracks. They're no longer perfect, and they might seem unreasonable, difficult, and at times, even toxic to be around, which they are.

But because of your initial concept of them, you might find it difficult to come to terms with the reality.

What's more, you've already seen what happens to people who might get on their bad side. Because most of your friends and family are theirs as well, you might feel compelled to avoid confrontation in order to protect your image from their onslaught and aggression.

Generally, you should want to stay away from narcissists at all costs because it's hard to get out of their web once you're intertwined. So, keeping these markers in mind when facing new people can help you determine narcissistic tendencies before you're in too deep.

But what about the people that you can't choose? What about those who have been in your life for a while, but you've only just now realized are narcissists? How do you deal with them and is it possible to keep them in your life without ruining your relationships and your reputation?

Chapter 2

Causes of toxic/Negative behavior

There are many reasons why you can attract toxic relationships but let me tell you the ugly truth first—no one is safe. Whether you are of good character or you are toxic yourself, toxic relationships are bound to be around you, circling like eagles eyeing a prey on the ground. It is a different question, however, if you allow them to come into your life and stay. In brief and precise words, I have explained the various reasons why you attract toxic relationships in paragraphs to follow.

Low Self-Esteem

Try to score your self-esteem. If you have any doubt at all, then you fit the profile of a person who will certainly fall prey to toxic relationships. If you doubt your self-worth and value, then you will welcome and give deference to anyone who seems to reinforce your suspicions and turn them into a conviction. Any of the teammates on Ridley's team could be like this, doubting their self-worth because they believe there is someone who is worth way much more than they are worth, and they bow to this person.

Victim of Bullies

Another reason you can fall prey to toxic relationships, especially the manipulative and aggressive types, is if you have been a victim of bullies and have never stood up against their oppression. Your mentality is one of immediate submission to a force you think is greater than yours. The manipulative toxic person preys on you because he sees a weakness in you, the longing for approval, for recognition from others. He flatters you into doing his bidding. The aggressive, toxic person finds you a willing prey because you have the tendency never to stand up for yourself, never to challenge the dominance of others over you.

Excessive Caring

If you are the type of person who cares very much about others and little about yourself, you are bound to keep the company of toxic relationships. The reason is simple: in caring too much for others, you become incredibly willing to please others and not to annoy them. You are ready to give up your seat to someone who even asks rudely for it. You are ready to inconvenience yourself for the benefit of others whose approval you seek. You are a fertile ground on which the seeds of toxicity will grow, and so the toxic relationships plant. When they harvest, you will be lucky to still have your life intact.

Good Upbringing

If you had a good upbringing, you might also fall prey to toxic relationships. That is strange, right? I will explain it. Recall that the causes of toxicity are all traced to poor upbringing of one kind or another. So, if you are lucky enough not to have been raised by parents who excessively pampered you, or by parents who scolded you all the time, or if your parents showed you adequate love and attention while you were growing up, then you have everything the toxic person was denied. You radiate a balance of character, a work of excellence, which the toxic person envies and would like to destroy. How is it possible, he asks, that you are naturally not interested in smoking crack or drinking too much? To the toxic person, this is an abomination, and he is determined to rid you of it. He only rests after he sees you indulging in what he indulges in.

Are You Toxic Too?

Birds of a feather flock together, they say. This is very true in the case of toxicity. Toxic relationships are attracted to one another. If you are the type of person who is willing to do anything to please another, to gain their approval and retain their attention on you and you alone, then there is toxicity in you, too. You will do anything to get what you want—that approval—and manipulating others is just one of the tricks in your bag. Another prominent one is throwing emotional tantrums. Someone like you will attract the narcissist or the nerdy toxic person who is self-centered. The narcissist's desire to be adored, glorified, and even worshipped by others plays into and fits your willingness to gratify others at all costs.

Now, tell me, is anyone safe from the tentacles of toxic relationships? If this is true, then you need to be able to identify the toxic relationships in your life. How do you do this? By asking them if they are toxic? By asking them to fill out a questionnaire? Is there a simple, easy way to identify toxic relationships, a method devoid of all the complexities a psychologist might employ?

Chapter 3

Setting boundaries

There are relationships we get into that offer us numerous benefits. They help us improve and ensure we are better than we were before the relationship. However, some relationships have the opposite effect. They make us lose our self-worth as individuals and change us into worse people than we were when we got into the relationship.

These sorts of partners tend to hurt you purposely or unknowingly until you begin to doubt everything. Many toxic individuals who could be your spouse, co-worker, or friend continue to manipulate you till you believe you are responsible for all the problems they are dealing with. These sorts of individuals deplete and drain all of your energy.

Regardless of where you find yourself, you do not want to be in a toxic relationship with anyone. For this reason, you need to learn to recognize a toxic relationship, and we will be teaching you how in this chapter. But first, why is it important to learn how to spot a toxic relationship?

Why is it vital to learn how to recognize a toxic relationship?

In relationships, the parties involved are expected to be of help to one another when things are not so rosy without having any expectation of a returned favor. You're supposed to help each other in times of need. When a lot of people hear the word "relationship," what comes to their minds is a romantic relationship involving two members of the opposite sex. Although very widespread, this is not precise. This is because any two individuals can be involved in a relationship, and toxic relationships do not have to be between people involved romantically.

Humans flourish when they have company and feel bad when alone. When one is in a toxic relationship, such a person might battle with inner conflicts which might result in depression, anxiety, or anger. It is vital that you can spot signs of a toxic relationship, as well as toxic individuals. This way, you can avoid unwanted emotional traumas. Below, we will be delving into a few signs of a toxic relationship.

You have Become Isolated

If you have started staying away from your friends and loved ones because of your relationship, then it is a red flag. If it seems your partner is discouraging you from spending time with people you love, suddenly your relationship has become toxic. This is a primary technique used by narcissists who have the aim of completely dominating you.

Isolation is usually not apparent. The toxic partner does it subtly via different tactics. These could range from taking charge of the events or activities the other partner takes part in, always calling to "check up" on them, or requesting that their partner stops other personal activities because their relationship takes priority.

Another strategy used by the toxic partner to isolate the victim is via financial abuse. Here, the toxic partner takes complete charge of how the other partner spends cash or earns it. A partner who uses this technique may request that you stop your job or get a new one because it is not giving you enough time to focus on your relationship. In the end, you may start to depend on the partner for financial assistance, which is their goal.

A healthy relationship consists of 2 mature individuals. As adults, you do not need to request permission from your partners when trying to do basic things. Compromise is essential in relationships, and it is vital to think of your partner when making massive life decisions, such as having to undergo extensive surgery or buy a new house. However, if it feels like you have to seek permission before doing minor things like spending time with friends or going to the store, or you appear to be uncomfortable when making fundamental decisions without your partner, it could show that there is something wrong and a clear sign you are in a toxic relationship.

Through the use of isolation as a means of cutting you off from your family and others around you, the toxic partner gets more control. Isolation can also be used in creating a vacuum in the relationship for the toxic partner to engage in other harmful and destructive behaviors. Eventually, victims may feel that they have no one to confide in about their experiences. This leaves the victim without a support system during perilous times.

If you observe all of these in your relationship, then it is a clear sign that you are dealing with a toxic relationship.

Asymmetric Relationship

Asymmetric relationships occur when one of the two partners in a romantic relationship has an excessively dominant role. In essence, one of the partners is more devoted to the relationship than the other partner.

Researchers grounded this concept on a theory established by sociologist Willard Waller. The theory was known as the "Principle of Least Interest." This theory connotes that the individual with a lower amount of interest in the relationship has a higher level of control. This is why many individuals urge themselves to act cool in social situations. It is also why many people take excess time in responding to texts even though they have an interest in the person (Stanley et al., 2018).

In a more recent study, researchers decided to try out this theory in romantic relationships. This was done to determine the kind of partners who keep the most control in relationships. Below are a few things they observed, which may indicate that you are in an asymmetric relationship (Stanley et al., 2018):

- Your partner believes that there are numerous fish in the sea.
- Your partner has issues getting attached and opening up to others.
- They have numerous exes.
- If your partner has cheated on you or does so continuously.

If you have observed that your partner does any or all of the following, then you may be dealing with an asymmetric relationship, which makes it a toxic one.

Other ways your relationship could be asymmetric include:

You are Obsessively Dependent

Codependency is categorized as a relationship where two individuals become so attached and invested in each other that they are no longer able to function separately. In this situation, the identity, happiness, and mood are determined by one of the partners. In these sort of relationships, one person has more dominance over the other. What's more, this individual gets a feeling of fulfillment from controlling the other partner and how they live. In this case, this is the toxic partner.

Dependence on someone you love and hope to spend the rest of your life with is not generally a bad thing. However, when you get obsessively dependent on your partner, who starts to show signs of control, this may be a problem. Being controlled by your partner and being excessively dependent on them don't go without one another. A toxic or controlling partner usually makes you dependent on them so you can help them satisfy their requirements. They may manipulate you until your entire life revolves around them, which gives them more control over you.

You need to remember that being excessively dependent on another individual is not due to love, but fear. When a toxic partner makes you responsible for them staying happy, their constant requirement to be validated begins to seem like an addiction. Your partner starts to control you, and it transforms into emotional dependency because you don't want to lose your partner. Being excessively dependent on your partner can lead you to totally let go of your identity to make your partner happy. Besides, your self-esteem may be centered on the relationship without your knowledge. If your relationship has started to feel this way, then it may have become a toxic one. If you are not sure about this, below are some of the general signs that can help you determine if your relationship is an emotionally dependent toxic relationship:

- You find it hard to make any decisions without your partner.

- You have trouble pointing out your feelings.

- You have low self-esteem and don't trust your judgment.

- You are scared of being abandoned and desire a constant need for approval

- You have problems expressing yourself in your relationship.

Individuals who are excessively dependent on others have a higher likelihood of transforming even healthy relationships into toxic ones. If you notice yourself portraying any of the symptoms listed above, then this is a major sign of a toxic relationship.

They Blackmail You

Emotional blackmail is an elaborate means of manipulation where individuals we are close to dish out threats to us because we failed to do their bidding. This is a prevalent strategy used by toxic partners. Many toxic partners who are apt at emotional blackmail understand the value we place on the relationships we have with them. They know your darkest secrets and know your weaknesses, which are typically not a bad thing in a healthy relationship. However, in the hands of a toxic partner, this can be very dangerous. If you observe that your partner is hurting and manipulating you as a means of punishing you, then it is a clear sign that you are in a toxic relationship.

There are many strategies used by the toxic partner to blackmail you emotionally. All of these are done to make you do their biddings. They include:

Capitalizing on your Fears

Fear is a feeling which keeps us safe from jeopardy. However, a toxic partner can take advantage of this feeling of fear to make you do their bidding. Below are the kinds of worries these toxic partners capitalize on to manipulate you:

- Fear of being abandoned
- Fear of getting others upset

- Fear of being abandoned
- Fear of confrontation
- Fear for your safety

Capitalizing on your Sense of Obligation

A toxic partner can make you feel obligated so they can do what they want. To achieve this, they use various strategies to make you feel bad about yourself if you don't carry out your obligations. For instance; if your partner requests that you do something you are uncomfortable with, and they remind you of all the times they went out of their way for you or tell you they would have done the same for you. Regardless of the way they go about it, you will feel a sense of duty to do their bidding, even if it is not your desire.

Guilt-Tripping you

Many toxic partners use your guilt to punish you. If you fail to do your obligations, they can use your guilt until you feel bad about yourself and do what they want.

If you have ever been blackmailed by your partner using any of the following methods, then you may be in a toxic relationship.

Chapter 4

Moving on

Now that we have already discussed what difficult behavior is, and the classically different types of person, let us now go to a serious and a very usual circumstance and event in that happens in any workplace: Conflict. Put it in simple words, it can be defined as direct opposition between ideas or interests. It arises when a person disagrees to the other person's point of views or beliefs.

In any conflict situation there would always be two important factors to be considered. The objective point in which the parties do not agree on and the emotions or personal perceptions that goes along the situation. Plainly speaking, you have to be aware that in dealing with conflicts in the office you must set aside the second factor and focus on the objective facts in which the situation is supposed to be based on.

According to Blaine Donais, author of Workplaces That Work published by Canada Law Book, the successful administration of work environment conflict obliges a comprehension of the nature and wellsprings of conflict in the work environment. It happens when there is a view of contrary point of views between work environment members. This ought to be recognized from arguments. They are simply a by-result of conflict. They are the outward explanation of it. Run of the mill arguments come as formal court cases, grievances, contentions, dangers and counter dangers and so forth. Conflict can exist without arguments, however it doesn't exist without conflict. In any case, this conflict may not be easily noticed. Much of it exists in every working environment without transforming into arguments.

For us to deeply understand workplace conflict we first must know its sources. Though in this book we would be mostly dealing with people conflicts these could help you have a better understanding of organizational setup which includes these conflict sources that includes interpersonal, change related, external factors and organizational.

1.   Interpersonal

Interpersonal conflict is the most apparent form of conflict in the workplace. It is not that difficult enough for you to be aware of the results of rumors, gossips and sometimes even office politics. Moreover, language and personality styles may often clash, resulting into a great deal of conflict. There are also strong racial and ethno-cultural sources of conflict as well as gender ones. These scenarios may lead to charges of harassment and judgment or at least the feeling that such things actually prevail. People also often bring their problems from home into the workplace resulting to further conflict. Another underlying reason for regarding workplace conflict can also be found in changing thoughts regarding individual achievements. The solid commute for business related accomplishment in a few members could cause conflict with members who don't underline business related achievement in their lives.

To help you reveal some sources of conflict, you may use personality testing instruments Personality Dynamics Profiles, Thomas-Kilman, FIRO-B and the very popular Myers-Briggs. Moreover there are other instruments you may use like forming of focus groups, conducting scheduled interviews and confidential surveys.

2. Change related (Trends)

Nowadays the workplace has increased noticeably the levels of stress and conflict due to many changes including critical downsizing and change of management. Other changes also include technological advancements and different work methodologies. Many professional are also aware of the constant reorganization that also leads to conflict. In relation to this reorganization, non-profit organizations sometimes find it necessary to shift their other work responsibilities to other related organizations. Those people who specialize in analyzing workplace behaviors of people must check the history of the organization going back as far as ten years to know the level of churn that has already occurred. Generally, the greater and recent the change is, the more significant the conflict will be expected.

3. External Factors

These factors could be sum up to evolving markets, effects of approving free trade amongst countries, foreign and domestic competition, and recession that also results to economic pressures. Conflict emerges with customers and suppliers effecting client administration and conveyance of products. Additionally, non-profit organizations specifically could face political pressures and demands form particular vested parties. Government change may have a great impact on every organization may it be public or not. Those organizations dependent on government funding could change their funding levels dramatically. Public philosophies could also have an effect on the system of treating employees and also on the way those who are in the higher management view them upon.

To search for outer elements of conflict, have an audit of the connections between the subject association and different associations. Organizations or government offices that have steady associations with outsiders will discover this to be a significant source of conflict for workplace members.

4. Organizational

There are various sources of conflict on this one. Those identifying with hierarchy and the lack of ability to resolve contradicting interests are very prevalent in many work environments. Due to power differences labor and employee tensions are heightened. The differences in management and leadership styles between departments can also be a source of conflict. It could also include seniority, pay balance and work style conflict. This type of dissonance may arise over the dissemination of responsibilities, resource allocation, types of work and benefits, distinctive levels of resistance for risk taking, and changing perspectives on responsibility. What's more, conflict can emerge where there are seen or genuine contrasts in treatment between divisions or gatherings of representatives.

A careful survey of the work environment is recommended for such sources of conflict. Again reviews, meetings and focus groups can help uncover these sources. Furthermore, organizational sources can be anticipated based upon best practices from comparable associations. All associations experience such conflict. Much can be found out from the lessons of comparative associations who have made an investigation of these sources of conflict.

Chapter 5

----- ❧❦❧ -----

Acceptance

We all find manipulating other people's minds unethical. This is because we consider it as playing with people's feelings as well as thoughts and emotions in order for it to benefit us alone. That is considered a very selfish move. Manipulators know how to play their cards well. They will make sure that they use all the available techniques to manipulate the targeted people. Whether manipulation is unethical or not mostly depends on an individual. This is because we are the ones with the final decision as to whether we should allow them to manipulate us or not.

One is therefore required to evaluate themselves every often in order for them to ensure that they have the required skills for them to be able to avoid manipulators. In this chapter, I am going to discuss some of the many manipulation techniques that one can use to manipulate, persuade and influence people.

Fear and Relief Technique

Fear and relief is a technique that is said to be very efficient when it comes to playing with other people's emotions. A manipulator is only required to instill some fear on an individual, which immediately makes them vulnerable. At the time when they are vulnerable, the manipulator does anything they want in their favor. The manipulator manipulates the individual at this point since they know that the victim will do anything to get out of the fearful situation.

The only challenge that the manipulator might encounter when using this technique is identifying the things that make them fear. They will, therefore, need to keep fearful situations to the every now and then until when they will identify it. The manipulators succeed in this situation since most people hate situations that make them fear. They would anything to make sure that they get out of the situation.

An example of how this technique is used is when the media wants to keep its viewers following the channel. They will put up a juicy headline, which will keep the viewers glued on the screen waiting for it. The reporter will then keep reporting that they need to keep watching the program in order for them to get the juicy news. Everyone will keep watching in the hope that the program will still come.

With fear and relief techniques, the manipulator is expected to instill fear until when they see that the manipulator is about to give up. It is at this point that they will be able to relieve them of the pressure that they are going through which makes them less stressful. The fearful situation that they have been through makes them obey the manipulator's orders anytime they give them since they would not want to go back to the situation they were in before.

Guilty Approach Technique

Through the guilty approach technique, the manipulator makes their prey guilty in order for them to be able to manipulate them. They will make sure that they blame them for things they did not do. One will want to compensate the manipulator without the knowledge that they will are about to be manipulated. A manipulator has to however make sure that their target is someone who is prone to feeling guilty.

Once you make the person guilty, you will be able to swing them in any direction since they are willing to do anything to make sure that you forget the things that they did to you. It works so perfectly since according to the victim, they will compensate for the moments that they were not nice to you but for the manipulator, it will be time to use them for their selfish gain. The guilt approach technique, therefore, works so well when one wants to influence other people since the victim will be feeling an obligation to make it up to you for the trouble they caused you. Little do they know that the manipulator was waiting for such a moment to strike?

Playing the Victim

This type of technique is somehow similar to the guilty approach technique. Playing the victim may however work against you if not careful when implementing it. You would be required to ensure that you do not overuse it. The trick is normally to ensure that you make the targeted person feel bad about a given situation. You will be required to ensure that the person actually made the mistake but for you, playing the victim shall be an exaggeration. The victim will feel bad about it and will want to compensate it by doing something different for you. They will, therefore, be nice to you, which will help the manipulator to use them to achieve her goals.

Love Bombing Technique

We all like it when we feel loved by the people around us. We will all appreciate it when the people around us make us feel appreciated and loved. That is why manipulators use love and attention to manipulate people.

This technique is mostly used for the purposes of manipulating people emotionally. A manipulator will mostly give a lot of attention to their targeted individual. They will show them a lot of affection, which would make them, not suspect anything from the manipulator. By doing this, they will be setting up a trap for them. They will be laying the ground, which they will use for their manipulation purposes. When the right time comes, they are able to easily execute their plan. This means that by the time they realize that you are manipulating them; they will have already been influenced to a place of no return.

Bribery Technique

This technique is said to work like a charm. This is because you will reward someone out of nowhere and they will automatically want to return the favor in a different way. It is an easy job since you are only required to find out what your victim needs and you get them exactly that. You will only be expected to look as genuine as possible. This will make the person really happy such that if you ever mention that you need anything, they will not hesitate to get it for you. By doing this, you will be able to make demands from them as many times as possible without them noticing that you are manipulating them. Through this technique, you will have influenced people to your system, which they may find it difficult to exit.

Becoming a Good Listener

A manipulator knows that people need good listeners in their lives. A good listener earns people's trust so easily. This is because they will come out as being very caring and concerned. This makes the victim trust them completely. A manipulator cannot manipulate people before gaining their trust. Once you have their trust, it will be very easy to manipulate them. You will only be required to discuss with them a few things that you may be going through and without even questioning, they will reciprocate for it since you were there for them before. Through the trust, the manipulator will be able to manipulate them for a long time without the victim noticing.

In as much as a manipulator uses these skills to manipulate, persuade and influence people, they all need to be good in some skills. Some of the skills have been discussed below.

- They need to have excellent verbal communication skills. No one will listen to someone who cannot communicate clearly. You would need to be able to express yourself well if at all you want people to listen to you. Most manipulators have mastered this skill very well which helps them to prey on people without them noticing. When one is good in communication, they are able to easily prey on the victims with the language that they understand. The victims will, therefore, understand the manipulator very well and follow all the instructions given without knowing that they are in the trap of being manipulated.

- For a manipulator to be able to manipulate and persuade people, they should look good before them. Your way of dressing and the way you present yourself tells a lot about you. People will only take you seriously when you look good. You will be able to earn their trust easily. People are normally impressed by people who dress nicely, who are well kept and also who have manners. They will easily like them and listen to them and in the process trust them. Once trust kicks in, the manipulators are able to easily persuade them as well as influence them in the direction that they want.

- When you are conversant about psychology, you will be able to read people's minds. You will be able to know how they feel, how they will react to certain things and also their mood. Knowing all this will be of great help in ensuring that you use their weaknesses to your advantage. You will be able to manipulate them without their knowledge.

Chapter 6

The roots of suffering

The chapter was keen enough to take us through the facets of manipulation. This chapter, however, focuses its radar on the art of persuasion. Before we indulge further into the major facets of persuasion, we will first have to comprehend the meaning of persuasion. Persuasion refers to the psychological influence which affects the choice that an individual ought to make. With persuasion, an individual is often inclined to make you buy his or her school of thought in a bid to change your thought process. In order for one to effectively achieve persuasion, there are a number of things that need to be put in mind. When we are able to go beyond the natural human framework and get a grasp of what moves others, then you are in a position to achieve effective persuasion. This is because you are aware of the pressure points and how best to manipulate them.

When exploiting the art of persuasion, there are various pointers that can come in handy. These are:

Mimicking

As human beings of reason, we tend to vary from one individual to another. The diversity of this is what makes us appear in the discrepancy of others. Owing to this particular fact, you will find that as individuals, we are more drawn to be warm and welcoming to those people who exhibit the same characteristics as us. It could be a physical trait or just the way an individual carries themselves out. This type of technique is said to elicit positive feelings that go a mile when it comes to persuasion. When an individual has the feelings of liking towards someone, he or she is in a position to be swayed by your influence.

In a bid to elaborate on this particular type of technique, we are going to employ the use of this scenario. In the hotel industry, especially in the most advanced and high-end ones, you will find that the allocation of a waiter is dependent on the customer. High-end hotels in the industry have high customer feedback and thus they tend to treat their clients in a manner that suggests so. A client, for instance, would be allocated a particular type of waiter who matches their description. For instance, French waiters are renowned for their exquisite service. Putting the client first is at the top of the list when it comes to this particular field. Many professionals have succeeded in this area owing to the manner in which they treated clients. This is because of the clients re the main source of business. Putting the client into consideration goes a notch higher to even saying the exact words that the client has said. With this, they are able to gather that you have aptly decoded what they meant.

In order to accurately achieve this particular technique, an individual ought to do a number of things. First, he or she may consider doing in-depth research into the particular field of the question in order to see to it that what is required of them is met. Before you are able to achieve persuasion by the use of this technique, one ought to be well versed with the individual that he or she ought to persuade. This type of expertise should be keen enough to make sure that it elicits major points that may come in handy during the process of persuasion.

Social Proof

When it comes to persuasion, social proof has repeatedly proven its dominance. Before we go deeper into the technique, we first need to gather the meaning of social proof. Social proof refers to the process by which an individual's feelings and thought process are affected by the way other people have reacted to the same issue. When it comes to social influence. An individual who is the persuader, draw his or her basis from the acts that others have engaged in time and again. It could be the norm. With human beings, the danger that occurs is the feeling of wanting to be associated with a group of people. Human beings want to accrue a sense of belonging either to a group of people or to a particular act and this is what puts them at a higher risk of being influenced easily.

Employing social proof when persuading an individual will mean that you have a basis of a norm that has been used repeatedly by the people whom we consider to be in the same class. This basis must be something that most people engage in and not a few numbers. Take, for instance, there are newbies in the estate who are looking for service providers. This newbie would first be inclined to know what other people in the estate are using. Although they might not settle on the same option as the rest of the estate, this will be somewhat a buildup on to what choice they may choose to settle upon. Rather they may end up embracing what others have used. With this technique, the trick lies whereby you ought to create a distinction in the manner in which an individual sees himself or herself as per against others. You will only achieve persuasion by convincing this individual that the desired option is one that has been embraced by a large group of individuals.

Reciprocity

When it comes to this type of technique, one needs to understand that a good deed was done to another individual no matter how remote, tends to go a long way. From the wording of it, reciprocity refers to the process by which an individual is able to respond to a good deed by performing a good deed in return. With this type of technique, we will find that most people fail to notice at its onset not until you are obligated to return the favor. In the world today, it is almost as rare as the sun rising from the west as it is to find someone who will extend feelings of warmness and care towards you. Save the people whom we are closely related, we tend to feel differently when an individual who is not even in your circle of friendship extends warm-hearted feelings.

The feeling of obligation arises as a result of being extended a good deed by an individual. This is the result of being extended with feelings of warmness. At this point, you are in a position to persuade the individual in the manner that you wish. This is because he or she would be obliged to follow in the direction of the wind. It should be noted that this particular type of technique ought to be time cautious. This is because the implication of reciprocity does not last forever. There are limits to this timeline and one should be cautious enough to make sure that these limits are not exploited. With the passing of more time, it weakens the wave of reciprocity.

In order to achieve this particular type of technique, an individual ought to play in the tone of offers and obligations. If your offer is worth it, then it raises an obligation effect on the other hand. Thus creating a win situation.

Consistency and Commitment

This type of technique is wired on an already formed perception. An individual is in a position to settle on a particular choice. The choice that this individual picks would be pegged on him or her for as far as they go. From the wording of it, consistency and commitment refer to the fact that an individual is in a position to make a choice and stick to it with sheer determination and perseverance. When it comes to persuasion, not all techniques may work and you may find that you hit rock bottom once or twice in your venture. When this happens, it is not advisable to give up. Consistency is what builds our character in almost every facet in life. This type of technique is vast in a manner that cuts across various fields not limited to the field of education and business. The first approach to an individual for purposes of convincing them may or may not end up in a manner that you wish. The first approach is often one that is characterized by rejection and in some cases mental torture. The best way to respond to this type of instance is by not giving up. The second encounter of individuals who first rejected your idea will see to it that you have an audience who understands what you are talking about.

The talk of consistency and commitment is one that does not go down the throat easily. This is because these are the most subtle facets to embrace because they tend to take a toll on an individual. You can imagine getting rejected severally. In order to achieve commitment, an individual ought to operate in a manner that is relentless.

Chapter 7

----- ❦❦❦ -----

Free at last

What happens to your brain and how to change

You cannot say an entire population is terrible just because a few people in it have done terrible things. There is a lot of hatred toward those with Borderline Personality Disorder, for example, and I am not here to further that.

The reason that I am incorporating so much about personality disorders is that when a person goes undiagnosed, or nobody confronts them on their problems, it leads to serious consequences. These words are only meant to inspire you to take action when you think somebody close to you is struggling. You are in no position to be throwing around disorders, however, so keep that in mind. This is only a reference tool to see if you spot any of the "psychological red flags" that would lead you to suggest the person seeks help.

There is also a huge difference between "sharing traits" with these disorders and actually having one. There is a reason that the DSM (the Diagnostic and Statistical Manual) is so black and white and puts serious limitations on diagnosing. Professionals in the medical field also have a strict policy against dealing with relatives or anybody close to them. You need to have an entirely unbiased opinion and at least four years of medial school behind you.

Now that the necessary pretext has been laid out, I think that it is a great time to start talking more in-depth about how, exactly, personality disorders are diagnosed. This goes for just about any type of mental illness, however. Even ones that are more "common," such as depression, normally have "high agitation" or "irritability" listed as a diagnostic criterion.

So, to the untrained eye, these disorders can look rather similar.

I am going to run down each one, as well as what the criteria are for diagnosing it. Earlier I talked about some of the "signs," as well as some stuff we already know about the disorders. This section is going to be far more scientific- but I will do my best to break it down so that it is easily digestible for you.

- Borderline Personality Disorder: This is a disorder that primarily affects the self-image that you hold. Those with Borderline tend to have long patterns of unstable relationships, high difficulty managing their emotions, and more. This is particularly hard to treat a disorder, but recovery rates are astoundingly high in many cases when CBT, or cognitive behavioral therapy, is used.

- The diagnostic criteria for Borderline Personality Disorder are fairly to the point. Unlike in some disorders, there is no specific number of months in which symptoms must happen. Instead, it is diagnosed based on the noted effects in the person's life as they grow into adulthood.

- The criteria are as follow:

- Using any means necessary to avoid abandonment, whether real or perceived

- Clear patterns of consistently unstable, and often intense, relationships

- These relationships will be marked by alternations between idealization and devaluation

- Having poor self-image and no real idea of "who" they are

- Showing signs of high impulsivity in relation to self-destructive behavior

- Frequent threats of suicide and self-harming behavior

- Extreme mood swings from one moment to the next

- Feeling chronically "empty" inside

- Poor control of temper

- Disassociation related to stress to the point of paranoia

- There are several different "self-destructive" behaviors that can be listed. Promiscuity, high spending, and excessive drinking are three ways in which this behavior can be engaged.

- Narcissistic Personality Disorder: This is a disorder that is mainly characterized by the excessive need for admiration and attention. Oftentimes, there will be little reason as to why this person "deserves" the praise that they seek. It is also notable that they will have a grandiose sense of self with a strong lack of empathy.

- Again, this is not a disorder that can be diagnosed by anybody other than a professional who specializes in the disorder. There is also a lot of work that people with this disorder need to put in before they improve. Oftentimes they will not show up to therapy because of their narcissism. Instead, they end up going for something unrelated and end up being referred to a specialist. It is normal for them to reject the diagnoses and refuse to engage with the process of recovery, as well.

- The criteria are as follow:
- Having a self-image which is grandiose
- Greatly exaggerating accomplishments or other talents
- Requires special treatment without reason
- Preoccupation with fantasies surrounding recognition for their brilliance, unlimited success, and other similar ideals
- Exceedingly high sense of being entitled
- Exploits and manipulates all of those around them as a means to their ends
- Very low levels of empathy
- Frail self-esteem and lack of confidence
- Those who suffer from Narcissistic Personality disorder can, absolutely, recover. The question is

not if they can, it is whether or not they want to. You will most likely find that they are entirely unwilling to take accountability.

- It is important to note, however, that this more so due to having to accept the damage they have dealt with. Accepting that means processing it and realizing that they have left a trail of wreckage behind them. The most dangerous time for a person being treated for NPD is this phase. Accepting what you have done, and actively developing the empathy to understand why it was wrong, is enough to make anybody suicidal.

- Anti-Social Personality Disorder: Perhaps the most often talked about, Anti-Social Personality Disorder is often also misunderstood. Most people use the words "Sociopath" and "Psychopath" in place of the disorder's actual name. If you take nothing else from this section, take away the idea that neither of those words is a disorder. In fact, they are only used to describe behavior which fits into different disorders diagnostic criteria.

- Those who have ASPD lack empathy entirely. As a result, they will have a long record of aggressive or violent behavior. They will also, as a general rule, have numerous run-ins with law enforcement and criminal history. Their inability to feel empathy translates into complete and utter interpersonal chaos.

- Understand that there are several different subtypes for this disorder. All of them are entirely dangerous. Part of the criteria for it says as much, as it turns out. I think that this will make more sense if I just jump into that part of it, however.

- The criteria are as follow:

- Refusal to obey laws, both social and legal, and engaging in unlawful behavior as a result

- Repeated patterns of lying, using falsified names, engaging in con artist behavior, and exploiting others for profit or pleasure

- Inability to plan for the future

- High levels of aggression and poor temper control

- Entirely disregards the safety of others or self

- Irresponsible behavior which leads to an inability to meet financial obligations or inability to hold down a job at all

- Inability to feel remorse as a result of their actions

- Please note that you must be at least 18 before this disorder can be diagnosed. Part of personality disorders is that before our brains finish developing, our personality is fairly fluid. Early intervention at the onset of symptoms goes a long way in putting the person on a correct path before they are too far gone.

Remember, these are extreme disorders that cause extreme behavior. While you may feel as though a toxic person in your life exhibits these behaviors, it may just be that they are "narcissistic" in personality, but do not have a disordered personality.

On the other hand, you may also be experiencing a toxic relationship with somebody who has been formally diagnosed. If you know that the person has the disorder, and has not just self-diagnosed themselves, this information is vital. On that note, this is something else you should look for as a red flag for toxicity. Somebody glamorizing personality disorders and claiming to have one, while having never been formally diagnosed, has become more and more popular. This is not necessarily a sign of a personality disorder, however.

In most cases, these are people who are highly toxic. They do not have an understanding of the extremity with which those who actually have personality disorders act. Many of these types of people are doing so for attention and fail to grasp the severity of the situation. This type of person is, absolutely, a red flag unto themselves. I recommend steering clear of anybody who makes light of mental illness in general, but especially those glamorizing it.

Now, I think it is important that I go over the science behind the personality types, as well. Earlier I went over them in a brief way and spoke about how they related to the topic at hand. Now I am going to get a little bit deeper into them, and why they are so great at classifying people. Our brains work in mysterious ways, but hopefully, yours will feel less mysterious after this!

INFJ

- What is the Myers Briggs Type Indicator (MBTI)?: This is a fantastic tool created by two women after thoroughly studying the work of Carl Jung. His theory of personality types is what inspired them to develop this system of identification. While neither were "scientists," they were absolute experts on interpersonal systems and the science of people.

- This is now one of the most commonly used methods of psychological evaluation. Many businesses have incorporated it into their offices in order to better understand employees. Many hold it in the highest of esteems, and it has proven time and time again to be highly effective.

- The Characterization of INFJs: Did you know that this is the rarest of all the personality types in the MBTI? INFJs are a quirky bunch and highly dedicated to the world around them. They tend to be driven to enact change and help the world become a better place. INFJs are generally predisposed to burning out because of their need to always be furthering their ideals.

- You will also find that INFJs are incredibly people-oriented. They want to spend time making sure the world around them is actively becoming a better place. While less than 1% of the population shares this personality type, they tend to be the people who leave the biggest marks on the world around them.

- Why this Type is Predisposed: As you can imagine, those who fall into the INFJ category are idealists. They often want to sympathize with others as much as possible and can be taken advantage of as a result. Since they are also predisposed to burning out, toxic relationships can take an extra toll on them. They do not want to "give up" on the person with who they are having trouble. Instead, they want to help them.

- This creates a toxic cycle in which the INFJ is constantly pulled back into the toxic relationship. They cannot "get away" from the person because they know that they can somehow help them. "Giving up" is not a phrase in the vocabulary of many INFJs, especially those who are devoted to the toxic person in their life.

Empathic

- What Makes People Empathic: This is a largely arguable question, with many entirely undecided on the answer. Scientists and laymen alike have been wondering for years what, exactly, empathy is. In fact, we really do not understand how it develops, either. Neuropsychology is a brand-new field, and because of that we are still in the infancy of the discoveries ahead. There are a few commonly held beliefs on the matter, however. Most of our evidence shows that empathy is largely learned.

- This is why early trauma and abuse can cause a person to develop low empathy. You must be taught by those around you to display emotional regard for others. It is part of learning to "share" and how to get along with others. When a person is not exposed to these ideas early on, it can create a seeming inability to feel empathy.

- Most of the normal play you see children engage in will cultivate empathy, as well. Play is important not only for children but also for adults. It helps us build understanding, work with others, and more. Building your emotional intelligence and empathy does not have to be difficult. That leads us to our next topic!

- Emotional Intelligence: There are several ways in which you can build your emotional intelligence. Most of them are not very difficult, too. It is important to consistently work towards understanding those around us. This is not just good for empathizing- it is good for protecting ourselves. Being able to spot red flags early because you have a great understanding of people is something that you need to hone. This will help you in all aspects of your life.

- Emotional intelligence refers to your ability to understand the emotions of others. It is kind of like the idea of "standard" intelligence. While standard intelligence is based on the ability to recognize patterns and solve problems, emotional intelligence is based on your ability to read people and understand interpersonal situations.
- I will be going over several different methods of building emotional intelligence later on in the book.

Highly sensitive

- What Constitutes "Highly Sensitive": This is a tricky one since all of us, at one point or another, could be classified as "highly sensitive." I suppose the best way to look at it is to understand the frequency of these scenarios. By that, I mean how often you feel like others do not like you, or how easily you cry. Timid, meek people tend to be highly sensitive and highly reliant on others for reassurance.
- Those who are highly sensitive do not act with aggression or lash out as a result of others inspiring these feelings within them. Instead, they tend to fall victim to depression or similar mindsets. Highly sensitive people are those who cry frequently

without much prompting. If you cry every time you see a video of a cute animal, for example, you are definitely highly sensitive.

- The problem with this is that those who are highly sensitive need partners who validate and uplift them. There is nothing wrong with having incredibly high empathy- and that is, generally, what highly sensitive people have.

- Some People are Predisposed: There are two sides to every coin. Many people who did not receive enough attention or love as children end up being highly sensitive. Neglect and abuse can cause this, as it oftentimes will cause people to be overly empathetic instead of lacking empathy. That is part of why neuroscience is so complicated- we really do not understand why some people go to one extreme, while others go the exact another way.

- Having strict or overbearing parents can cause heightened sensitivity, as well. And, of course, some people are just born the way that they are.

- Overcoming High Sensitivity: Becoming more aware of yourself is the best way to begin overcoming a highly sensitive personality. You also need to begin engaging in confidence-building activities and exercises. There are several ways to do this, and most of them are incredibly easy. I will go over this far more in-depth later on in the book. For now, just understand that you can, in fact, rewire your brain. You do not have to be subject to the directions in which your brain pushes you.

- In order to overcome being highly sensitive, you need to push yourself to take part in challenging activities. There are so many things out there to help you, such as mindfulness or self-defense. High sensitivity is something many people struggle with.

Codependents

- How Codependency Forms: There are many ways in which a codependent relationship can form. One of the largest is that one of the partners begins to look for validation from the other in a way that is entirely inappropriate. Codependency generally happens if the two partners are on "different playing fields," so to speak. What I mean by this is that if one is significantly further ahead in life than the other, there is a high risk for that partner to become codependent on the other.

- The problem with codependency is that it is not just about the one partner who has become codependent. The "co" is key here. Both partners will become intertwined in such a way that breaking free from the toxicity can be incredibly challenging.

- While it may begin with one of the partners leaning on the other, the fact of the matter is that at one point or another, both people become toxic. For example, the partner who is supporting the other may feel like they need to give that support because it makes them feel validated. They might also do it out of an innate sense of needing to "fix" others. And still, they may also just drive everybody around them away, and so a codependent relationship is the only one that can be successful for the person.

- Changes in the Brain: Like with any relationship, this has some serious consequences for your brain. This goes for all toxic relationships, however, and we'll get into that a little later in this chapter. In fact, it will be the rest of the chapter so we can get really down into it. I just want to preface the more complicated science with brief overviews.

- Essentially, you can become, quite literally, addicted to the other person.

- Overcoming Your Codependence: I want to impress upon you as much as possible that you do not need to stay in a codependent relationship. You also, however, do not need to reject relationships that you have. There is a chance to turn them around and choose a healthier way to intermingle with the person. It takes a lot of effort, and the setting of boundaries, but it is not impossible. The brain is constantly changing and making new connections. It is just about harnessing those connections!

I hope that was a much more thorough rundown on the science behind all of this information. My hope is that you have a solid foundation off of which to work. I highly encourage you to take the Myers-Briggs Type Indicator test if you have not already. It is a great way to figure out what kind of person you are and give you some more insight into how your mind works. There are a lot of people who encourage the usage of the MBTI in workplace environments, too, in order to soothe interpersonal clashing.

The MBTI can also help you understand how predisposed you may be too toxic relationships. Perhaps more importantly, it will, on top of that, key you in to whether or not you yourself are toxic.

There is a lot of blame which gets thrown around at victims caught up in toxic relationships. This is very unfortunate because, as science shows us, there is far more to it than just the "choice" to stay. If you are currently stuck in this kind of situation, know that my sympathy is with you. There is hope, and you are not a weak person. In fact, you are taking a very large, brave step by reading this book.

One of the biggest reasons people believe that people who stay in a toxic relationship is weak is that they do not understand the core of the matter. Just like with drug addiction, for example, it is hard to understand from the outside looking in. Having an addiction is no laughing matter. It can be almost as dangerous if that addiction is a person rather than a drug.

The brain makes connections constantly and is always rearranging to process and hold new information. This brain structure also largely mirrors those we surround ourselves with. This is why surrounding yourself with positive, forward-thinking people is so important. You need to make sure you are setting yourself up for success. This is always what comes first. Dealing with toxic relationships begins with dealing with yourself. I will talk about a bunch of exercises and such to help with just that later on in the book.

For now, let us get into what makes your brain tick and why it is so hard to detach yourself from people. Again, this is especially true for those who are stuck in abusive relationships. If you are one such person, I definitely recommend that you exit the relationship immediately. Abuse leaves a huge marker on your brain and can set you up for failure in the future. Nobody deserves to be in a relationship that is abusive. Seek help, because it is out there.

People stay for a variety of reasons. For example:

- Being underage (18 and under)
- Marriage
- Children
- Familiar relation
- Sharing a friend group

There are many more reasons- just as many as there are people! Each situation is unique and has its own set of challenges. Yours will, undoubtedly, be vastly different than any other person. You need to understand going into this that this will be generalized information. However, this is on purpose so that you can apply it to yourself as an individual.

In psychology, there is a concept known as "trauma bonding," and it is one of the reasons why people cannot see their abuser for what they are. Manipulative people have a way of using emotional abuse to get the same reaction out of their victims. Trauma, after all, does not just relate to physical violence. In fact, emotional trauma goes a long way in affecting the brain. You can easily develop PTSD related to emotional trauma.

You should note that PTSD from long-term emotional abuse is different than something which occurs due to a sudden, traumatic event. In fact, psychologists have begun to differentiate the two. C-PTSD, which is a complex post-trauma stress disorder, is a diagnosis all unto itself.

This happens in a few different steps. First, the abuser will have a "honeymoon" phase in which they treat the person incredibly well. Once this honeymoon phase is over, they begin to engage in abusive behaviors, which can range from emotional abuse to physical aggression.

Fear is what it all comes down to.

I am excited to share this knowledge with you, however, so let me get right into it.

Chapter 8

----- ❧☙ -----

The toxic termination process (TTP)

We all think we've chosen wisely when it comes to those people who are our friends and who make our lives easier and more fun to experience. However, sometimes, despite our defenses, a toxic person manages their malignant manifestation.

If you keep your wits about you you'll soon detect them. Over a period of time their continuous backbiting and attrition becomes wearing. Or they do or say something so odious and reprehensible that it creates a tipping point, and you know that they deserve no place in your life.

So how do you deal with them? Once you've exhausted any attempts to negotiate with them, the straightforwardness of the approach given is breathtakingly elegant in its simplicity. It may require the qualities of determination, resolution and perseverance in how you play it out – qualities that are very useful to develop in any case and are replicable for other situations.

Consider it as a character-forming act.

Tell them you will have nothing further to do with them. Then ignore them. Don't engage with them again however much they entreat you to do so. Ensure that they understand this and secure their unqualified commitment if you can.

It may also help to have a few things to counter them with just in case they fail to get the message and act upon it. This should only be considered as a last resort and is best done through a legal representative, depending upon whether the other party's actions escalate into the murky and illegal worlds of harassment or stalking.

Remember, people who add no value to your life have no right to be in it. All these individuals are inimical to your physical, mental and emotional health. They are not worthy to be your 'friend'.

" Life shrinks or expands in proportion to one's courage."

— Anaïs Nin

The following Toxic Termination Process or TTP can work face to face or via email or social networking. An elegantly penned letter can be used if you wish to practice your skills in the fine art of calligraphy. You may like to print the TTP as an aide memoire for what you need to do.

Be assertive, direct and polite and ready to counter any arguments. If all goes to plan, this will be your last interaction with this person, so it's important to get it right. What you are about to do should resonate within their mind and psyche.

And get them out of yours.

Rehearse the scene in your mind and focus on the outcome you want. Consider how they might react, based on your knowledge of their behaviour and psychology.

Will they try to make everything your fault and play on any residual guilt? Will they try to drown you in a lake filled with their own emotional incontinence? Will they resist your logical entreaties vigorously and beg for 'one last chance'? Unfetter your imagination, write down every potential scenario and come up with a range of responses. Use visualisation to practice your reactions and clarify your objectives.

If you have any suspicion that the person might resort to physical violence, exercise extreme caution. You may wish to avoid any physical contact with them. Raise your concerns with a family member, legal representative, law enforcement official or a friend who used to be in the military.

Always stay safe.

Once the person is out of your life, move on and don't pay any mental attention to them. You might find this difficult initially, so have a number of things to do that will enable and facilitate this process.

Your engagement with this person may have formed some neural connections within your brain – remember the expression 'neurons that fire together wire together'. Luckily neuroplasticity (the ability of the brain to create new patterns of thinking) and neurogenesis (the brain, in particular the hippocampus, creating new brain cells) are your friends here.

You are looking to create new, powerful, associative and transformative neural patterns, which, as a fortunate and serendipitous by-product, also serve to terminate any negative associations with a toxic person.

Take this as an opportunity to do different things and give your brain a real workout. Find new friends, challenging and stimulating things to do, practice mindfulness meditation. Read 'The Power of Now' by Eckhart Tolle, a book that will nicely root you in the eternal present, free from the grasping encumbrances of the dead hand of the past and pointless speculation on the unborn future.

You are looking to get rid of any trace of this person that lingers around your mind to ensure any effect on you is eradicated.

Identification

You've been through the Friend Ranking Quadrant (FRQ) and worked out whom you want to keep in your life and, by process of elimination, which you want to permanently extract.

You will have a hit list of at least one Toxic to contend with. If you have several Toxics, run through the exercise again to ensure that your first analysis is correct. If you do have more than one to contend with you have two options.

The first is to perform TTP on all of them, more or less simultaneously; the second is to target them one at a time. Both approaches clearly have their pros and cons. If you can eliminate all of them at the same time you've achieved something quite dramatic and should feel very proud. However, if there is any linkage between the Toxics, they may try to gang up on you.

Picking them off one by one and keeping them isolated is a longer-term process that may require more time, effort and energy. The end result, however, is what you are looking for and this may be a 'no pain, no gain' scenario that you can't avoid.

Life sometimes throws you challenges to toughen you up and sharpen your insight and experience. Some people welcome them – which is not an excuse to invite more Toxics into your life.

SWOT Analysis

This is a classic situational analysis tool used by many business organisations to identify their strengths, weaknesses, opportunities and threats. This can include market position, financing, quality of personnel, effectiveness of management, systems used, competitive analysis and so on.

You can use this as a tool to plan TTP. The SWOT analysis should cover both you and the Toxic, which is why knowledge of their backstory may be useful. Try also to factor in any environmental or contextual issues – where you will perform TTP (physical or remote), other parties involved and so on.

Strengths:

You – motivation and intent (you know the person is toxic and want them out of your life). Technique – you know the process and how and where you will apply it. You have a strong personality, which you have worked on, and have planned every conceivable variation on events.

Toxic – you don't quite know how they will behave and they can be quite tenacious. Even now, it's unclear what behaviours they will utilise. Evidence and analysis leads you to believe that they will move on to vex another party, but you are only eighty five percent sure.

Weaknesses:

You – slight feelings of guilt that some of this may be your doing, and that the Toxic is behaving the way they do because you didn't communicate earlier that you wanted nothing to do with them. Therefore they could argue that you were sending misleading messages and try to work a guilt angle on you, which, due to your upbringing, you know might be effective.

Toxic – they are very over emotional. As an analytical person, this is a trend you detest and usually handle by being cold and indifferent, which they find very difficult to deal with. The more emphatic they get, the colder your response. They already have this pattern formed, so if necessary, you are comfortable with exploiting it.

Opportunities:

You – you know what you want and can set the meeting or email sequence as soon as possible. You know the Toxic dislikes change and surprises, so you can wrong foot them by acting quickly and striking with your carefully honed TTP missive when they are least expecting it.

Toxic – unclear what their options are at this stage, you've factored everything you can think of into the mental dress rehearsal you've performed, and are sufficiently savvy to counter anything that, short of them pulling a gun on you, comes leftfield.

Threats:

You – nobody can predict one hundred percent what will happen in any give situation. You've planned as best as you can and thought it through and can see no downside. Once again, your flexible mindset should serve you well. You'll be meeting in a public place, so the worst you can expect is a series of teary tantrums and childish and noisy displays of disquietude.

Toxic – you have been the centre of the Toxic's obsession for far longer than you wish to remember. You are now absenting yourself permanently from the Toxic's life and this will hit them hard, perhaps harder than you or they know. What the Toxic will do next is unclear, probably to them as much as to you. You have decided that they are bad for you to be around and ultimately your happiness and peace of mind are all that matters to you, so you have no choice but to continue with the strategy you've committed to.

Negotiation (Optional)

This is the very reasonable 'one last chance' stage of TTP. You are telling the Toxic that it's your way or the highway.

Note that this stage is optional. If you know that you definitely want the Toxic out of your life, you should go straight to Final Rites and Burial. If you think there is some remote chance that the Toxic will change their behaviour in a way that is acceptable to you, negotiation is your only realistic option. Make sure that you are choosing this in a clear-headed analytical way, and are not allowing emotion or sentiment to cloud your judgment.

If the negotiation fails and the Toxic, verbally agreeing to everything you say, reverts to their old behaviour as soon as they get the opportunity, you have wasted a lot of time and energy and give the Toxic more power. This could make the rejection stages of TTP more difficult than they need to be. So exercise extreme care if you go this route.

When negotiating, let them know there is a problem and that they are the problem. You don't want to get into long-winded circuitous arguments as to who's at fault. All you are focusing on is that they are bad for you, their behaviour is unacceptable and that, unless the behaviour changes, you do not want them in your life. You can expect a degree of argument and bluster;

especially if the Toxic is of the mentation that nothing is ever their fault.

Make it clear, concise and unambivalent to ensure that they understand that this is their very last chance. Furthermore, that you are setting a period of time in which you are expecting them to make the required changes.

Accept that you may need to modify some of your behaviour – negotiation is a matter of give and take and trading concessions. However, make them aware that there are boundaries that they must not cross and that if they do, that's it. They're out of your life forever. Get them to understand the consequences of transgression and commit to change. A written statement or email to this effect is an effective way to seal the deal.

The Toxic, gushing in agreement, may want a hug or some physical reassurance at this stage.

Should you do it? It depends on your reading of the Toxic. They might think that they've got away with something and that you are not serious. So on balance, don't – keep everything professional, cordial and business like. Also make sure they know that you are monitoring their progress, and that any transgression on their part will prove fatal.

Stage One – Final Rites

Step 1.

It's time to cut this individual out of your life forever. They've had multiple chances but won't change. They just can't make the effort to change and will never redeem themselves, so let them go. You've completed your analysis and made the decision. It's time to initiate the Termination Sequence.

Step 2.

The message can be delivered in person, by letter or email. Work out what you are most comfortable doing and what, given your knowledge of the person, will be most effective. Remember, this is non-negotiable, so craft your message thoroughly so that even the densest Toxic will understand and act upon it.

Step 3.

Tell them how the way they treat you makes you feel and that you won't accept this from anyone. (Rehearse this a few times – be strong and assertive.) Show them who the boss is and lay down the rules. Advise them how toxic they are and how you refuse to continue to tolerate them. Your communication should be direct, polite and balanced. Whatever they do, you do not descend into being ignoble or over-emotional, and you therefore retain the moral high ground.

Step 4.

Make them aware that you no longer wish to communicate or spend any time with them. Ensure this message is short, crisp and to the point. Get them to agree to this – you want a commitment from them that they will never contact you again in any way, shape or form.

The majority of people have a sense of honour, if so bring out this fine quality by reminding them of it. They might even feel better for the duration of your conversation. But clearly don't let them use this as an argument to stay in touch.

Step 5.

Cut off their oxygen supply by being succinct. Don't give them any information they might use to hang a counter argument on or interpret in a way to suggest there is any hope for them. Just say no if they ask for something. Don't take anything they offer so you can avoid any potential guilt trips. Ensure you control the interaction and dialogue at all stages.

How should you craft your argument? It needs to be effective and concise. You could see yourself as a barrister finalising their case and presenting it to both judge and jury. If necessary, you need to be very focused, determined and even brutal – whatever it takes to reinforce the message and get rid of them. You don't want to make them into an enemy, though sometimes this is unavoidable.

And, though tempting, you may not want to go as far as the following quote from an awesome TV drama (though if you are dealing with a particularly aggressive and abusive long-term Toxic, you might find parts of it inspirational):

Stage Two – Burial

Step 1.

Now deliver on your promise and cut them out of your life completely – don't answer emails or calls, do nothing to encourage them. Blank them. Just get rid of them.

If the person has any decency, honour or integrity, they will respect your wishes and leave you alone.

Step 2.

Be aware that some people will try every trick in the book to argue against you and insinuate their way back into your life (this is why you need to gain their assent and commitment, outlined in paragraph 4 above). So dress-rehearse your strategy and work out their possible responses. Don't fall for guilt trips, hoovering or anything else they might try in the future.

Step 3.

Feel no guilt or remorse. You are doing what's best for you to make you happy. Toxic individuals are full of poison for your mind and soul, so getting rid of this unnecessary negative force empowers you to live your best life.

To you, this person no longer exists and is effectively dead to you. Resurrection is not an option.

Step 4.

If necessary change your email addresses, sites you often frequent and so on. If you are a social networking aficionado, ensure your security is set at the absolute maximum. Or just do something more interesting in the non-virtual world.

Step 5.

You want to ensure that this individual cannot communicate with you in any way. If you need an existing email address, just set up a rule to move any communication from them into a designated folder so that you don't even read it. You may choose to keep a record of their communications but do you really need to read them?

Step 6.

Be very wary of any online request to be your friend from someone you do not know. Vet everybody. A degree of vigilance will work wonders for your self-interest and reduce the possibility of the Toxic sneaking back into your life.

Step 7.

Obviously you do not follow the toxic individual on any social network, blog or similar site. Your objective is a clean, clear break so you don't do anything to compromise this. Out of sight is out of mind, right?

Step 8.

You may consider retaining copies of any existing correspondence in case you need it for your legal advisor, authorities etc., depending on the legal framework within your jurisdiction.

If you don't want this material polluting your house or PC/Mac/tablet/phone, keep it elsewhere, on a memory stick, with your legal representative or on a secure cloud server. Treat it with caution and quarantine it – like a piece of malware.

Step 9.

If the person proves intractable and attempts to get in contact, consider rerouting any further communication to your legal representative to establish if there are grounds for proceedings to be taken.

Step 10.

You want the toxic individual out of your life permanently - this means physically and psychologically. This entails not thinking about them, not fuelling them or giving them any headspace. You could do a short rite of exorcism if this works for you, spend more time with your real friends, sing a song (ding dong, the Toxic's gone), tell a joke, have a drink, or go for a decent meal at a good restaurant.

Step 11.

Ultimately, live the best life that you can.

Enjoy yourself, be creative, have fun, make new friends, learn how to fly and get your pilot's licence, master a musical instrument to really engage all parts of your brain (keyboards are good), get a different job, travel extensively.

See the departure of the Toxic as a wakeup call to change your life.

Do things that fully engage you in the moment so that you don't feel any compulsion to ruminate over the past. You won't be moping when you're bobsleighing around St. Moritz at 90 mph or leaping rooftop to rooftop in Paris whilst you perfect your parkour skills.

Choose whatever works for you. Moving on and being your best self is the most effective way of disengaging and distancing from malign toxic influences. And you can do the truly spontaneous Duchene smile. You know they'll just hate the fact that you are having a happier, more successful time without them than they could even begin to conceive.

Step 12.

Be vigilant and self-aware so that you do not attract such people in the future. Work on your self-esteem and self-confidence if you find that prolonged exposure to a Toxic has caused you to lose confidence in your ability to read people. Building your self-esteem and self-confidence will help immeasurably when it comes to attracting the right friends and creating healthy relationships.

Be Aware

That ditching your Toxic may cause you to lose other friends especially if the Toxic has managed to make you appear toxic for ditching them. There's little if anything you can do about this. Sometimes freedom comes at a cost.

Perhaps you need a new set of people in your life anyway.

Chapter 9

Exercises to try

While one on one time with a therapist is going to be required in order to make it through the complicated process of recovering from a lifetime of dealing with a narcissistic mother, it is important to understand that change is possible thanks to a concept known as neural plasticity. While you work on dealing with your larger issues in the long-term the following exercises can help you cope with the symptoms of these issues in the short-term.

Watch for cognitive distortions: In order to restructure your thoughts, the first thing that you are going to need to do is become aware of when your thoughts are distorting the truth of the matter. These types of distortions can come in a wide variety of shapes and sizes, but the one thing they will have in common is that they will try and force you to see the world differently than it truly is. As such, the way to ensure that this ceases to be an issue is to become more aware of when they are affecting the way you respond to specific situations.

Once you are more aware of when cognitive distortion is occurring, you will then be able to more easily respond to the situation in a way that is productive, instead of simply being along for the ride. To start, you simply need to ask yourself how else you could be thinking about whatever it is that is going on. You may also find it helpful to consider what the worst-case scenario in the current situation could be. With that in mind, you will likely find that you start to feel better when you consider how likely that scenario is to actually occur.

With this done, it is important to act upon the information that you have gained, especially if you have determined that the cognitive distortion is invalid. Going through the process of determining the accuracy of a cognitive distortion is meaningless if you don't follow through on what you have learned. The change doesn't need to be immediate, after all some distortions will likely have been with you for a very long time, however, as long as you acknowledge what you have learned and remain open to new experiences moving forward, you will find that your old cognitive distortions can give way to a new way of seeing the world.

Cognitive restructuring: If you looked at another person's cognitive distortions you would likely find them easy to dispute. For example, no matter how much a friend of yours feels as though they are absolutely the worst, you can see why this is untrue. However, when it comes to your personal cognitive distortions, you will likely find them much more difficult to overcome which is why they persist in the first place. You will find that, without help, you will continue to believe in your own cognitive distortions no matter how they actually differ from the way the world really is.

Luckily there are several different ways to tear down your cognitive distortions, no matter how deeply held they might be. These techniques can be used at any time you find yourself coming up against a cognitive distortion and, with enough practice, you will find yourself coming up against them less and less often and they will be replaced with balanced, accurate thoughts instead.

For starters, you are going to want to utilize what is known as Socratic questioning to determine the validity of your thoughts out of the gate. The Greek philosopher Socrates always emphasized the importance of questions as a means of exploring otherwise complicated ideas and uncovering inherent assumptions. To make use of his method when it comes to cognitive distortions, you will want to assess that you are looking at things through their filter by asking a number of different questions of yourself. These questions include:

- Is this a realistic thought?

- What is the basis for the thought, is it feelings or is it facts?

- Does this thought have any evidence to back it up?

- Is it possible that I am misinterpreting the evidence based on cognitive distortion?

- Is this situation more complicated than simply black or white?

- Is this a habitual thought or is it supported by the facts of the current situation?

When you come across a negative thought that you just can't shake, take the time to test it out instead. This is a great way to take whatever it is that you are thinking about and figure out an answer, one way or another. For example, if you are angry because you feel too stressed at work to take breaks, then this is something that can easily be tested. You would simply act normally one week and rate your overall effectiveness, and then take more breaks the next week, rate your overall effectiveness and then compare the two. This takes the entire process out of the theoretical and puts it fully in the realm of something that can be tested with results that can be taken to the bank.

If the thought process that you are stuck on can't be easily tested, then you may instead find it useful to look at all the available evidence and see where that gets you. To do so, all you need to do is to take a long hard look at the situation in question and then write down everything that supports whatever your thought process says is going on and then everything that supports the idea that your perception of the situation is warped. When you are staring at the evidence in the face you will find that it is much harder to hide from the truth than when everything is simply floating around in your head instead.

Break common patterns: Finally, knowing what you now know, the only thing left to do is to break out of the patterns that have formed around the cognitive distortions you are trying to break free from. This is going to be much easier said than done, however, especially if the habits are extremely deeply ingrained. As such, you may want to start by changing small aspects of the negative habits first, before working up to a full-blown change. This will give your ingrained neural pathways some time to start expanding before jumping to something entirely new and different.

Remember, it takes about 30 days to build a new habit from scratch, which means that once you have reached the point where you are ready to give the old habit the boot for good, you should be ready to immediately start something new to take its place. Having a new habit to replace the old one with directly will give your mind something new to latch onto, giving it a place to put its focus while you focus on the more serious task of kicking the old habit to the curb. Keep in mind that forming a new habit is a chance to improve some aspect of your everyday life, choose wisely and keep it up once you start. While the going may be tough in the interim, in just one month you will be settled into your new routine and it will have all been worth it.

Positive self-talk: If you have ever heard a little voice in your mind telling you that you aren't good enough, smart enough, strong enough or fast enough to complete a given task then you have experienced negative self-talk. While most people hear this voice occasionally, and more or less ignore it, for those with lingering issues related to a narcissistic mother, this type of negative self-talk often never stops. While most people will be able to ignore it for a time, eventually it starts to work as a mantra and seep into the very fabric of your thought processes.

That is to say that this level of repetition can have a far greater impact than you may initially realize as eventually, you may come to believe it is true regardless of what the true state of the world might be. If you aren't careful, what starts out as simple heckling could ultimately redefine the very way you see yourself, how you think about yourself and how you define yourself with thoughts and actions.

In order to combat this insidious tendency, your best defense is its opposite or positive self-talk. Positive self-talk is an exercise you can do whenever you feel the need or whenever you are having a particularly negative thought about yourself. Getting started is exceedingly simple, all you need to do is mentally deny the negative thought and replace it with a positive one instead. The denial is an important step in the process as it is important that you get in the habit of actively denying the negative self-talk for the best results.

The first step towards fixing the problem is being aware of it, if you have already practiced meditation than the concept of seeing thoughts without interacting with them will already be familiar to you. Basically, what you want to do is take the time to become fully aware of every thought that passes through your mind. Common forms of negative self-talk involve the phrases "I can't" or "I have never been able to", these are common answers to fixed mindset patterns and should be avoided at all costs. If you find that you mind to be full of these sorts of statements, respond to them by asking "why can't I" and see where this train of thought leads you.

It can be easy to let thoughts exist in the background while another task is front and center but for this exercise, it is important to focus on those other thoughts for long enough to ensure that they aren't harboring thoughts which might promote a fixed mindset. The trick is hearing these thoughts without interacting with them, the goal is to find them and let them go without giving them any extra mental real estate. While you are working on not interacting with these disruptive thoughts it can be helpful to instead think, "Abort, abort" after any negative self-talk has been perceived. This command will break up whatever thought process you were currently working through and allow you to eject the negative thought more easily.

If you find yourself having difficulty with this particular tip, another option is to wear a rubber band or hair tie around your wrist so that every time you catch yourself in negative self-talk you can snap your wrist. This will serve two functions. The first is it will draw your attention to the negative self-talk so that you become aware of it and can then deal with it accordingly. The second is to distract your mind from the negativity long enough that the negative thought does not have time to propagate.

Mindfulness meditation: Meditation can work wonders. Mindfulness activities including meditation can bring about a high volume of the hippocampus and amygdala and reduce stress. One research project showed evidence that just 27 minutes a day of meditation or other mindfulness techniques can accomplish improvements in hippocampus and amygdala performance and relieve stress.

While the ultimate goal of mindfulness meditation is to quiet the mind in an effort to find a state of internal calm despite the hustle and bustle of the outside world, many people find it difficult to achieve this state right out of the gate. Instead, you will likely find it easier to start to supplant any thoughts you might have by focusing all of your attention on the signals that your senses are relaying to you to the exclusion of everything else. While you might not feel as though you are receiving much data on the physical world, especially if you are practicing in a quiet, temperate space, the truth of the matter is that your brain naturally filters out approximately eighty percent of everything it receives, you just need to get in the habit of tapping into it.

With practice, you will learn to tune out your more common thoughts and to instead tune into what is going on around you. When you do this, it is important to simply take in the information your senses are providing without thinking about it too deeply or passing judgement on what you perceive. Judging tends to lead to additional thoughts or, even worse, comparison of the present group of situations to those of the past which is more likely to pull you out of the moment and make finding the state of calm you are looking for even more difficult than it is likely to be, especially when you are just getting started.

Remember, the goal with mindfulness meditation is to get as close to existing at the moment as possible and ignoring everything outside of your current surroundings as much as possible. To reach the required state you are going to want to start by focusing on your breathing, the feel of the air slowly entering and exiting your lungs as well as any smells or tastes that go along with this practice. From there you can then expand the sphere of observation to any other sensations that your body might be experiencing, all the while going deeper into yourself in search of the point where your mind ceases to form new thoughts and simply exists in a state of peaceful relaxation.

Mindfulness is not necessarily quieting the mind or finding an eternal state of calmness. The goal here is simple. We want to pay attention to the moment we are in without judging. When we judge a thought or something we may have done in the past, we tend to dwell on it. That isn't living in the moment and is not conducive to mindful meditation. While this is easier said than done, it is a crucial step to mindful meditation. With practice, it will be easy to achieve. Be mindful of the moment, of your senses and your surroundings.

Take notice of the times you are passing judgment while practicing. Make a note of them and move on. It is easy for our minds to get lost in thought. Mindfulness meditation is the art of bringing yourself back to the moment, over and over, as many times as it takes. Don't get discouraged. In the beginning, you will find your mind wanders a lot. Reel it back in and keep moving forward. Even if your mind does happen to wander—and it will—don't be hard on yourself. Acknowledge whatever thoughts pop up, put them to the side and get back on track.

Keep it up: This list is by no means exhaustive, and sometimes a setback can really upset your plans to solve some very real problems in your life. Think of the destruction, the lost friendships, and maybe the lost opportunities. Opportunities to make more of yourself or the opportunities to get to know people throughout your life somewhat better.

Remember not to get discouraged. Remember that you do not need to be perfect all the time and don't ignore your feelings too much. Cut yourself some slack. Do not be so hard on yourself. You want to form new habits, new coping skills.

There's no way to find out more about yourself if you do not put in the hard work. Try to sweat it out and try some of the ideas here that require you to leave a seated position. A runner may stumble in the field sometimes, but he gets up and continues to run until he reaches the finish line. The true winner is not who reached the finish line first, but those that didn't give up. At times you may still have difficulty managing your emotions and holding back your anger, but that's normal and understandable. We're not perfect and may go the different way sometimes. But always remember what your goal is and how much improvement you've made so far.

Chapter 10

Public and private images of narcissists

Narcissists are good actors. This is one of their manipulative skills. They need histrionic skills to gaslight their victims and assert their dominance. The better you understand their good acting skills, the better you'll be able to deal with them.

Narcissists can be charming when they want to. I mean, they are great charmers! They have the uncanny ability to sweep you off your feet on a first encounter. You'll love them! They are astute in reading their scripts and in interpreting their roles perfectly well. That's why they are good actors!

And what's their scripts? You and me. Their scripts are people they meet and situations they find themselves. They will enchant you if they need something from you. They may like something or dislike it, depending on the script. For example, a narcissist may actually dislike your taste of music, but can tell you she loves in order to get into you.

A narcissist can pretend to like your favorite celebrity if that will help her cause. I have to warn you, narcissists are good actors—better than Angelina Jolie and Dwayne Johnson combined. Okay, that may be an exaggeration. But you get my point? Good, that's all that matters.

You really have to understand this aspect of narcissists, because this is one aspect people don't really know about them. And this is why people, even some relatives and friends, don't know the ordeal a child is going through at home. The reason is because the narcissist is playing the role of the best mom outside and villain at home.

So I'll be devoting this chapter to reveal their various images and roles. I could write a whole book on this alone. To help you have a concrete understanding of the acting skills of narcissists, I'll be using tangible imageries to explain.

The human chameleon

Narcissists change attributes more than chameleons. That comparison may be hyperbolic, but it's not that off, if you've met a narcissist. Chameleons change color for various reasons: to adapt to their environments: to adjust their body temperature to that of their environment, to trap unsuspecting preys and to protect themselves from predators.

Does this sound familiar? Narcissist acts in order to:

Adapt to their environments

Like chameleons, narcissist need to properly adapt to their environments before they begin their operation. This is the first thing they do. Don't let their self-absorption and insensitivity fool you into thinking they don't know what's going on around them. They do!

They do more than you realize, and this is one of their advantage. It takes dark wisdom to foster division between people. It takes some ingenuity to gaslight and exploit others for selfish purposes. So wake up from your slumber! Narcissists are much more alert to their environment.

They are great readers of situations and good calculators. They may appear slow like chameleons, but their shrewdness makes up for their seeming tardiness. To adapt to their environment, narcissist do a lot of scripts reading.

Adjust their body temperature to that of their environment

While chameleons adjust their body temperature to match that of their environment, narcissists adjust their mood and character to match that of those around them who they stand to benefit from. Narcissists will never adjust their mood for those they can bully.

This ability endears narcissists to outsiders. A woman can be a narcissist in her home and no one in her church may know anything about it. They are that good! Your narcissistic mom may put up her best behavior in public, to the admiration of everyone—including you. You may find yourself wondering if this is actually your mom. She has mastered the art of playing the mood.

Trap unsuspecting preys

Have you seen the chameleon's tongue before? It's a long thingy that's super-fast. The chameleon uses it to draw in unsuspecting preys into the vaults of its stomach. Narcissists are like this too. They may not be fast as chameleons, but like their reptile counterparts, their attack is sudden and fast.

They first start by disguising as good people. They will make every effort to make their victims feel comfortable before they strike. It's like the proverbial folklore in which the animal kingdom decided to kill the proud elephant. The only way to do this was to make the elephant the king.

Amidst pomp and pageantry, they led the elephant to the throne that was placed on a very deep hole. Thud! The big guy crashed into the hole trumpeting as he went down. That was the end of that elephant. Moral of the story: The narcissist doesn't mind making you a king if that's how he'll get rid of you.

Protect themselves from predators.

Though narcissists live in imaginary world, they understand the dangers of real life. This is to be expected since the trauma of real life was what encouraged their narcissism in the first place. If pretending to be who they are not will protect their dominance and selfish interests, they will do it.

They can even obey or submit themselves for the time being to protect themselves. But be assured that they will strike at the opportune moment, and they will strike hard.

Having multiple images is very essential for the survival of narcissists. It's their way of being in control. They require a public image and a private image to be on top of their game. The public image is a nice, easygoing, and lovely one. This isn't their true nature. It's a false projection of their true self. The private image, on the other hand, is who they truly are. Your true character is the quality you exhibit when you're alone. It's pure and unpretentious.

Typical Images of Narcissists

Narcissists can be compared to many things. Narcissists are:

Like the earth

Narcissists are like the earth. How? Glad you asked. The earth is dark on one side and bright on the other side. This explains night and day. When the United States is sunny, the United Kingdom will be moony. As the earth spins around its own axis, one side faces the sun and the other side backs the sun. The side that faces the sun is the day and the other side is the night.

Narcissists spins around their own axis too! They show good side to some and bad side to others, depending on their mood, relationship, and selfish interest. Their public image is sunny, lovely and beautiful to behold. You'd love it. But their private image is often dark and freezing cold. This is their true nature.

Their dark side is insensitive, emotionless, abusive, divisive, domineering, cocky, and every other trait I've addressed earlier about NDP. This is the side that's hidden, but it's the side that's venomous.

Demons at home

On their good day, narcissists can be very cruel, but on their bad day they can be monstrous. This image is of course shown to those close to them. It's their private image. They are venomous monsters that victimize their victims. They are unstoppable in their quest to assert their dominance.

They are merciless and vicious. They will do almost anything to achieve their objectives. They will gaslight, victimize, traumatize, and even pauperize to have their way. Show me a more formidable monster!

Angels outside

Narcissists are angels outside. They are likable and social. They are good actors, remember? Outsiders see them as those who can't even hurt a fly. They are congenial and fun to be with. This unreal side of them is part of their divisive strategy. They need to put on a show so that outsiders won't suspect a thing.

Chapter Summary

Image is everything to narcissists. They need this talent for survival and dominance. Please, never underestimate the acting skills of narcissists. If your mom is a narcissist, or you know a narcissist, you've already seen it in action.

Narcissists must have two images: a public image and a private image. The images you see are the ones they want you to see. They are like chameleons, so they can neatly hide their flaws. They can pretend to be who they aren't perfectly, because their whole life is imaginary. You must be very careful when you're dealing with them.

Chapter 11

A narcissistic mother's daughter

Symptoms in a narcissistic mother-daughter relationship are not exclusive to the mother. Daughters who have been raised by narcissistic mothers are also subjected to experiencing many of their painful symptoms that can lead to many problems in the future. You need to take the time to look at yourself as a part of the equation to see what symptoms you are experiencing, and to understand how they may be influencing you to experience more problems or abuse in your adult life.

Looking at your symptoms can be painful because you are going to have to face everything that you now experience and understand that this was all due to your mother. You might feel an intense amount of rage, sadness, pain, grief, guilt, or other emotions relating to these discoveries, so I strongly encourage you to make sure you can speak to someone you trust after reading this chapter. Being prepared to receive support as soon as you need it when difficult emotions or memories come up can be helpful in your recovery from this abuse.

You may be chronically ashamed of yourself

Daughters of narcissistic mothers are known for experiencing chronic shame in their lives, particularly around everything relating to who they are and what they do. It may feel like there is no limit to the shame that you experience, and that you tend to experience it in many different ways.

The shame that you experience now stems from always being made to feel inadequate as a child. Narcissistic mothers tend to be especially threatened by their daughters, which means that the level of abuse that you have experienced in terms of being put down and bullied is likely enormous. There is a good chance that your entire childhood was spent with you being told the many reasons as to why you were a bad person, and why you were not good enough. You were probably told that you were not deserving, not pretty, not smart, not worthy, and many other untrue things that were said to get you to stop bringing attention to yourself.

By making you feel horrible about yourself, your mother could feel confident that you would stay quiet and hidden all on your own so that she did not have to attempt to do it for you. She also would not have to take responsibility for dragging your name through the mud or spreading bad rumors about you, which is a common narcissistic behavior known as "smearing." In some ways, your mom may have even used your low self-esteem to increase her sense of importance, such as by bragging about how she had to stand up for you or try to build you up in certain situations because you lack self-esteem. Of course, she would never mention that your lack of self-esteem came from her in the first place because this would take away from her perfect image.

As an adult, you may now experience chronic shame around everything in your life even when you know it is not needed. You might hold yourself to unreasonably high standards, feel guilty about things that are normal human experiences, and attempt to behave like a superhuman because you have been told that you are not good enough. These behaviors are likely both an effort to be seen as a good person and an effort to avoid being abused any further because in your childhood you would be abused if you did not fight to achieve these unreasonable standards. This shame is extremely toxic, painful, and life-altering, which is why we are going to spend so much time addressing and healing it in part 2 of this book.

Childhood abuse may lead to adulthood abuse or toxic relationship patterns

Any form of childhood abuse can lead to children growing up and entering abusive and toxic relationships, and a child abused by a narcissist is no different. It is possible that as an adult you are now finding yourself in many toxic relationships, or relationships that are even downright abusive. You might feel like you have some sort of hidden "signal" that somehow calls in people who will take advantage of you, bully you, or abuse you through narcissism in your adult life. Many daughters of narcissistic mothers feel as though they cannot get away from narcissism, even though they were sure that leaving their childhood homes would suffice.

The reason why you may be experiencing toxic or abusive relationships now in adulthood is that you have never been taught boundaries or important self-care steps in life. Being raised by someone who commanded you to live your entire life based on her needs and desires has resulted in you not knowing how to fully stand up for yourself and take care of yourself in relationships now. This may be painful to admit, but, indeed, it is likely the reason why this is happening. If you notice that you seem to be surrounded by people who abuse you or take advantage of you and you cannot seem to understand why this happens, there is a good chance that it is a product of your groomed behaviors.

You may reflect some of your mother's symptoms

As a daughter of a narcissist, this can be one of the more scary symptoms that you may face. It is one thing to feel unsafe with others, but to feel unsafe within yourself and to recognize yourself behaving in ways that you do not like can be downright terrifying. There is a chance that now as an adult you reflect some of your mother's symptoms, and this can lead to an intense fear that you are going to become abusive toward someone you love just like she did. You may not understand why these behaviors or exist or have any clarity around how far they will develop too, leaving you feeling powerless and as though it may be inevitable for you to follow in her damaging footsteps.

Believe it or not, even though many people do not like to talk about this point, it is quite common in those who survive narcissistic abuse from a parent specifically. The reason for this symptom is that as a child you are supposed to be raised by a nurturing guardian who can guide you to learn how to navigate various parts of life. Ideally, a healthy guardian should have taught you how to deal with difficult emotions, conflict, expectations, self-esteem, insecurities, and other natural parts of life. Unfortunately, you were raised by a mom who did not know how and who regularly modeled extremely poor examples of how an individual should deal with these things. As an adult, you reflecting this behavior is unlikely to be you displaying true narcissism and more likely to be you displaying poor coping methods in life. With proper healing and efforts, you should be able to identify new ways for you to cope with things in life, enabling you to move beyond the patterns of repeating your mothers' behavior due to not knowing a better way.

There may be the feeling of a deep void in your life

One of the most painful things that I have experienced as a daughter of a narcissist, even to this day, is that void that you feel in yourself and your life around your mother. As an adult, you may now find yourself longing for a positive relationship with your mother, possibly to the point where you keep attempting to have a better relationship with her only to find yourself trapped in the cycle again and again. This is a common experience for daughters of narcissistic mothers and I want to tell you right now that this is not a poor reflection of you, instead, it is a painful reflection of your reality.

Even when you heal yourself from your mother's abuse, you are likely to find yourself in moments where you wish you had a healthy, supportive mother to rely on. You might even recall the times your mother showed you her charming mask, leading you to feel like maybe you can call her for support on just this one thing, hoping that she will offer that type of charm and support once again. It can be painful when you realize that your mother is unavailable to offer you the support and the love that you need, and even more painful when you realize that she has no idea why you feel so disconnected and alone in the world due to her treatment. This is a natural part of the recovery and healing process, and in time it does become a lot easier to navigate. While the pain itself is always there, you will find that you become much stronger in healing that pain and coping with it when it rears its head. This way, you do not put yourself in a game of yo-yo with trying to get your mother to be the woman you need her to be when she truly can't be.

Chapter 12

Beating the narcissists at their own game

Now, we're going to look at the various techniques you can use to foil the narcissist at every turn. I did promise I would give you these tools. If you'd like to learn how to drive the narcissist nuts and beat them at their very own game, then let's proceed.

Be Unpredictable

The narcissist expects you to behave in certain ways every time they do something manipulative or hurtful to you. More often than not, when the narcissist provokes you, you have set ways of responding. You've both done this song and dance long enough that you don't even realize that you have the option of reacting differently.

The one thing the narcissist is never quite prepared for when they attempt to hurt or provoke you is indifference. They also don't expect you to be happy, or joyful. They don't expect you to be stubborn about what you want, or to act from a place of security when they torment you.

What you want to do when the narcissist is tormenting you is the exact opposite of whatever you'd like to do in that moment. For instance, rather than cry, or lash out angrily, you can choose to smile or laugh instead. It helps you feel a lot better, and will get rid of all feelings of anxiety and stress. Let's make this as practical as possible.

Say, at the moment, the narcissist is triangulating you. One thing you can do is simply keep your facial expression neutral, while you switch to a different topic. Another thing you could do is simply choose not to engage in the conversation to begin with. If the narcissist is triangulating you with a stranger in your presence (one the narcissist has no sexual or romantic ties with, to be precise) then you could be extra friendly and warm towards the stranger the narcissist is trying to triangulate you with. Or, you could simply leave the room. Choosing to take the high road by leaving will definitely not go unnoticed by the stranger. One way to tell for sure that the narcissist is triangulating you is to focus your attention on someone else besides the person the narcissist is actively engaging with in your presence. If the narc is triangulating, her attention will turn from her conversation to yours.

If the narc is stonewalling you, then it's certain they expect you to try to claw through their defenses to get to them. Rather than anxiously struggle to get back in their good graces, choose that time to do something for yourself. Do something you enjoy. Go tend to the garden, or pick up a book, hit the gym or take a walk, call a lovely friend, or see the nice neighbors. Keep your phone off while you do whatever is the opposite of what they expect from you. If you used to beg for mercy in the past, just stop. It's a great chance for you to get some practice going No Contact. So, do that instead.

Is the narc trying the hoover maneuver in the hopes of sucking you back in? Doubtless, he expects you to fall for the empty apologies and the crocodile tears. He thinks your No Contact thing is for show, and nothing more. You'll be back to him in no time. Well, this time, choose a different course of action. Block him on all your social media. Ignore him. Act like he does not exist. The more the narcissist attempts to hoover you, the more obvious it becomes that she has lost her hold over you.

Become A Mirror

Let Narcissus see himself in you. What do I mean, exactly? You want to mirror the narcissist. When it comes to dating, pretty solid advice is to mirror your love interest. This way, you won't wind up becoming a little too invested in someone who doesn't care all that much for growing a relationship with you. You can employ this same tactic with the narcissist.

When it comes to mirroring the narcissist, you do not want to reflect his false, charming self to him. What you should mirror instead is his cold, cruel side. When you mirror the narc, what happens is you reduce the level of investment you have in the relationship, and at the same time, you prevent the likelihood of fresh trauma. This will give you the room you need to gather your strength and leave when you're ready. So, when the narcissist grows cold, give her the same treatment. When she withdraws, do the same thing.

Using the Silent Treatment

If you're in a relationship with a narcissist and are preparing yourself psychologically to leave, if the narcissist has just recently abused you or is giving you the silent treatment, it would behoove you to take advantage of that. Encourage the silent treatment to go on. Mirror the narcissist. The time you spend not talking to each other can be invested in taking care of yourself, and nurturing your connection with others. This is a great step to take on your way to full No Contact, by the way.

Put Yourself First

This is the ultimate revenge. The narcissist is used to being the big kahuna, the top dog, el jefe, numero uno. Well, for a change, put yourself first. What this will mean is you've got to be willing to say *NO* to the narc, and you've got to yes yourself back to feeling worthy of the good life has to offer. Do this so you can heal. Do this for yourself. Do this to pay back the narc for all the times they put you in second place, if you ever were on their list of priorities to begin with. From now on, when it comes to you and the narc, you come first.

Step Into The Future

It's good to be mindful and present. However, you need to consider the future. As a victim of narcissistic abuse, the tendency is to keep flipping from the present to the past and back, constantly replaying past trauma, and focusing on how bleak the present moment is. Rather than do that, focus on your future. Ask yourself, if things are this bad now, how much worse will they get? Because, bet your bottom dollar that abuse gets worse over time, not better. Ask yourself what the impact will be on your body, and soul. Ask yourself what dreams you may never accomplish if you don't get out while you can.

Ask yourself if you really want to bring kids into the world with this person as a co-parent. If you've already got kids, ask yourself what your abusive, toxic relationship is going to your kids' psyches. Ask yourself if you'd be willing to put up with the narc's behavior when they are old and ugly. The fact is that part of their charm is in their attractiveness right now. Would you still look at them in their twilight years and find them beautiful or handsome with that shitty behavior? It's not shallow if you answered no.

If it's a narcissist you're putting up with at work, ask yourself whether it's worth the risk to your career. If it's a friend, ask yourself if it's worth it to stay friends with them when all they ever do is drain you.

Cut Down On Social Media

It almost seems that social media was made for narcissists. They just love to use social media to find ways to make you feel terrible. They make themselves seem like something other than what they truly are, and they enjoy the fact that you can actually see them in action as they triangulate you with others. When you withdraw from the narcissist, it would serve you to keep clear of all social media. Do not give in to the temptation to stalk the narc. You can temporarily disable your accounts on all social media, so you don't fall for all the manipulation. It might not be easy in the beginning, but over time, you'll find you're craving to be in the loop will die down, and you'll feel more relaxed and at ease, which will facilitate your healing from the trauma bonds the narcissist has created between you two.

Meditate

Meditation is a great way for you to come to terms with everything that has happened to you so far, as well as to reconnect with who you really are. Chances are you've forgotten who your true self is, on account of all the abuse you've suffered at the hands of the narcissist. However, when you meditate, you begin to find the lost pieces of yourself, so you can put yourself back together again. It's a great aid on the path to recovery and rediscovery of your authentic self. It will also help you become more and more detached from the narcissist, reducing any impulse to return to your vomit.

No More Rewards for Terrible Behavior

The narcissist is an adult toddler, plain and simple. If you keep giving them sweets every time they do something terrible, what do you expect them to do? Of course, they're going to keep acting terribly! In this situation, after the narcissist has discarded you, when they come back to hoover you and you let them have their way, you have given them some candy again. The best thing for you to do should be to completely ignore them. Stay silent. Don't give them even the start of a word. When you remain completely nonreactive to whatever they say or do, this will drive them nuts. Don't just do it to drive the narcissist nuts, though. Think of it this way: When you were in the narc's life, she never respected you. She never valued you being there. So why bother going back?

Rather than allow the narcissist to idealize you, you idealize yourself for a change. Love bomb yourself. You want to please someone? Please your own self. Why feed the narcissist's illogical, nonexistent fantasies? Channel that energy into your own realistic, attainable dreams. Stop giving your energy, time, and emotion to the narc. No more treats!

Is the narc shedding fake tears again to get you to stay? Come on. You've seen this show before. It happens after every abusive incident. It's at worst, boring and, at best, pathetic and hilarious. You can see through the act now. Pack up and leave. Is the narc going on and on about some prized thing he just acquired or purchased? Look as dull and uninterested as you can. A blank stare ought to do the trick.

Validate Yourself

Stop seeking validation from the narc. It's nice to have validation, true, but you must learn to give it to yourself. This way, you're not giving your power away to others. You don't need to please people to receive validation. You can deliberately choose to congratulate yourself. Become more sensitive to all the wonderful blessings in your life. Become thankful for all your achievements, past and present, great and small. Keep the focus on you, and learn to be comfortable with that.

Get It On The Record

Always save the horrific messages that the narc will inevitably send you. You might need them later. If the narc is out for blood, trying to bring you down with a smear campaign, as a last resort, you could release those messages. However, it doesn't have to come to that. You could simply screenshot the messages and save them to remind you why you never want to have anything to do with this person again, on the off chance that you start to think they really have changed. Document everything: videos, voice notes, chats, emails, and texts. Whenever you're tempted to go back to that horrible drug that is the narc, pull these up and go through them. You'll remember why you don't want to be with them or around them anymore.

Write It All Down

Get yourself a journal. In this journal, you'll make a list of all the terrible qualities the narcissist in your life has, as well as the experiences you've had with them where they were gaslighting you, or manipulating you in other ways. Keep this journal somewhere the narc won't see it. Keep notes of everything, including the discrepancies between their version of events and yours. Make sure it's all dated. Note your feelings, and note the episodes of abuse. This journal will help you see you're not the crazy one whenever the narc begins with the crazymaking.

In Summary

As the narcissist idealized you, you must idealize yourself. The difference is because you are capable of empathy, you will come from a place of true love for yourself. Do not waste even a smidge of energy pining over the narc. Idealize yourself, and you'll find that what you've been looking to get from the narc, you could have given yourself all along.

As the narcissist devalues you, you must also devalue what he tries to make you believe about yourself. Understand that the narc sees you as an extension of himself, and as such, the image he's force-feeding you about who you are, is really who he is. So, devalue all that by ignoring it, laughing at it, and seeing it for what it is: futile attempts at manipulation by a pathetic, powerless person.

As the narc discarded you, you must also discard her. Let her go. She is not worthy of you. That's the whole reason she keeps cutting you down. She knows she is not worthy, and she knows she could never measure up to you. So, she hopes to deceive you into forgetting who you really are. Don't fall for it. Discard her.

Now, should you attempt to hoover a narc? The answer to that is no. Hoover yourself. Get to know you again, so you can be reminded of all the many ways you are an awesome badass. It's about time you started treating yourself like the beautiful soul you are.

Chapter 13

Statistics on narcissistic personality disorder

Narcissistic personality disorder is prevailing in the ever-growing population of the world, especially in the population of United States. Narcissistic personality disorder can be diagnosed by certain therapies, rehabilitation sessions and treatments, but the problem is that a lot of people, teenagers and specially the parents fail to consult a psychological professional.

A lot of cases have been reported regarding the narcissistic personality disorder and a lot of people are consulting the psychological professionals to get out of this disorder. Narcissistic personality disorder is not inherited or an in-born disorder. Instead, the people develop it over time due to the inferiority complex or due to the societal pressure. The people with narcissistic personality disorder, especially the parents of the children as they have to nurture and raise the children according to the cultural norms.

Narcissistic personality disorder was the subject of many researchers in their studies. So far, they have gathered little data based upon the various cases of narcissistic personality disorder and the types of faces of the maternal or paternal narcissism. Here is the statistical data or findings of the carried out results.

United states statistics on narcissistic personality disorder

According to the data gathered, approximately 0.5% of the general population of the United States is suffering from narcissistic personality disorder. Moreover, 2-16% of the population who is seeking help from the medical professionals is reported to have a narcissistic personality disorder.

Almost 6% of the forensic population is suffering from narcissistic personality disorder. But, most of the narcissistic traits present in the general population and in the forensic population are not referred as actual narcissistic personality disorder. Actual narcissistic traits are found in the veterans or the people in military. Almost 20% of the military population is suffering from the narcissistic personality disorder. All six types of narcissistic issues have been reported to the psychological professionals by the military population.

In United States of America, more than 17% of the population of the medical students (first year) is suffering from narcissistic personality disorder. The founder of the IRHRPPE (Institute of Relational Harm Reduction and Public Pathology Education), Sandra L. Brown describes in her online journal at almost 60 million people living in the United States are suffering from the narcissistic traits of the people or the family members around them.

She further says that there are at least 304 million people who are suffering from narcissistic personality disorder in the United States. However, this narcissistic personality disorder population also includes the people with psychological issues and anti-social personality issues. She gives an estimate that at least 12.6 million people are suffering from narcissistic personality disorder with no conscience. It means that the 12.6 million people have no moral values to judge themselves. They comply with what they are feeling, without thinking about the right and wrong.

More than 60.8 million people are adversely affected in the United States by the narcissistic behavior of the narcissistic parent, narcissistic spouse, narcissistic friend or any other narcissistic family member. Furthermore, she makes a clear statement that the 60.8 million people is just a rough estimate as it does not include the children who are secretively being affected by the narcissistic behavior of their parents. Maternal and paternal narcissism is very common in United States.

According to the DSM-5, prevalence of the narcissistic personality disorder in the population of United States is 6% while the prevalence of the anti-social symptoms in the personality is as high as 3.3%.

According to this data, there are more than 326 million in the United States (the population is ever-increasing) and the 6% of the total United States population is suffering from narcissistic personality disorder. This means that approximately, 19,560,000 people are suffering from the narcissistic personality disorder. So, if we combine the population is suffering from the narcissistic personality disorder and the population suffering from anti-social personality disorder. Approximately 697,500,000 people lack empathy or have no conscience. As estimated by Brown, these people affect almost 80.8 million people.

Moreover, the DSM-5 proceeds to inform us that almost 50-75% of all the narcissistic patients are men. The remaining narcissistic patients are women and teenage kids.

International statistics on narcissistic personality disorder

Globally, the DSM-5 states that almost 6.2% of the total world population suffers from the narcissistic personality disorder. Narcissistic personality disorder is recognized outside the United States just like in United States. However, the ICD-10 lists 8 faces of narcissistic personality disorder globally.

Narcissistic personality disorder should not be considered lightly as a high unknown percentile of children and adults from around the globe are suffering from the bad effects of maternal narcissism and paternal narcissism. However, despite having narcissistic issues, many parents and fathers are seeking help from the professional psychologists so that they can raise their children in a safe, protective and a healthy environment.

Maternal narcissism symptoms

Narcissism is a common human practice of feeling important, needing admiration, attention from others, desiring success and love. To an extent, this is quite normal and in most of the situation, it is being considered as an important personality trait which every person must possess but only until it is occasional and mild. It is because it is perfectly fine to be

Narcissist to the extent which could not be classed as a disorder.

However, on the other hand, if there is a person who is characterized by Narcissism quite strongly, or the Narcissist personality traits have gone to an extreme in someone, then this is a personality disorder and it will become highly important to pay attention to its treatment. It is because in such situations Narcissism will have the ability to cause functional impairment and distress and even the situation can last for a longer period of time with ease.

If a person possesses a pattern of abnormal behavior for a longer period of time which are particularly characterized by the feeling of self-importance, lack of empathy and excess need for self-admiration. His constant behavior of seeking excess attention and constant admiration can frustrate other people who are in a relationship with the sufferer of this disorder.

Well, to get a better idea about Narcissistic personality disorder it is important to have a look at its basics to get a better idea about the things. Knowing this will surely help you to understand more facts in an effective way with ease.

Narcissistic personality disorder

A narcissistic personality disorder is one of many other personality disorders. It is a mental sense of suffering from an exaggerated sense self-admiration, self-importance, deep urge of extreme attention, etc. Such people who are suffering from this may have trouble with their relationship because they also have a lack of sympathy and compassion for others.

Such people always feel that they are superior or better than the others who are around them and therefore, they should be treated in special manners accordingly. Well, the fact which remains behind this extreme situation are, this excess confidence is just a mask. Actually, these people have flimsy self-esteem which is vulnerable to even the slightest criticism.

Narcissistic personality disorder can be best defined as a paradox. It is because such people who are suffering from this may act confident and superior but they are lacking at self-esteem and are not actually confident about themselves. They are just craving to seek attention from others and want everyone to praise them only.

Due to their superior attitude, most of the Narcissistic personality disorder sufferers are unable to build positive relationships with others. The Narcissistic personality disorder can become a cause of great disaster not only for the person who is suffering from this but also for the people who are living around that person. These affected persons more often spend much time thinking about themselves only. They often think about the ways to achieve power and success or about the ways to improve their appearance. They try to take advantage of the people who are around them most of the time. The abnormal behavior in most of the people normally begins early in their adulthood or occurs across a different variety of social situations such as in relationships or work life.

Most commonly people who are suffering from this problem are being characterized as self-centered, arrogant, demanding and manipulative. Most of them may also have some sort of splendid illusions or fantasies or could be convinced that they need to have special treatments. In some cases, these people also try to associate themselves with the people they think are unique or have some special capabilities.

It means such people want to be linked with the ones who have been gifted in some way and this is also only for the enhancement of their own self-esteem not to praise the next person. Such people tend to seek excessive attention and admiration and have difficulty when it comes to bear any kind of criticism or defeat.

Fast facts:

Here are some facts about Narcissism which you must know:

- Narcissism is a term which has been come from a particular character named as Narcissus in Greek Mythology.

- Narcissism is being characterized by an extreme sense of self-admiration and self-worth. Features of being prone to irritation, quick to anger and vulnerable to criticism are also associated with this situation.

- For its diagnosis, symptoms or signs of Narcissism must be chronic and persistent.

Causes of Narcissism

Well, the exact cause behind the Narcissism is yet unknown because there are different theories about the cause behind Narcissism. Some people think it is a mix of the things which can be ranged from how a person has been raised or how he or she handled different stressing situations.

However, most of the experts tend to apply a biopsychosocial model for this which means that a combination of social, neurobiological, genetic and environmental factors may have played their roles in formulating a Narcissistic personality.

There is also some evidence that this personality disorder can be heritable individuals are likely to develop Narcissism disorder if they have any family history of this disorder. However, in some cases, a specific gene interaction can also contribute to the development of Narcissism personality disorder.

While on the other hand, social and environmental factors are also having a prominent influence on the development of Narcissism disorder. In some cases, Narcissism could develop a weakened attachment with their parents or primary caregivers. This can cause a sense of unconnected and unimportant to others in a child. In some cases, the child may tend to believe that he has some defects in his personality which are making him devalued or unwanted. However, permissive parenting such as over-controlling or insensitive behavior can also play an important role in influencing Narcissism disorder.

Although to find out the exact cause of this personality disorder is complex to figure out but, the children who have been raised by a Narcissist are more likely to develop Narcissism disorder. Although parental narcissism can affect the children but even with few maternal narcissistic traits has the ability to affect their daughters in deceptive ways.

Well, if you are new to the realization of a maternal narcissism then you need to keep learning about what you have to deal with. One of the worst things which you may come to know is the fact that your narcissist parent will never change until she finds a way to bring healthier change in her life.

Well to know what signs and symptoms of maternal narcissism can be and how it can affect you, it is highly important to learn about this in a proper way. Well, here we have brought major and most common symptoms of maternal narcissism which are surely going to be better for you to know in this regard.

Conclusion

Energy vampires – they'll make you feel like you owe them the world, including your own sense of security, self-esteem, and confidence. They'll make every day an obstacle course, an elaborate maze to navigate with extreme caution. Make the wrong turn, and you could be face to face with their demons.

Much like the typical image of pop culture vampires throughout the years, real-life energy vampires can be seductive, admirable, pleasant, and charismatic. They ooze an appeal that begs to be praised, and we just can't help but give them the attention that they so obviously deserve... at a glance.

It's because of their superb capability to present themselves in the best way possible that makes it easy for the rest of us to feel captivated and fall in love. We gravitate towards them, we offer ourselves up to them, we try to be a part of their life because we want that perfection to rub off on us. But when the smoke clears away, and the mask is pulled off, the real narcissist shows its true form.

Behind closed doors, these individuals can be the worst to deal with. They'll make you feel like everything is your fault and they'll make you doubt your own capabilities and talents. They'll destroy your reputation and your relationships without thinking twice, and they'll laugh at you when it's all over. They'll control you and take your identity, they'll force you to toe a tight line and whip you back in shape when you make the tiniest misstep.

They're not easy to deal with, and they're definitely not yours to fix.

At the end of the day, the narcissist in your life will not change. Accept that. Don't think that it was ever your responsibility to make them a better person. It never was. What you need to think about is your own self-worth, your emotional wellness, and your mental well-being.

You are your own responsibility, and you need to protect yourself from the vampires around you.

So, take this information as your wooden stake and drive it through the heart of the relationship you've been trying to save. Before anyone else, save yourself from the abuse and give yourself the chance at a better life and better relationships – there are far more people out there who would gladly give you what you truly deserve without any strings attached.

Is it easy to live life without the abuser you've come to know and love? Absolutely not. But remember, you can't pour from an empty vessel. Restore yourself first and do away with the people who sap you of what you have to give. This should help you find your way to more fruitful, more loving relationships that will reciprocate the affection and positivity you have to share.

Narcissist Abuse Recovery

SEPARATING AND HEALING FROM AN EMOTIONALLY NARCISSISTIC RELATIONSHIP. DISCOVER HOW TO SAFELY CREATE BOUNDARIES FROM TOXIC PARENTS AND OTHERS. A GUIDE TO TAKE BACK YOUR LIFE

HOPE UTARAM

Table of Contents

Introduction..**418**

Chapter 1 Defining narcissistic behavior in simple terms..**421**

Chapter 2 Overcoming negative personality traits..**436**

Chapter 3 Understanding your thinking.................**449**

Chapter 4 Choices and self discovery......................**455**

Chapter 5 Narcissism in Families...........................**460**

Chapter 6 How did i get this way?...........................**471**

Chapter 7 Unlearning unhealthy patterns..............**482**

Chapter 8 Can i choose a new way of thinking?......**496**

Chapter 9 Does genetics play a role?.......................**511**

Chapter 10 Freedom at last.....................................**516**

Chapter 11 How to heal from narcissistic abuse......**532**

Conclusion...**548**

Introduction

----- ❧☙ -----

Unless you live under a rock you've definitely heard the word narcissism. In fact, the World Narcissistic Abuse Awareness day, usually celebrated on the first of June, clearly shows that the world acknowledges narcissism to a high degree. Due to the increased spread of information among the public from every corner, the meaning of narcissism has become so diluted such that even harmless people are labeled narcissists based on what they share on social media.

It is ironical that despite the popularity of the word, only a small percentage of the population understands what narcissistic abuse really is. Lambe et al. (2018) in analyzing how narcissism leads to violence and aggression, define narcissistic abuse as a form of psychological and emotional torture which is inflicted by people associated with a lack of conscience and who have antisocial disorders. Narcissism is the condition where one possesses an inflated sense of themselves. A narcissist seeks gratification from their unrealistic self-image hence they have trouble maintaining relationships. The same love and attention that they seek from others, they are unable to reciprocate. They lack empathy and have troubled relationships. Their idealized self-image covers a great vulnerability that is sensitive to the slightest criticism. Narcissism develops from a troubled childhood exposed to traumas, in which one feels unloved and develops a deep sense of inferiority. Therefore, narcissists seek validation from the people they identify as the most appropriate targets who will worship at their feet. They disguise their hidden motives with love for the would-be victim and after trapping them, they manipulate them to fulfill their selfish motives. Narcissism is real, and it has wounded various people in society. People who had their life together become off course and if one is not careful, they end up in great harm.

It is difficult to comprehend how someone professes to love you then goes right ahead to abuse you, but the truth is, love and loyalty do not always exist together. In an era where various people find their partners from social networking sites, it is easy to find yourself under the embrace of a narcissist because you can hardly assess their background or anyone else, they have dated in the past. Online matchmaking businesses are on the rise and anyone not in a relationship seems interested. Those who want to love and be loved are being targeted by these businesses ready to hook everyone up with "like-minded" individuals. First, this boom of the business shows that people are increasingly and desperately looking for love. Second, it has greatly increased the risk of encountering imperfect matches.

This book aims at showing you how you can fully recover from the abuse of a narcissist and resume your original self. It equips you with the knowledge to understand when you are in a relationship with a narcissist and how to end it. Notwithstanding, you will be able to help other people you know who might be in such abusive situations. It brings to you the good news that most narcissists are predictable, and you can use their vulnerabilities to your advantage.

Chapter 1

Defining narcissistic behavior in simple terms

Understanding how narcissists think and who they are most likely to target for narcissistic abuse, you are now in a much better position to deal with any narcissists in your life. Whether the narcissist in question is a spouse, romantic partner, family member, friend, or boss, these tips and strategies will help you keep a clear head and respond effectively.

Effective Responses

There are a number of effective responses to narcissistic abuse, but they all have one thing in common: an understanding of what the narcissist really wants. No matter what seems to be happening at the moment, the narcissist is always looking for power. The most effective responses are those which allow you to keep your power rather than giving any more of it away to the narcissist. This means not allowing the narcissist to disregard your boundaries, but it also means not reacting emotionally in ways that might make the narcissist more powerful in the situation.

Clarify Your Boundaries

The first and most important step is to clarify your boundaries. For a codependent person, developing clear boundaries is always difficult. One of the defining characteristics of codependency is a lack of clarity about where the self ends and where others begin, so you may need to clarify that for yourself before you can begin to establish boundaries with the other people in your life. You are not responsible for how other people feel, for what they do, or for the consequences of their actions. You are only ever responsible for your own actions.

To start the process, make a list describing how you want to be treated by the other people in your life. The list should have clear statements about the kind of behavior you aren't willing to tolerate. For example, "no putting me down" or "no guilt-tripping."

Making a list might be a little challenging, especially if your self-esteem is badly damaged or if you've been conditioned to feel that you don't have any rights. If you feel like you're always responsible for other people's emotional reactions, you might feel guilty about setting boundaries.

If this is how you're feeling, remind yourself that you have the same rights as anyone else. First and foremost, you have the right to say, "no." One way to write your list of boundaries is to ask yourself what you wish you could say "no" to. Everything you wish you could say "no" to is a boundary you can set.

For instance, if your mother always calls you on the weekend and asks you to run errands for her no matter what else you had planned, you probably wish you could say no in that situation. The truth is that you can—you just need to establish a clear boundary. Add "not doing errands for Mom without advance notice" to your list of boundaries.

Once you have your list, attach a realistic consequence to each boundary. For example, "if anyone tries to make me feel guilty, I will not do what they are asking me to do," or "if anyone shouts at me, I will leave and go someplace safe."

The consequences should not be retaliation, just basic and logical steps to protect yourself and your own boundaries. For every situation in your life that feels abusive or manipulative, you should have a clearly-defined boundary and a clearly-defined consequence. The goal is to know just what you will do ahead of time, so you don't need to react emotionally when the situation comes up.

Assert Yourself

Asserting yourself is not the same as being aggressive or hostile and is completely different from being passive-aggressive or resentful. In order to assert yourself effectively, it's essential to stay calm. Stand up for yourself but don't let the narcissist push your buttons. He will almost certainly try!

Be as direct as possible. For example, if your partner launches into a tirade about your shortcomings, don't respond with a counterattack or a resentful hint about how you're feeling. Instead, just tell them that you aren't willing to participate in a conversation where you're being put down, then walk away from the conversation.

If someone is trying to guilt-trip you into spending time with them, tell them you aren't available and leave it at that. If they tell you that you don't care about them because of the boundary you're setting, tell them you disagree, or you see it differently.

Whenever you assert yourself, be as clear as possible about what you are willing to do and what you aren't willing to do. Stick to the boundaries you've set and refuse to engage with any attempts to manipulate you.

If the person you're talking to is being abusive, confront what they're doing in the clearest terms. For example, "I don't like it when you call me stupid. If you want to continue this conversation, don't do that again."

To establish clear boundaries may take a little while because the narcissist has to see that you really mean it. He will try to push it, testing to see if your resolve will weaken. Follow through with your consequences every single time, and the narcissist will either learn to respect them or leave the situation.

Projection

Projection is simple if an immature psychological defense mechanism in which negative emotions and self-criticism are projected outward onto another person to avoid having to face them directly. Narcissists use projection all the time because their true or inner self is the complete opposite from the false or ideal self they want others to see.

Whenever anything reminds them of how they really feel inside, they defend themselves by projecting the negative emotion onto another person. When the narcissist is feeling incompetent, he will accuse you of incompetence. When the narcissist is feeling ugly, he will call you ugly. When the narcissist is feeling worthless and unlovable, he will do everything in his power to make you feel worthless and unlovable.

Understanding this process is the key to not being controlled by it. If you have unclear boundaries, it's hard not to absorb what the narcissist is saying. When your boundaries are stronger, you can see that the narcissist isn't really talking about you at all—she's talking about how she feels inside.

You can deal with sniping and minor put-downs by refusing to react the way the narcissist is hoping for. The narcissist is always looking for an emotional response because no matter what the emotion is, it demonstrates the power the narcissist holds in the situation. If you respond calmly and don't take the bait, you can avoid giving them any more power. For example, if your partner says, "the house is a terrible mess, you never do anything around here," you can say, "yes, it could stand to be picked up, should we do that now?" without reacting to the accusation.

It's sometimes better to ignore anything hinted or implied but to respond directly to insults or put-downs by setting a firm boundary. Either way, the key point is to not react in any way that will give the narcissist more of the power he craves.

Remind yourself that he isn't really talking about you in the first place. He's really describing his own inner self—the self that he can't stand to face or deal with. Don't take it personally, but don't let him use it as an excuse to mistreat you. The narcissist's actions may be driven by suffering, but he has no right to inflict suffering on you as his coping strategy.

Codependency often makes it difficult to deal with projection because the codependent person also has a painful relationship with the inner self. You may have received toxic messages in childhood that gave you a distorted sense of who you are. For instance, you may have such a negative self-picture that you find it easy to accept criticism and almost impossible to accept praise. When someone tells you something good about yourself, you can't hear or it or believe it. When someone tells you something bad about yourself, it feels like the truth.

Your negative self-image comes from your own experiences and has nothing to do with whatever criticism or blame the narcissist is throwing at you. It might feel like he sees the horrible truth about you, but that really isn't what's happening at all. The narcissist cannot see the inner you, for good or bad, so his comments can never represent some special insight into who you really are. No matter what terrible thing he says, he's always describing how he feels about himself. It's always a projection.

It's important to work on your self-esteem, which may mean getting therapy to deal with the toxic beliefs you absorbed in childhood. Whether you're in therapy or not, understanding projection is essential in dealing with narcissistic abuse.

Dealing with Narcissistic Parents

For many people with codependency, the first narcissist they ever met was their mother or father. Establishing boundaries can be much harder with family than with other people because family usually knows you a lot better and has a lot more practice pushing your buttons.

Some people choose not to deal with their parents at all because they can't establish boundaries in any other way. If you still want to maintain a relationship with your parents, learning how to have better boundaries may be the only way to do it.

The key is to detach, which doesn't mean to move far away (although that works for some people) or to stop caring but to stop taking on the responsibility for your parent's feelings. Just because your mother wants something does not mean it is your responsibility to provide it. Just because your father expects you to prioritize him at all times doesn't mean you have to.

For example, if your mother expects you to take her phone calls even when you're busy, you may feel like a bad child if you don't take the call. However, you're not responsible for managing her emotions. Take a step back and detach emotionally, then tell her you'll call her when you're no longer busy. That doesn't make you a bad child—it just means you have to manage your time like everyone else.

Your mother or father may try to guilt-trip you for not going along with what they want. For instance, they may send you texts or leave voice mail messages to blackmail you emotionally. Set clear boundaries when this happens: "If you want me to spend more time with you, I need you to stop sending me this kind of message."

Some people find it easier to establish healthy boundaries when they can keep a little more distance between themselves and their family members. For instance, it might help to stay with friends or at an Airbnb when you're visiting home, rather than to sleep at your parents' house. This allows you to take a little space when you need to withdraw while still spending time with your family.

Ineffective Responses

Some tactics are effective when dealing with a narcissist, and some are ineffective. Remember to avoid these common but ineffective responses, especially if you have a history of codependency:

- Placating the narcissist
- Arguing with the narcissist

- Defending your own actions
- Criticizing the narcissist
- Begging or pleading
- Blaming yourself
- Making empty threats
- Excusing, minimizing, or denying the problem
- Avoiding conflict
- Trying to get the narcissist to understand you

Don't Placate

Placating the narcissist will only backfire because he will interpret your attempts to appease him as a victory. Narcissists see interpersonal conflict in black and white terms—every disagreement has a winner and a loser. If you appease the narcissist, he will only take this as an admission of defeat, encouraging him to continue with the same behaviors. Once you draw a line with a narcissist, you have to stick to that line.

Don't Argue

Arguing back and forth with a narcissist is a lose-lose proposition because it's based on the false assumption that the narcissist shares your desire for eventual agreement and mutual understanding. In reality, the narcissist only cares about who wins and who loses. Facts are irrelevant to the narcissist, so debating things like who said what or who did what can only play into the narcissist's hands. Deflect every attempt to draw you into a debate. The narcissist isn't arguing in good faith anyway, so trying to win an argument or prove your point would only waste your time and energy.

Don't Defend

It's only natural to defend your actions or your motivations when someone is criticizing you, but defending yourself is always a mistake when you're dealing with a narcissist. Why? It's because the narcissist is assuming something that she doesn't have any right to assume, which is that she has the authority to judge your actions as acceptable or unacceptable. The same thing goes for explaining yourself, which tells the narcissist that she has the right to demand explanations. As an independent person, you have the right to make your own decisions. You don't have to defend or explain yourself to anyone.

Don't Criticize

Criticizing the narcissist is a mistake for several different reasons. First, it assumes that the narcissist actually cares about doing the right thing, when in reality, he only cares about getting his own needs met. Second, it opens you up to the narcissist's counterattack—after all, if you can judge him, then he can judge you. Third, it can trigger an explosive burst of narcissistic rage. Narcissists cannot handle even a hint of criticism because it exposes the vulnerability and pain of the inner self. Rather than criticizing the narcissist for his selfish actions, it's better to establish and enforce your own boundaries.

Don't Beg

In the black-and-white mental world of the typical narcissist, those who beg and plead are weak and contemptible, while those who receive these pleas are strong and powerful. When you plead with a narcissist to change his behavior, he sees this as a clear confirmation that he is strong and you are weak. Instead of doing whatever you're begging him to do, the narcissist will simply view you with even more contempt and disregard. It can be hard to remember this, but you are only ever in control of your own actions. Focus on what you can do—not on what he should do.

Don't Blame Yourself

If you cannot control the narcissist's actions (and you really can't), then you cannot be responsible for them either. The only person responsible for any action is the person who commits that action. When the narcissist yells or gets drunk or punches holes in the walls, those actions are his and his alone. It's impossible for you to provoke them or bear any responsibility for them whatsoever. Remember, codependent people have a hard time understanding and establishing boundaries between themselves and others. It may feel like you are somehow to blame for what the narcissist says or does or feels, but you are two separate people and can only be responsible for your own life.

Don't Bluff

Don't ever make a threat you aren't prepared to carry out because the narcissist will take this as a sign that you don't really mean it and that he can ignore any boundaries you try to set. For example, don't say "if I catch you cheating again, I'll move out" unless you fully intend to do exactly that.

Don't Deny It

Denial is one of the strongest instincts the codependent person has, and you'll have to fight against it for a long time if that's part of your history and your personality. When you know something isn't right, it won't help at all to pretend otherwise. It's better to face it and get it dealt with, even if you find that painful or difficult. This includes making excuses for the narcissist's behavior or minimizing how bad the problem really is.

Don't Avoid It

Avoiding a problem is a lot like denying it and will do nothing in the long term to regain your power over your own life. Fleeing the scene of a conversation you have lost control over may sometimes be necessary so you can get your emotions under control and stop playing whatever game the narcissist wants you to play. However, you can't establish boundaries by simply avoiding any conflict, so in the end, you will have to address the situation one way or the other.

Don't Look for Sympathy or Understanding

Trying to get the narcissist to understand where you're coming from or even to sympathize with you is a losing fight. The narcissist isn't interested in understanding other people, only in getting what he needs from them. He may express sympathy under certain conditions, but his ability to actually feel it is limited or nonexistent. The goal in dealing with a narcissist is not to be understood, but to establish boundaries and make sure they're respected.

Dealing with Physical Abuse

Physical abuse is not always the most psychologically damaging form of abuse. Many people find that emotional abuse is more harmful to their overall wellbeing. However, physical abuse is dangerous in a different way because it almost always escalates over time. Many abusers will express intense shame and remorse over their violent acts in the immediate aftermath, but that doesn't mean they won't do it again. They almost certainly will, no matter what they say—and it will almost certainly get worse.

The abuser may try to evade the responsibility for their own violence by blaming it on you, so boundaries are especially important in this type of situation. You can't be responsible for the other person's actions, so if they say you provoked them or drove them to it, they are simply trying to dodge responsibility. It is never your fault.

If your partner is physically abusive, threatening, or violent, it's important not to minimize the problem. Denial can literally be deadly. Seek help immediately and make a plan to ensure your own safety. No matter how strongly you feel about the other person, don't kid yourself about a violent relationship. It's never acceptable for anyone to hit you, and if you don't take steps immediately, it will happen again.

Chapter 2

Overcoming negative personality traits

There are several different tactics that narcissists use to manipulate and abuse other people. The list that will be used in this chapter is not comprehensive, by any means, but it does cover the most commonly used tactics that narcissists employ. Each of these manipulation tactics can be harmful in their own ways, and each is meant to keep you in line for the narcissist, doing whatever it is that the narcissist wants you to do, and providing him with a steady stream of narcissistic supply.

The false self

As briefly touched upon earlier, the narcissist creates a false self in an attempt to manipulate others into liking him. The false self is used to draw people in and is constantly changing. Perhaps one of the most unnerving things about watching a narcissist from a distance is watching him change as he goes from person to person. He may have certain quirks and mannerisms with one person, but then as soon as he moves to the next, his mannerisms change completely. This is because he is constantly mirroring their mannerisms in an attempt to get them to like them more.

Remember, people like those they relate to, and one of the easiest ways to build rapport or a relationship between people is through mirroring. People naturally mirror people that they like or are close to. You can see this if you watch a couple at a restaurant for a date. You may see them choose to take a sip of their drinks at the same time, or both prop themselves up on their elbows as they talk. This is because they are in sync. If you had the ability to view their breathing and heart rates, you would likely be met with the surprise that they are both quite similar as well. The narcissist preys off of this way of synchronizing with others, using it to his advantage to create bonds where none would naturally develop. It is perhaps the closest thing to empathy that the narcissist is capable of.

The false self serves another purpose as well—the narcissist uses it as a shield between his fragile inner sense of self and the world around him. He pretends to be someone more confident, so people do not realize the truth about him. He uses it to be charismatic, in hopes of drawing more victims near, or in order to develop enough of a positive reputation that there is no way for his victim to leave and actually get anyone to believe that the narcissist was abusive.

This goes one step further and allows the narcissist to feel better about himself as well. He feels more comfortable and confident in the skin of another because he, himself, has a very fragile, fractured sense of self. The person he is inside is not one to be proud of, and he is aware of that. When he takes on the persona of someone else, however, he is able to better live with himself. He acts as if he is another person, and he gets valuable information from this. He learns what works and what does not, which traits are more and less desirable, and more. By learning this information, he is better able to manipulate others in the future. He knows how to tweak his behaviors by watching the people he emulates and how they manage to get through the world. This makes him more effective in general.

Idealization-devaluation-discard cycle

The idealization-devaluation-discard cycle is the cycle in which the narcissist puts you onto a pedestal and then knocks you off of it just as quickly, leaving you reeling and unsure of your place in his life. It is used to manipulate and hook you onto the narcissist, where he will keep you until he has decided you have done your job and he is bored with you.

Idealization

The first stage, idealization, involves what is referred to as love bombs. This stage seeks to build you up, showering you with love and affection. The narcissist pushes for the relationship to move quicker than you may be comfortable, and comes onto you with more tenacity than is typically expected early in a relationship. He wants you to feel the most intense whirlwind romance you have ever felt, and he mirrors exactly the person you want him to be. The persona he creates is everything you have ever desired at this stage, and he will show you how loving and affectionate he can be.

At this stage, he is listening closely to everything you say, learning all about you and your insecurities. Any information you provide at this stage when you are confiding in someone that you think you can trust, can, and will, be used against you later on. The narcissist will be attentive now, but it is only to learn what he can use to manipulate you when the time comes.

The idealization stage continues to pick up the pace over time, and the narcissist grows more clingy and affectionate. He always wants to spend time with you, and you quickly explain this away as passion or try to perceive his overzealousness as romance. You quickly find yourself hooked to the intensity, enjoying every moment of it, and you eventually want to seek it out yourself. You find yourself just as willing to spend time with the narcissist as he is to spend time with you, and your relationship with him slowly begins to consume other aspects of your life. You start spending more and more time with the narcissist and less time with others around you.

Devaluation

Just as quickly as the spark in your relationship caught fire, you quickly find it burning away. The narcissist seems to be pulling away at this stage, and you cannot figure out why. If you ask what is wrong, the narcissist denies there is a problem at all. He insists that everything is fine, but the distance has been put between you. He may begin to demean you or call you names, implying that you are wrong about things, or that you are unworthy of his time.

Confused, you find yourself desperate to figure out what changed so suddenly. You do not understand why the narcissist suddenly withdrew affection from you and replaced it with this. The reason for it is he has decided to devalue you. The purpose of this is to get you yearning for more. You do whatever it takes to get back into the narcissist's good graces, knowing that is where you want to be. You want to be with the narcissist when he is loving, not when he sees you as invaluable. He takes advantage of this and realizes that you have, effectively, been ensnared into his web and you will be willing to put up with his mistreatment. He may move back to the idealize stage at this point if you have done a sufficient job of proving that you are willing to do whatever it takes to keep him happy, or he may move on to the discard stage.

Discard

Eventually, the narcissist decides that he no longer wants you around. Maybe you were not willing enough to put up with his abuse, or maybe he has found someone else that puts up with it better. Narcissists prefer not to work much for what they want and will often take the path of least resistance to getting their narcissistic supply. If you are no longer the path of least resistance, you will be discarded.

At this point, the narcissist essentially cuts you off. He likely will not respond to messages you send or your attempts to reconcile with him. He instead moves on just as quickly as he flew into your life, ready to move on to other victims.

Sometimes, the narcissist will eventually move back from discarding you to idealizing you again. This may happen if he decides that he wants to keep you around as a backup, or maybe he has decided he wants something you have to offer that other people do not. Regardless of the reason, the cycle will begin again at this point, starting with idealizing.

Gaslighting

Gaslighting is one of the most dangerous manipulation tactics narcissists use. This one involves the narcissist convincing you that you are crazy or incapable of understanding the reality around you. When the narcissist decides to gaslight you, he wants you to discount your own perception of what happened and instead focus on the one he insists happened. Of course, the narcissist is trying to instill a false narrative into you rather than the truth.

He does this over time to weaken your perceived grasp on reality. If you are questioned repeatedly on whether your memory is faulty or not, you are prone to believing it eventually, especially when it comes from someone you love and trust not to hurt you. This is what makes this abuse so insidious—the victim has trusted the abuser, and it has been betrayed so thoroughly that the victim feels as though he or she can no longer trust reality as he or she perceives it.

The narcissist most frequently does this through denying your account of what happened. If you say that the narcissist started a fight, he will either vehemently deny that a fight happened at all, saying you must have imagined it and asking if you are okay, or he will say that you did something to instigate it rather than allowing the blame to remain on him. Either way, the perception of the truth has been altered in some way, and the narcissist is counting on you trusting the narcissist enough to disbelieve yourself rather than disbelieving the narcissist. After all, most people would not think that someone would attempt to make them think they are insane, especially if it is someone they think loves them.

Frequently, the declarations of something being false or having never happened will be matched with the narcissist pointing out some other times where you really did forget something. If you forgot all about an appointment you had last week, for example, the narcissist might point that out and then look at you in concern and ask if you are doing okay. He may imply that you need to see a psychologist, or that you seem to be losing touch with reality, which is terrifying to most people. You are then left feeling doubtful about what had really happened. Rather than speaking your mind about it, you instead nod your head and agree with the narcissist, not wanting to push the point or come across as crazy. To people who are not abusive, the idea of playing with someone's mind in this manner is absolutely abhorrent, so you do not think that the narcissist may be manipulating you, particularly if you do not know what the narcissist is at this point.

The ultimate irony here, however, is that the narcissist is the one with the skewed perception of reality. In fact, he may have even gaslit himself to believe what he is convincing you of, and that is what makes him so credible—he may literally believe what he is saying if it fits his narrative better than what actually happened. Ultimately, when in doubt, you should trust your gut. Especially if you have been wondering if you are being abused, you should never trust what the narcissist may be saying to you. Your own perception

Smear campaigns

Smear campaigns involve the narcissist attempting to absolutely destroy another's reputation through any means possible. The ultimate goal is to entirely and irrevocably tarnish someone's image that they feel as though they have been cast out of their social circles. This most typically happens when you have somehow enraged a narcissist in one way or another, and the narcissist feels the need to seek revenge on you and make sure that you are ultimately the more injured party.

Imagine that you have just cut off your narcissistic ex after finally divorcing. The narcissist, feeling as though he cannot possibly allow someone to tarnish his own image through cutting him off, he instead creates a story in which he has actually divorced and cut you off. Usually, his reason for having done so is one that most people would find absolutely abhorrent, and it may even be the reason you have chosen to divorce him. For example, if you divorced him because he cheated on you in your own home, going so far as to bring the other women into your own bed, that you, personally bought, and then he proceeded to attack you or physically assaulted you after you confronted him, he would spin that story around to everyone else instead. You would be the one having an affair in his bed, and you had attacked him when he walked in and started crying because he ruined the mood.

The narcissist would then spin this tale to everyone who would listen. If you live in a small town, he will tell everyone: The grocer, the gas station attendant, and even random people he passes walking his dog. The point is to ruin your image, and he holds nothing back. He even spins things around to say that he is such a great person for not pressing charges because he just loves you so much and wants the best for you, even if the best is not him.

The lies may not stop there and include stories about how you had been on drugs, or that you stole a car when drunk one night and that you gave him several STIs. He will stop at nothing to destroy your reputation in order to protect his own and damage yours.

He will insist on all of this so adamantly that some people are likely to believe him, and that can be the end to you being able to find work in a small town, where reputation is everything. At the end of the day, the narcissist does this to regain control of a situation that spiraled out of his control. You may have cut him off, but he got the final word in by ruining your hometown for you. You can either deal with the rumors and attempting damage control, or you can move on with your life and hope that the narcissist does not find you again.

Remember, even though the narcissist has flung this at you, you can be the better person and choose not to engage at all. You will probably be happier in the long run if you refuse to confront him about his lies. All that would do is prove to him that he could get a reaction out of you, and he will remember that tactic for future use.

Triangulation

Triangulation involves three people who are interacting with each other, in which one attempts to manipulate, deceive, and abuse another person through weaponizing a third person. It involves three different people: the persecutor, the rescuer, and the persecuted.

The persecutor is someone who believes that he has been victimized in some way, shape, or form. He feels as though he has been hurt somehow, though his internalized victim role is most likely unjustified in this instance. As you have learned, the narcissist thrives on victimizing himself, even when he has been the one that hurt other people.

Typically, the triangle begins when the narcissist wrongs the persecuted, who responds unfavorably. The persecuted may call him out for such egregious behavior and request not to be disrespected again. Even though the persecuted could have said that in the nicest way possible, with a smile on his face and offering the narcissist a friendship bouquet, the narcissist takes some sort of fault with what has been said. He feels ashamed that he was called out, and he uses that shame to say he is the victim.

The narcissist then calls out to the rescuer to come to his aid. He does not see any issue using someone else to fight his battles, as the ends justify the means every time for the narcissist. The narcissist tells the rescuer some sort of lie about what has happened, skewing it just enough so that the story is compelling enough for the rescuer to get involved. He may say that the persecuted has been talking badly about both the persecutor and the rescuer, or he may say that the persecuted has been intending to take advantage of you both. No matter what he says, it is fabricated in order to get the rescuer to also seek to discontinue a relationship with the persecuted.

The persecuted, much as the person who was a victim to a smear campaign, finds his reputation completely destroyed and may have even lost a relationship or job due to the narcissist's actions. Meanwhile, the narcissist happily sits in his corner, content that his own vigilante justice has been served. He does not care about the implications of his actions, or that the persecuted if he has lost a job due to the narcissist's behaviors, can continue to feed his family. The narcissist does not care about anyone involved beyond himself.

The persecuted is then left trying to pick up the pieces of his life that are left behind, particularly if the consequences of the triangulation were devastating, and trying to move on with life. The narcissist is then able to get away with this behavior, despite how unfair it was, and how wrong the narcissist's behaviors were. He can try to defend himself, but he is likely only going to be the victim of a further attack from the narcissist and the narcissist's rescuer in response.

Chapter 3

Understanding your thinking

How that you have learned about the healing process and how spiritual healing works, it is time to move onto the next aspect of healing.

Just like a house that has four walls, you are also made up of four walls. These four walls or pillars are what make you the person you are and help you in creating an identity for yourself.

The four pillars are as follows:

- self-esteem
- self-worth
- self-trust
- self-love

You must have noticed that throughout the book, these words have been used generously. These are the four pillars on which every human being stands. These pillars offer the support to live life, to tackle problems that life throws at you and to finally experience a fulfilled life.

Relationship with a narcissist hurts so much and causes internal damage because a narcissist methodically attacks all the four pillars. He ensures that he leaves no stone unturned in damaging every small part of all the four pillars leaving no option for you other than to fall.

To help you understand this better, imagine a storm that is raging through. Have you ever seen the destruction a storm causes and have you wondered how long it takes for the people and homes affected by the storm to reclaim their life back?

You are exactly similar to the person caught in a storm. A narcissist attacks you unannounced just like a storm when you least expect it or are least prepared. He attacks all your pillars and disturbs the foundation on which you are standing, so you fall and collapse just like those houses that fall in a storm or massive trees that get uprooted. The destruction is so much that it takes months and in some cases years for the pillars to rebuild.

There are some basic practices that you can do to help rebuild the pillars.

Self-Esteem

Self-esteem essentially means supporting yourself. It is how much control you have over yourself, your mind, your body, and your behaviors. Self-esteem is also about the perception you have about yourself and how you see yourself.

The opposite of self-esteem is self-sabotage or self-damage. During the process of healing, it is important that you build your self-esteem.

You can begin by doing simple things that will tell you that you are in control of the situation. You can start by tackling basic things such as hygiene that you might be ignoring right now because of your PTSD or depression. Something as simple as having a daily routine to take a shower or to dress decently even when at home can help you regain a sense of control. These baby steps will help you tackle the bigger problems.

Self-Worth

This is about knowing your value and respecting your worth. It is believing that you are worth the respect, love, and affection. The exact opposite of self-worth is shame and unworthiness.

After the abuse, the narcissist would have ensured that you feel a deep sense of shame and hate yourself. Self-worth is also about speaking up for your rights and standing up for yourself and what you believe in.

You need to focus on the courage to build self-worth. Courage does not mean trying to scale the mountains or running in the wild. Courage means taking measures to change your life actively. It can be applying for another job, being able to negotiate a good pay that you deserve, applying to school if you always wanted to finish school, etc. It means identifying something that you wanted to do but have never done because you believed that you were not worth it.

It also comes by not compromising on your values or doing things you are uncomfortable doing. You would have compromised on your values while trying to appease the narcissist. Once you develop courage, you will not compromise on your values and thus will develop self-worth. Regardless of what you have come to believe about yourself, God our father has a very different view of who you are. I choose to believe that his word and it changed my life completely. I went from feeling lost, to finding hope in his promises. If you haven't read that book yet, I suggest you do. If you have tried everything else, and years after leaving your abuser you still feel stuck, angry, and broken, I suggest you start by getting a bible. Read as frequently as possible and I guarantee you would see a change in your life.

Self-Trust

Self-trust is about trusting yourself, your judgment. It means having faith in yourself and being confident about your decisions. It means not second guessing every single decision and worrying about it.

When you lack self-trust, you live in constant fear and doubt. During the relationship with the narcissist, you slowly start losing self-trust without even you realizing. It happens silently, and before you know it, you will be second-guessing everything. The narcissist achieves this by gaslighting and deflecting blame.

The only way to rebuild self-trust is to listen to your intuition. The gut feeling that everyone talks about is what you must pay attention to. If something does not feel right to you, then trust that instinct and let it go. Gut feeling is more tangible than some more forms of intuition. Gut feeling is never wrong, as it is your inner voice trying to guide you and protect you from danger or from something that is not right for you.

Your gut feeling and intuition stop working once you start ignoring them. It is like ignoring your best friend who has nothing but the best intentions for you. Once you start ignoring your intuition and gut, they no longer guide you, and that is when you take the wrong steps.

Get it back by listening to it. Follow whatever your gut says and see the change.

Self-Love

Finally, the fourth pillar, self-love is about caring and nurturing yourself. It is about treating yourself well. Self-love takes a back seat during the relationship with a narcissist because the narcissist wants and demands all the love. When you are in a relationship with a narcissist, you cease to be in a relationship with yourself. You slowly stop loving yourself and go into self-denial and self-judgment mode. You judge yourself poorly and try to rationalize all the bad behavior being shown by the narcissist. When you do not love yourself, you go into a people-pleasing mode and develop a savior complex. By now, you know how dangerous savior complex is to your health and sanity. You start believing you are ugly and stop taking care of your health.

The medicine to this lies in loving yourself back. This can be accomplished by taking small steps such as cooking your favorite meal, eating healthy food, and eating regular meals. It could also be treating yourself at a salon or spa and just pampering yourself.

You can focus on things that you want to change about yourself and more importantly accept what you cannot change. Self-acceptance is a part of self-love because if you do not accept yourself just as you are, then there is no way that another person or the world will accept you the way you are. This is because others will treat you just as well or as bad as you treat yourself. By treating yourself well, you are teaching the world how they must treat you and conveying your boundaries and wishes to them.

How long does it take to heal completely?

This is a question that haunts most victims because it can seem like forever with no end in sight. A lot of days you may go to bed wishing that you do not have to get up the next morning because you are afraid how bad the day will be. You will constantly feel like there is no light at the end of the tunnel.

Do not drown in this hopelessness because this kind of negative thinking will quickly take you back to victim land. The journey to victim land is a free airplane ride where you will reach the deepest levels of fear, hatred, and disgust within minutes, but remember that journey to victim land means no return.

Hence, hold onto your horses. Take comfort in the fact that God has given you this amazing opportunity to heal you, and you can start by drawing closer to him. Healing that comes from your spirit, is exactly what you need for psychological abuse, just because a lot of the scars you have are not physical ones.

There are countless women who spend their entire lives trapped in victim land and never live a happy and fulfilled life.

The truth is that there is no timeline for healing. It is not a mathematical calculation with definite results. Do not trust anyone who is telling you that it takes no more than a month or two to recover. Neither must you pay attention to fellow victims who claim to have healed in record time. You are not in competition with anyone, this is about the rest of your life, and healing needs to be thorough and deep to be sustainable.

This journey is a spiritual journey, and the destination is you, so it can be one month for some; it can take one year for some, and some people can take several years. Healing depends on various factors, but above all, it depends on how committed you are to the process. At times you will see no progress at all. There will also be times when from one forward stage you will take two steps back for reasons you cannot understand yourself. Despite this, persist. Persistence works magic. Keep a journal and write down everything so that when you feel demotivated, you can turn back the pages and see how far you have come.

Celebrate each milestone and make a note of it. Acknowledgment helps develop self-love and will bring you to acceptance. Again, you need to understand that you are not in competition with anyone but yourself in this and this not a race. Healing from narcissistic abuse is not like running a sprint, but it is more like a marathon. Hence, pace yourself and keep the momentum going.

It does not matter whether it takes a few months longer, but it is important that you heal completely and come out of the marathon with flying colors.

Chapter 4

Choices and self discovery

When adults mistreated by their abusers begin to develop a positive feeling towards people abusing them, it's referred to as Stockholm syndrome. As the whole abusive situation progresses, you find yourself being childlike and overly reliant on your abuser. You start becoming grateful for even the smallest sign of affection and approval they show you. Eventually, you end up bonding with your captors and end up loving them more.

But again, how do all these apply to a narcissistic relationship?

Stage 1: Continuous rewards with nothing given in return

At the very beginning, the one thing that you have to notice is that your narcissistic individual targets on getting hold of you. That is why they will start giving you emotional pellets in the form of love, validation and affection, sweet gestures and even praises. They make you believe that you are a wonderful person and this makes you right.

The truth is, you are not alone; we all enjoy getting stroked and loved by someone that we like. This is necessarily what we refer to as 'love bombing' all that they are seeking for in return is for you to continue giving them a chance to prove their love for you.

Stage 2: Performance rewards

Once the narcissist feels secure enough with you, they suddenly stop rewarding you continuously. The only thing that you now get is simply positive attention especially when you soothe their ego and do things that make them feel good.

The truth is, you get enough positive attention that you do not realize that now the only time that you get a reward is when you 'press the food bar' so to speak. In other words, the narcissist is grooming you so that you can please them continually in your life.

Stage 3: Increase in devaluation, a decrease in rewards!

During this particular stage, the narcissist starts abusing you and becoming overly critical of you. They want to control you and put you down whatever chance they get even if it means doing it in public. You may get occasional 'rewards,' but the truth is that at this point they are quite unpredictable. The bad stuff is beginning to outweigh the good stuff. In other words, you are now on 'intermittent reinforcement.'

Stage 4: They set you in flames

At this particular point, if you have never been in a narcissistic relationship before, there is a high chance that you will be puzzled by the whole experience wondering how and why this is happening. The answer is with your narcissistic friend who thinks that you are the cause of all the problems. They blame you and think that if you would do a, b, c and stop being 1, 2, 3, everything would be perfect. You end up doubting your perception of reality.

All you can now do at this point is get addicted, leave and hoover. You are addicted to narcissistic validation and approval. The truth is, you have stopped thinking rationally and rather than projecting your hate at the abuser, you become terrified at the thought of losing them to someone else. Due to what we mentioned above about 'trauma bonding' you cannot see the obvious and no longer care how you feel and what damage this is doing to your life.

If you start summoning your inner strength so that you can quit, they suddenly change their tactics. They try all means to make sure that they suck you back in the same way a vacuum cleaner does 'hoover.' They start doing something minor like buying you a small gift, commenting positively on your dressing, linking your social media posts among others. If that does not seem to work, they work harder by simply going back to the 'love bombing' In other words, the more you are resistant, the harder they try to win you back.

At this point, the sad thing is that many of us are vulnerable and we end up getting sucked up into the relationship again. Mostly it is because we start second-guessing whether there is change or if you will end up regretting this decision for the rest of your life and blah blah blah. In other words, what you are doing is ignoring everything that you know about your abuser with the hope that they might have magically transformed into someone more loving, decent, stable and reliable!

The truth is, it is indeed good to feel loved and wanted. But you have to realize that they are just soothing salves for your wounds. Do not forget that they have destroyed you and caused you so much pain yet you invested all your time and resources into the relationship. They did not see that, but they discarded you like trash anyway.

Before you can start making rash decisions and justifying why you are still in the relationship with this narcissist, ask yourself what makes you so sure that they will not do it again and maybe this time, even worse. Just know that, once you get sucked back, they will soon stop rewarding you and the cycle of abuse starts all over again. Understand that narcissist can train even the strongest of people into believing and submitting to them by using the right combination of praise and punishment. Are you ready for that again?

Chapter 5

Narcissism in Families

Dealing with a narcissist is incredibly difficult in the best of times, but there are many different ways to manage your relationship. Regardless of whether you are interested in severing all ties for good or you are in a position of having to continue some degree of contact with a narcissist, understanding some of the ways to deal with the narcissist's toxic behaviors can help you minimize your risks of harm and abuse. You can also cause the narcissist to lose interest in you and move on to other targets when you prove yourself invulnerable to his manipulative tactics.

Keep in mind that this will be a trial and error effort, and not every method discussed here may be useful or productive in your unique situation. Consider each method carefully to decide if it meets your needs and can help you, and once you have chosen a method, it is important to remember to keep it up. No matter how much the narcissist may push and try to get your attention back, be consistent in order to get the best effect from your actions. None of these methods are easy, and each will take a gargantuan amount of effort, but when you finally make it to the other side and realize how very free you are from the narcissist's abuse, you will recognize that it was worth every ounce of effort you put into it.

Cutting off the narcissist

The easiest way to avoid harm from a narcissist is to end the relationship entirely. Refuse to engage in the relationship at all costs. Taking a huge step back from the relationship may be necessary so you can clear your head and see things for what they are. This is typically a permanent change and decision and is the only surefire way to make sure that the narcissistic abuse stops. If you refuse to play the game at all, the narcissist cannot manipulate you.

Furthermore, by refusing any sort of engagement or communication with the narcissist, you are able to deny the narcissist's strongest motivator: Your attention. You suddenly remove yourself as a reliable source of narcissistic supply, and if you continue to deny the narcissist, ultimately, he will have to go elsewhere to meet his need.

Keep in mind that when you do this method, there will be a period that, in psychology, is called an extinction burst. Consider an experiment in which a rat is taught to press a button to get a small nibble of candy. The rat very quickly learns to expect that candy every time the button is pressed, and the behavior of pressing a button becomes positively reinforced. The rat does this to get the candy and does so repeatedly. If the rate goes up and presses the button and one day, it just stops giving out candy, the rat will be confused. It will press the button again and again, with increasing fervor, as it desperately tries to force the button to do what was expected of it and provide more candy. Over time, the rat will lose interest when it becomes clear there is no further reaction, but it will go back to the button occasionally and try to press the button.

Think of the narcissist as the rat and the narcissistic supply as the candy. You are the button to get it. As soon as you cut off contact, the narcissist will suddenly resort to every last strategy that has proven successful in the past in order to try to get your attention and that narcissistic supply desired. He will attempt everything, ranging from love bombs to promises of change and even threats of abuse or suicide if you do not give in. The most important thing to remember is that you cannot give in. No matter what the narcissist says or does, refuse to give him what he wants. His behaviors will escalate more, just like a toddler throwing a fit over having routine broken unexpectedly, and he will not stop at anything that he thinks will be effective. Eventually, however, you will weather the storm, and the narcissist will stop trying. The need for narcissistic supply is too strong, and he will seek it out elsewhere if you continue to refuse. At that point, remember that he will likely come back again in the future to try again, but each attempt will be weaker than the last as he learns that it is useless.

Remember, the period of leaving an abusive relationship is the most dangerous, and the narcissist likely will rely on every physical and emotional threat he can think of. He may threaten to kill himself, you, or other people, or he may begin stalking you. No matter what he does, refuse to engage, and report erratic or dangerous behavior to the appropriate authorities.

Take a break from the relationship

Similar to cutting off the narcissist, taking a break from the relationship involves a refusal to communicate. In this case, however, it is not permanent. The break is intended to allow you to clear your head and reevaluate whether you want to continue the relationship. Regardless of what he may accuse you of, remind yourself that this is not a punishment. You did not make this decision to hurt him; you made it protect and care for yourself. You are entitled to controlling who you communicate with, and if you decide that you do not want to talk to the narcissist, you are within your rights to make that choice.

When taking a break from the narcissist, it is appropriate to tell him once that you are taking a break and you will discuss things with him when you are ready. You do not have to provide him with a timeline, no matter how much he may pester you for one, and at that point, you refuse all future contact. You are giving yourself the chance to cool off. You are ensuring that you do not say something that will make the situation worse or inflame the narcissist into doing something harmful.

Do not let the narcissist goad you into responses with accusations of abuse or through playing the victim. You are making a choice that works for you, and ultimately that is the most important part. You need the breathing room and you are taking it. Remind yourself that you owe it to yourself to care for yourself, especially when no one else will. You cannot care for others if you are not caring for yourself.

Healthy boundaries

Sometimes, cutting off a narcissist is not a viable option, and that is okay. When you have no choice but to continue contact, such as if you are bound by court order to continue a co-parenting relationship, or you work with the narcissist and are not in a position to leave your job, you can focus on mitigating as much harm as possible and protecting yourself from the toxicity the narcissist seems to naturally exude.

Healthy boundaries are one of the easiest techniques to minimize harm from a narcissist, but they are difficult. These boundaries represent a line between what is acceptable and unacceptable to you, and they are to be set at your own prerogative. Boundaries are a healthy part of every relationship, regardless of whether it is a marriage, a friendship, or even with your children. Without boundaries, you will find yourself constantly stepping on toes and breeding resentment.

Unfortunately, narcissists see boundaries as the ultimate insult. It is irresistible to the narcissist, and he will try to stomp on them at every turn. The boundaries set are nothing more than challenges; games to get rises out of you and exert control over your emotional state. When you set these boundaries, you must be prepared to enforce and defend them at all costs.

When the narcissist challenges a boundary, give him one warning. Tell him that if he continues to test your boundary, you will provide a consequence. Tell the narcissist what that consequence for stomping on your boundary is, and every time it is done, you need to enforce the consequence. If you tell the narcissist that you will take an extended break in the event that your boundary is broken, follow through when he stomps on it. If you tell him you will stop talking to the narcissist if he calls you names in anger and he calls you names, you must immediately disengage and walk away. The key here is to follow through with the entire consequence, no matter how much the narcissist may cry, beg, or threaten.

Disengage

When cutting off is not an option, the next best thing is disengaging emotionally. If you do not invest any emotional energy into your interactions with the narcissist, he will eventually lose interest in you. You can keep your interactions relatively unchanged, but do not pay any attention to the words said, no matter how hurtful they may be. Try to keep in mind that people with NPD are stuck in a developmental stage of a child, unable to feel empathy and wired to be selfish, and remind yourself that if a child had said the things the narcissist spewed at you, you would likely not be very upset or offended at all. After all, children are impulsive, emotional, and irrational. The narcissist hits all three of those traits on the nose, and you should not take the narcissist's actions personally at all.

Disengaging does not mean ignoring or bottling your feelings, however. When you disengage, acknowledge what was said and give it the consideration it deserves, which is, admittedly, very little. This can be particularly difficult if the narcissist is a loved one that you trusted, but remember to try to disregard the emotional reactions to the words protects you. You do not fall into the narcissist's trap, and you do not let the narcissist regain control over your emotions, and in return, the narcissist will slowly lose interest.

The grey rock method

Similar to disengaging emotionally, the grey rock method involves minimizing emotional reactions, but in this case, it is ignoring all interactions, both good and bad. You are aiming to avoid as much interaction as possible, and when you are forced to interact, you should keep it boring and meaningless. The name alludes to a grey rock on the side of the road. Consider how often you notice and remember all of the rocks you walk past in a given day—the answer is most likely none. People do not pay attention to something as mundane and worthless as a grey rock on the side of the road. Your goal in this method is to be as mundane and useless to the narcissist as the grey rock. If you can achieve this state of mediocrity, the narcissist will slowly lose interest in you.

The trick in interacting is to tell you to be robotic in responses. No matter how angry you may feel in response to whatever was said, respond in as few words as possible, and make sure it is never immediately after the message was sent if it does not warrant an immediate response. For example, imagine that he messaged you saying that you are beautiful and he loves you. This should be ignored. Five minutes later, he messages asking how your shared child is doing. Give him the bare minimum answer while still being comprehensive. List what she is doing, whether she is sick, and maybe what she ate for dinner, but keep the interaction as emotionless as possible. Do not emote, no matter how tempting it may be.

Be realistic

Keeping your interactions with the narcissist realistic will keep you from setting up high standards that she will never meet. Telling yourself that she will never be emotionally supportive with you and that it is a personality limit that she lacks empathy will help you keep reality in mind when dealing with a narcissist. If you are fully prepared for the narcissist to respond in typical narcissist fashion, you will always be prepared, no matter how she responds, and you may even find that you are surprised on occasion. This is key when you are maintaining a relationship with a narcissist, whether romantic, platonic, workplace, familial, or co-parenting. You are protected from the disappointment of narcissistic behavior.

Keep in mind that being realistic does not excuse abuse. It is never okay for someone to hurt you or step on your boundaries. However, if you know that narcissists do those, you will not be as blindsided when it does happen, and you can better prepare in advance to protect yourself. You should absolutely still correct negative or unproductive behaviors, even if it is unpleasant or you would rather avoid doing so.

Focus on the positive

Likewise, when continuing to interact with a narcissist, remembering to focus on the positive can aid you in recognizing things that you enjoy about the person. After all, something must have attracted you to the narcissist at some point, and you may be happy to see tiny semblances of that person in the narcissist in front of you. While the personality is still likely vastly different from the one you met at first, there still may be parts of the narcissist that at least make her tolerable. For example, she may be horrible at being emotional support or anything but the center of attention, but she may also genuinely be a good cook, and she loves to cook for all of your friends' get-togethers, or she may be incredibly smart and you enjoy the intellectual conversations you have over coffee, even if they involve occasional snide comments about how you do not understand because you did not go to school for politics, or whatever the two of you were discussing. Reminding yourself of the positives can help you in moments when you are ready to lose your temper with the narcissist but it would be detrimental to do so.

Decide your hill die on

The last important tactic to remember is to choose your hill to die on wisely. This is a fancy way of saying choose your battles carefully. Though narcissists seek out confrontation-avoidant people on purpose, choosing to avoid conflict can actually be a way to avoid detection too. For this reason, you should always pick your battles wisely and only be prepared to engage in a conflict if you truly want to deal with the aftermath. While some things are absolutely worthy of a conflict, such as a co-parent choosing to drive with children in the car while drunk, an argument over who said something first is petty, and the narcissist are not likely to ever concede or admit that he is lying. For this reason, you should only choose battles if you are willing to fight for them. If you are unwilling to deal with the aftermath and ultimately, whatever the narcissist did is insignificant, do not bother fighting over it.

Chapter 6

How did i get this way?

Codependency is a part of the reality of an unhealthy bond or relationship that can manifest in a variety of ways, not only in the narcissistic relationship, and will always show up with a narcissistic partner. So, what is codependency anyway, and who is to blame for it?

No one is to blame, and accusing one partner of being more at fault than the other, is just a product of unhealthy relationship dynamics, both with the self and others. By definition, codependency is essentially a condition of behaviors in a relationship in which one partner will facilitate or enable the other partner's irresponsibility, addictive tendencies, mental health issues, immaturity, and even their under-achievement.

Typically, if you are in a codependent partnership with someone, you are likely in need of something from it as well. Oftentimes, the narcissist will need all of the affirmation, accolades, and praise, while the partner is need of someone to take care of and nurture, allowing them to have a sense of fulfillment by meeting someone else's needs.

This can be just as problematic as being a narcissist because it requires that you are dependent upon another person to make you feel worthy of existence. The codependent partnership is just a loop of the same behaviors and patterns being repeated over and over again until someone breaks the pattern. A codependent partner works well with a narcissist because they exist to feel helpful to someone to feel loved for their efforts, and all the narcissist wants is someone to fulfill all of their needs without having to give anything in return.

So, if you are a codependent partner, you may be interested in asking what kinds of traits you might exhibit if you are in that type of personality spectrum.

Characteristics of Codependency

To understand the relationship dynamics prevalent in the narcissistic relationship, having a grasp of the other partner, who is not the narcissist, will be helpful. In the end, it takes two to tango, and if you are in a long-term or even short-term partnership with a narcissist, you might need to start asking the questions of why you might be drawn to that person in the first place.

So, a codependent person will often work to meet the needs of others in the sacrifice of their needs. This act is an assumption of responsibility that is not required but will offer the codependent a sense of purpose, as well as the narcissist someone to meet their every need.

An increase in self-esteem for the codependent comes from controlling their emotions, and by proxy, those of their partner, effectually keeping the peace and making sure that everyone feels satisfied; however, the state of control over emotions prevents the real feelings, issues, or personality disorders from being identified, leading to the behavior loop between the codependent and the narcissist.

Codependents will often feel anxious, worried, or have boundary confusion revolving around intimacy with their partner. This is realized in their attempts to have their needs met by their narcissistic partner who only offers intimacy when it will benefit them, and so the codependent will often have a distorted view of their attractiveness, desire, or right to feel intimacy with their significant other.

One of the greatest indicators of someone being a codependent partner is enmeshment. When you are unable to have authority or autonomy within your relationship, you may decide that you are not whole without the other person and will enmesh yourself in their reality, feelings, and circumstances, blending your realities.

Additionally, codependents will usually, unconsciously, choose partners with addictions, abusive tendencies, mental or emotional disorders or issues, and impulse disorders. These are not the only circumstances, of course, but they are common attributes of a codependent partnership. The reason is that there is a lack of definition of the self, for both the narcissist and the codependent. The codependent feels a sense of self when they are caregiving or controlling another person.

A codependent person will deny their feelings, or that there is anything amiss in the relationship, because of their patterns of thought or belief about what a good partner does for the other. A narcissist will easily convince a codependent that they need to continue to be self-sacrificing, and so, the two work well together to continue manipulating these realities.

Here is a list of some of the common characteristics of a codependent partner and if you or someone you know can check off three or more of these, then you are likely in a codependent state in your partnership:

- Depression
- Compulsive activities (i.e., food binges, shopping sprees, constant house cleaning).
- Holding in emotions
- Constricting feelings
- Anxiety

- In a regular or excessive state of denial
- Overly diligent, of hypervigilant
- Abuse of substances
- Sickness or illness caused by stress or anxiety
- Victim of physical, sexual, or emotional abuse (recurring)
- In a relationship with a person for over two years who has an addiction, without ever asking for help, or seeking therapy
- Can't handle being alone and will make extreme efforts to avoid being alone
- Perfectionism
- Extreme desire for affection and/or acceptance
- Low self-esteem or self-worth
- Feeling a lack of trust
- Dishonesty and/or manipulation
- Overly controlling behavior
- Severe feelings of emptiness and/or boredom
- Intense relationships that are often unstable

- Subordinating your needs for the acceptance of the person you are with

These are some of the hallmarks of a codependent partner, and there are certainly a few more characteristics that can manifest, but these are the core characteristics. You may need to sit down and make a list of some of these qualities and try to determine if these concepts are reflected in your relationship. If so, you will need to understand how a codependent partnership is an unhealthy way to experience love and that there will need to be some shifts and changes in your reality to help you identify your true feelings and desires with your relationship.

Relationship Dynamics of Codependency

A codependent person will often seek out or involve themselves in relationships in which they play a particular role, and it is one that they are the most comfortable with. Their main role is to act as the supportive confidante or rescuer of the other person, and a codependent partner is characterized as being a "helper" type. The reality is that a codependent is dependent on the low, poor, or disordered functioning of their partner to satisfy their emotional sensitivities and needs.

This kind of relationship, especially between a codependent and a narcissist, is colored by lack of healthy boundaries, ineffectual and dysfunctional communication skills, issues with intimacy, patterns of denial, controlling behavior that manifests as caretaking (or various other forms of control), high levels of reactionary behavior, and dependency on these positions.

There is a distinct imbalance in the partnership so that one person is in control, abusive (emotionally/physically/mentally), or enabling, such as in someone else's addiction, immaturity, or in the case of this book, narcissistic tendencies.

The dynamic for a codependent and a narcissist is that one's sense of purpose is to make regular, extreme sacrifices to uphold, or satisfy their partner's needs, while the other maintains the attitude of being superior and worthy of being fawned on and "served" by their partner. Usually, as a result of this dynamic, one partner will lack personal autonomy and self-sufficiency, or authority, while the other will have an overabundance of these qualities to the point of hubris. Some other dynamics include:

- Excessive clinginess
- Needy behaviors
- Dependence on personal fulfillment from their partner

- Mood swings determined by how they perceive their partner currently feels about them (the codependent)
- Self-inflicted self-sacrifice (codependent)
- Getting their partner to "buy into" their vision of life (the narcissist)
- Obedience and attentiveness (the codependent)
- The need to make someone feel important to receive their love in return (the codependent)
- The need to receive love without giving anything in return (the narcissist)

There are a lot of versions of this reality because every relationship is unique and has a beginning, middle, and somewhere, an end. When we are involved with another person, whether or not there is codependency or narcissism, it can be a challenge to maintain your sense of self and reflect through your needs and emotions what you want to support in your relationship.

The codependent and the narcissist share a similar desire or need, but it is reflected in different behaviors. Either way, these dynamics result in unhealthy, imbalanced partnerships that can have a detrimental impact on the core reality of a person's true needs, emotions, and desires. Some people who end up in codependent partnership with a narcissist are empaths, without understanding or knowing this about themselves.

Chapter 7

Unlearning unhealthy patterns

After going through torture and trauma for many days, narcissistic abuse victims may suffer PTSD commonly referred to as Post Narcissistic Stress Disorder PNSD in this case. Although many individuals may suffer post narcissistic abuse stress disorder, only a few can tell what they are going through. Most victims of narcissistic abuse can barely tell that they have been abused. When they experience stress and anxiety, they relate it to other circumstances in life.

Every individual that has experienced narcissistic abuse at any level must be helped to heal. The people around a person that has experienced abuse must take care of the victim to ensure that he/she gets complete help. Given that most people do not even know that they are suffering, friends and family must help the victims come to terms with reality. Some of the actions done by post abuse victims are subconsciously instigated by their previous experiences. Here are some signs to look out for when dealing with narcissistic abuse victims. These signs are a clear indication that the victim is suffering from PNSD.

- Physical and Emotional Responses to Traumatic Recaps

Victims usually have a way of responding to flashbacks of the traumatic events. In some cases, individuals may undergo deep emotional traumas. A victim suffering from PNSD may start crying for no reason. Remembering the traumatic events they went through may bring back emotions leading to tears, fear, anger disgust, etc. They may also show physical signs of traumatic recap such as shaking and shivering even when they have not been hurt.

- Disturbing Thoughts or Memories

Victims usually experience disturbing memories. A person that has undergone the ordeal of narcissistic abuse may never have peace in life. The stress disorder manifests through disturbing nightmares or visions. The person may start talking in dreams, screaming or wake up sweating. Victims may also hallucinate during the day and keep on seeing images of people trying to hurt them

- Difficulty in Focusing or Falling Sleep

Individuals suffering from post-traumatic stress disorder develop problems with concentration. A victim of narcissistic abuse may find problems focusing on anything for long. They are often found wandering off in their mind. They cannot pay attention at work or school. They are often seen to be in their own world. The patients may stay for long hour's overnight thinking about the trauma. In some cases, insomnia is brought about by the fear of experiencing nightmares related to the ordeal.

- Conflicting Feelings

People who suffer from PTSD are unable to trust themselves or others. They tend to have conflicting feelings due to fear of being hurt again. A PTSD patient may appear to be so much in love in the morning just to start showing remorse and hate a few hours later. If a PTSD patient does not stay with an understanding partner, it often leads to relationship problems. The best medicine for such individuals is reassurance. A person suffering from narcissistic abuse stress must constantly be reassured that the trauma is over and that they're now in safe hands. Given that it takes so many years to publish negativity in the minds of the victims, it also takes a lot of time to wash away the effects. Constant support from family, friends, and colleagues is the best way to get healing for PTSD patients.

- Distorted Sense of Blame

Narcissists train their victims to always find blame for anything happening. As a person stays with a narcissist, he/she becomes the center of blame. The victim is often blamed for failure and success. The victim is never sure what is wrong or right. Every action may lead to abuse even if the victim did the action with good intentions. As the victims try to heal from such trauma, they may show some tendencies of blaming individuals. PTSD patients are quick to blame others to avoid consequences related to the mistake. They are quick to shift blame because they believe the person to blame is the person to be punished. They do all these subconsciously, without thinking about it.

- Social Retreat and Isolation

It is common to see individuals who suffer from stress and anxiety sitting in isolation. Post narcissistic abuse victims also go through the same scenario. In most cases, the victims believe that staying away from people is safer. In other instances, retreat and isolation is a strategy of escaping the shame. As mentioned early, narcissistic abuse patients always blame themselves for the abuse. The patients may find it difficult to associate with people due to the fear of being ridiculed.

- Detach From Reality

Most victims of narcissistic abuse show signs of PTSD by detaching from reality. They avoid tendencies associated with feelings, situations or people. They want to live in a world of their own, where they cannot love or hate. This is a sign of stress disorder associated with traumatic events. The mind subconsciously tries to lock away feelings, tricking the victim to think that lack of feelings is equal to safety. The victim believes that if they do not experience love, they may never have to experience the pain of heartbreak. The victim locks all the feelings that try coming up in order to reduce direct interaction with people. The victim subconsciously assumes that all people are evil and associating with them may eventually result in painful experiences.

- Hyper-Vigilance

Individuals suffering from PNSD show fear and anxiety. They are easily startled and angered. They may be angered by the smallest of actions. They may also be frightened if someone appears from behind or by hearing a loud sound. Most of the victims are always on the lookout; they are in a desperate need to have a 360-degree view of their environment. When thy are in the house, they prefer locking all doors and windows. They may be frightened even at the sound of movement made by an insect. They always look at strangers critically and may respond aggressively to people they do not know. All these factors are indications of stress and anxiety that is deeply rooted in the trauma experienced during narcissistic abuse.

- Fear or Panic for No Apparent Reasons

Individuals suffering from traumatic stress disorder often show fear. They may show fear even when there is nothing threatening around. They are usually afraid of the unknown and often panic when in stress or left alone. They are very protective of everything they find valuable such as children. They are always afraid that everyone around has intentions to harm or to steal anything they own.

- Inconsistent or Conflicting Beliefs

Most post narcissistic abuse victims are never sure of what is true and what is false. They do not have firm ideologies to believe in. They constantly waiver their thoughts and end up believing what people say. Most patients tend to lack self-esteem since that have been made to believe they are not worthy. Even when they try coming to terms with the fact that they are just victims, the idea does not stay around for long. Most victims easily find themselves going back to old thoughts.

How to Analyze People

Everyone can be a victim of narcissistic abuse. The first line of defense for all victims is having the ability to analyze people. By analyzing individuals, a person is in a position to tell whether someone is narcissistic or not.

Parents

In the case of parents, the victims are more often unfortunate. Being born or adopted by a narcissistic parent is the most unfortunate thing that could happen to anyone. In this case, the victims are unable to analyze people or to make any decision. They are innocent and vulnerable. In the case of parents, it is the neighbors or other family members that may be able to spot narcissism and rescue the child. However, as a person matures, he/she might be able to spot narcissistic tendencies in parents. Narcissistic parents are abusive and controlling even when their children are adults. They control a person's life to the extent of choosing a life partner. If you feel that your parent has some narcissistic tendencies, analyze their motives in every action. Narcissistic parents use their children to achieve pride. They punish their children for failure and demand that the children maintain high standards that the narcissist deems success.

Partner

Since most narcissistic abuse victims are romantic partners, it is important for all people to have a third eye when dating. Some clues can help a person spot narcissism in their partner. First, narcissists idealize their partner. If you happen to date someone that is 100% ideal for you in all ways, be careful.

Another very clear sign of narcissism is obsession and possessiveness. Narcissistic individuals do not give up on pursuing a person. They do not take no for an answer and keep on coming with enticing gifts. They may show desperation and even manipulate the victim just to have them.

The next sign of narcissism in relationships is separation. The narcissist separates the victim from friends and family. If you are in a relationship and realize that you are being separated from friends and family, start being critical.

Spot this pattern and stay vigilant every time you start a new relationship. It starts with Idealization then obsession, separation, and abuse. These are the most common and visible factors to observe to avoid getting trapped in narcissistic relationships.

Friends

In friendship, narcissists only come in for social or material gain. If you suspect that you are in a narcissistic friendship, ask yourself what could it be that the person wants from you. Narcissists often fail to hide their true intentions. If you look closely, you may be able to realize that a person only associates with you because of your wealth or status. Such individuals may sound genuine at first, but manipulation soon crops in. To avoid falling into such traps, cut links to such individuals. Avoid creating long-lasting bonds or making investments together with an individual you do not know well.

Children

Children can be narcissistic too. As a parent, you have to analyze your child for tendencies of narcissism. Unfortunately, most parents groom narcissism in children. Narcissistic children may come out as confident, assertive, and natural leaders. The parent has to help the child realize that they are not better than the rest of the world. On the contrary, most parents encourage their children by telling them that they are the best. If narcissism can be spotted in a child at an early age, the parents may be able to help the child. It is easy to help a child learn their true personality and get rid of any fears. In many instances, narcissists are just afraid of the unknown and have low self-esteem. Being able to help someone understand that failure is part of life and being weak is okay helps the person start accepting their true personality. They eventually get rid of the self-glorified false personality and live their life according to the truth.

How to Deal With a Narcissistic Partner

Dealing with a narcissistic partner is not a walk in the park. The best way is to spot the signs and avoid falling into the trap. However, if you realize that you are already in the trap, you need to be very technical in your escape strategy. Running from the hands of a narcissist is never easy. The abuser will keep on pursuing you and using manipulation to have you on their side. To deal with a narcissistic partner, follow this basic guide:

Basic Guide to Recognize and Handle Narcissists

Step 1: Gain Knowledge

The first step to dealing with a narcissist is gaining knowledge. Do extensive research by reading books such as this one and watching videos. Gaining knowledge will help you understand every principle used and applied by narcissists. If you are already in a narcissistic relationship, you must be careful in your quest to gain knowledge. The narcissistic partner should never know you are gaining such knowledge. Make sure you clear your browser history after searching such topics online. If the partner realizes that you are gaining knowledge on the subject, he /she may block all the possible ways of gaining such knowledge.

Step 2: Understand the Cycle

Understanding the narcissistic abuse cycle will help you know where you stand. If you are not in a narcissistic relationship, the knowledge of the cycle will help you avoid falling into the trap. If you are already in a narcissistic relationship, understanding the cycle will help you know the phase of abuse you are at.

Step 3: Learn to Analyze People

It is not possible to escape a narcissist if you do not know how to play the mind games. Narcissists thrive on mind games. You must find a way out by playing the games better than the narcissist. Emotional intelligence is a whole subject on its own. Invest in learning emotional intelligence. Learn to study people's emotions and manage them. Start understanding the actions that narcissists take and what makes them take such actions. Once you understand analyzing people, you will be ready to beat the narcissist at his/her own game.

Step 4: Mend Relationships

Narcissists are often successful because they manage to alienate their victims. If you choose to mend fences with friends and family, you may have someone to trust. After you finally understand that a narcissist only intents to hurt and harm, you must be able to retrace your route. Find people you can trust and those who trust your words. Find the people who love you genuinely. If you have not yet been captured by a narcissist, your first clue is to always maintain friendships. No matter how sweet the relationship may sound, make sure you maintain friendships and family relationships. Do not let a new person in your life take over your relationships or control the way you interact with people.

Step 5: With Help from Friends and Family Uncover the Narcissist

The only way to escape the traps of a narcissist forever is to ensure that the truth goes out. You must ensure that there is sufficient evidence to convict the abuser for the crimes committed. You should also ensure that the community and people around believe everything you say about this person. One reason why narcissists never get caught is that they create a very self-righteous public image. In some cases, they are powerful individuals with respected leadership roles in society. When you say your word against theirs, you might not be recognized.

To ensure that your word holds ground, you must first get some incriminating evidence. Gather evidence by the help of friends and family. Look for people who may have your best interests at heart. You may even be required to stay in the abusive relationship a lot longer in your quest to find the right information. Collect written, video and audio evidence. To ensure that the abuse does not notice your actions, you must be skillful and use help from close friends. When you eventually decide to stand up to the abuser, be sure you have evidence to convince the entire community. If you give the abuser a chance to escape they may be very manipulative with their words. Make sure you show their personality publicly so that they do not have anywhere else to hide.

Your Brain in the Abusive Relationship

The brain is the most affected part of your body when you are in an abusive relationship. As already mentioned, the pain threshold for physical and emotional abuses on the brain is the same. This means that any emotional or physical abuse directly affects the brain. The key to surviving any traumatic events and abuses is protecting the brain. Any individual who undergoes narcissistic abuse can only survive by protecting the brain from the trauma. If you are in a relationship that keeps inflicting pain, you must find a way of protecting the brain.

The only way to protect the brain is learning the truth. Emotionally intelligent people know how to differentiate facts from fiction. If you can train your brain to know the truth and live in reality, you will have very strong mental power. In fact, narcissists are not in a position to break anyone who stays within their mind. The first thing anyone in the clear state of mind should understand is that the narcissist is a liar. You must understand that the narcissist thrives on lies and capitalizes on your emotions. The narcissist hurts the emotions to make the victim feel worthless.

If you know what the narcissist is trying to do, you will not allow your brain to accept the message. You must train your brain to reject such negative information and only accept positive information. You must train your brain to only accept what is true and reject what is a lie.

Protecting your brain during narcissistic abuse also depends on your ability to control emotions. If you can differentiate between the truth and lies, you will not be affected by lies. If a narcissist keeps saying you are stupid, you will not be affected by their words because you know clearly, you are wise. The only fighting chance any individual has in a narcissistic relationship is staying sober. This includes the ability to make decisions that are not influenced by emotions.

As a victim, you must know that you are being victimized. You should be able to analyze your abuser and understand that he/she is suffering from a mental disorder. You should be in a position to analyze the personality disorder and start capitalizing on the abuser's weaknesses. You should be in a position to unravel the hidden personality of the abuser and shame their ego.

Although maintaining mental stability in such situations is not easy, every person can control their minds. If you have something you stand for, start from that point. Although narcissists distort a person's way of thinking, there are a few constants that remain. Every victim must be able to recognize the available constants and start utilizing them to overcome mental trauma. For instance, a narcissist may sabotage a person's path to success but they may never sabotage a person's past achievements. Even if he/she makes you believe you are incompetent, find one thing you can do very well.

Start building your strength and confidence from that aspect. Start reaffirming your thoughts and abilities. You must be in a position to remember your past success before you met your abuser. Think of the important steps you made in life and the milestones you have achieved. Remembering your old self gives you the desire to want to achieve again.

The victim must also be on a constant quest to enrich their brains. Feed your brain with the right information. The victim must ensure that the positive ideas that go into the mind outweigh the negative ideas that the abuser tries to instill. The victim should enjoy reading books, watching TV, playing mental stimulation games and d keeping up with the trends. Gaining knowledge that the abuser lacks puts the victim in a position of control. The victim can counteract negative energy being built by the abuser.

The victim starts differentiating facts from lies. The abuser may try to sabotage every effort made to gain knowledge. However, we live in an era of freedom. Every person has the freedom to gain knowledge. Even if you are confined to a house, you can still gain knowledge by reading books and magazines.

Chapter 8

----- ❧☙❧☙ -----

Can i choose a new way of thinking?

Life may not be all sunshine and roses for victims who manage to escape narcissistic abuse cycles. Many struggle to heal for years afterward, experiencing intermittent periods of growth and rehabilitation peppered with bouts of emotional relapse. Even so, recovering victims often report an overwhelming feeling of relief and a surreal sense of calm once they start to get used to the rhythm of their lives under the rules of No-Contact with dangerous narcissists.

Even through the difficult periods, it's important for any victim to consistently forgive themselves, appreciate their own strength and resilience, and throw themselves enthusiastically into a self-care routine. They must also try to consistently look towards the future rather than ruminating too heavily on the painful past. The most insidious legacy of narcissistic abuse is that it attempts to corrupt the victim's ability to enjoy self-esteem, interpersonal love, and all the other beautiful things that an empathetic life can offer, even after the abusive situation has been left behind. The best and most powerful form of revenge you can seek upon a narcissistic abuser is to deny them that possibility. Take the reins of your life; make the conscious choice to be happy and compassionate; give and receive honest, authentic love with joy and optimism. Don't allow your victimhood to define you.

Hypersensitivity

Many victims of narcissists are already self-identified empaths, or highly sensitive people (HSPs) before they even meet the narcissist in question. Some, though, only become awakened to this reality after leaving the narcissistic relationship or regime.

Hypersensitivity comes in many forms and varying degrees of intensity. Many people grow to see it as a superpower, though it needs consistent training, rest and care, just like a muscle. Intensive boundary work is a necessity for empaths, as is the establishment and maintenance of a self-care routine. It does not need to be costly--it simply needs to remind the victim on a regular basis that they are worthy of care and attention, and that they are responsible for creating their own happiness.

Some unfortunate victims may not find the support that they need in healing from this abuse. Many empaths and HSPs find themselves in frequent conflict with highly individualistic people, who invalidate their experiences of narcissistic abuse by calling them normal, and dismissing their feelings as overreactions. They might advise the victim to "grow a thicker skin" or to "toughen up," whether or not they realize that these words essentially serve to blame the victim for the abuse inflicted upon them.

If this happens to you, remind yourself of the person you were before the abuse started. You were not perfect--no one is--but you were strong. You were your own person. There was nothing wrong with you. You didn't deserve to be targeted, manipulated, exploited, shamed, or used as an emotional punching bag.

Try to remind yourself that the person who's telling you to toughen up may mean well, but that they are ignorant. They might buy into the "just world" fallacy--the idea that people get what they deserve in life, so people who are suffering have usually done something to deserve this punishment--and lack the perspective necessary to provide you with helpful advice. While this can be extremely frustrating, or infuriating if it's happening repeatedly, try not to bear anger towards these people. Put yourself in their shoes.

Imagine two empty water glasses set down on a table top with standard force; one stays unaffected by the impact, while the other shatters. It would be easy to deduce that there was something inherently defective in the glass that broke. But what if you came to learn that the intact glass had previously been cocooned in bubble wrap, while the broken glass had been repeatedly heated and cooled and then struck with a mallet, forming thousands of tiny invisible cracks?

A victim of prolonged narcissistic abuse is a shell of a person, a glass with thousands of tiny invisible cracks throughout. They need to be handled gently for a while, in order to heal. They may not be able to handle adversity that most people can take in stride. But that doesn't mean they started out defective; it means they are in need of repair, and patient understanding.

One place where this analogy fails, though, is in the aftermath; unlike a broken glass, a hypersensitive victim can mend all those little cracks, and eventually come out even stronger than the glass that was protected by bubble wrap all along. Empaths and HSPs can grow into emotional warriors, beacons for other victims in need of role models, and powerful healers. Hypersensitivity does not make people weak; it teaches them incredible strength.

Imagine those two glasses side by side again. This time, you're fully aware of what each has been through, and the abused glass does not break. Now, which one do you find more impressive?

Echoism

Echoism is defined as a phobia of narcissistic traits within the self. It's common in victims of severe narcissistic abuse, who become afraid of expressing their own needs, appearing selfish, or receiving special attention of any kind, most often because the narcissist in their life would punish them for doing these things.

One important test for victims of narcissistic abuse is this: are you able to enjoy your own company for a day, or a full weekend perhaps, without having an emotional meltdown? If not, there's no need to feel ashamed, but it may be wise to seek help for further recovery. There's nothing at all wrong with being social, but victims of narcissistic abuse may use their busy social and professional lives to distract themselves from unresolved pain or difficult emotional sensations that need to be addressed. Victims also are typically trained to be codependent, which means they may struggle to make decisions, grasp their true opinions and preferences, or even recognize their own emotions, without a dominant personality present to dictate these things for them.

Isolation can be painful and challenging, but it can also be a powerful tool for emotional growth or spiritual awakening. When you choose it for yourself, rather than having it thrust upon you, it can be extraordinarily empowering.

Stay mindful of the fact that this is your life, no one else's, and it's entirely possible that you only get one of those to live through. Make sure you're living it for yourself--not to please some ungrateful and apathetic narcissist.

Reframing memories

Unfortunately, victims of narcissistic abuse are often haunted by an unfounded sense of shame, even after they've cut ties and moved on from the narcissist who hurt them. It's important to work with someone--a therapist, counselor, healer, or spiritual guide--to reframe your memories of the relationship you shared with the narcissist, to start to untangle and alleviate the stress of this shame.

One especially effective technique that narcissistic abusers use is to react to a victim's bid for equal and fair treatment as though it is an unreasonable and narcissistic request. The narcissist's voice may haunt the victim, even long after they've cut ties, asking: "Just who do you think you are?" or "It's always about you, isn't it?" This is a combination of projection and gaslighting that can truly disrupt the victim's ability to assert or defend themselves in life. They become paralyzed with self-conscious fear, struggle to advocate for their own personal interests, and often get stuck in a cycle of further generosity towards the narcissist, all in a vain attempt to prove their own capacity for empathy. Somehow, by trying to stand up for themselves, the victims are tricked into bowing down yet again, and even more deeply, to the narcissist.

So when the relationship is over, the victim is left carrying the shame of the abusive behavior that they tolerated, as well as the shameful fear that they were somehow guilty of the same narcissistic behavior that their abuser displayed. This can impact the victim's future relationships, smothering confidence and promoting phantom anxiety.

If feelings of shame are haunting you, the best thing you can do for yourself is find a therapist or counselor to help you reframe your memories and rewrite your narrative. You'll need an objective third party to help you see the parts of your own memories that you've gotten into the habit of blinding yourself to: namely, the parts where your abuser crossed lines, and treated you in dehumanizing ways. These memories can be extremely painful, which is why many victims' brains automatically edit them out, or alter them, for the sake of self-protection. Victims should not expect to be exclusively self-reliant during their recovery processes; a good support system full of empathetic people with good judgment and strong moral character will be necessary, and the assistance of a licensed mental health professional should be included if it is at all possible.

Reconnecting with your true self

In the long term, purging narcissism from your life feels a bit like taking off a corset that you've been wearing your whole life and never even knew it. On the one hand, there's an enormous sense of relief, and the sudden ability to breathe more deeply than you ever realized you could. On the other hand, this corset may have been holding in some unsightly baggage that now is free to roll around and bounce and jiggle. This corset also may have been masking some pain that you've been normalizing for years, pain which now suddenly feels unbearable. And everything mundane that you never used to think about, like how to hold your rib cage when you walk, stand, or sit? Now, you find you have to think long and hard about every move you make, because everything feels so unfamiliar, foreign and awkward.

Removing narcissism from your life frees you from a lot of toxic nonsense, but it also sometimes means getting rid of your emotional safety net, which can be very scary. Without these dominant personalities around to tell you what to do, how to think, and how to feel, you'll have to decide for yourself, and take responsibility for your own behaviors. Reconnecting with your authentic self--the person you were before the abuse rewired your brain--can be a lengthy process, so you might as well dive in and do your best to enjoy it. Ask yourself: what do I like, when no one else is telling me what I'm supposed to live? What do I detest? Where do I want to be? How do I want to feel? How do I want to designate my time?

The most important question to ask yourself is what you want. Guided meditation practice can be enormously helpful in pondering that question, as well as silencing all the voices in your head that aren't your own. Society is full of narcissistic talking heads, telling us all what we are supposed to want, and what goals are worth striving for. But if you ignore them, you can open yourself up to a world of possibilities. For example, what if you really don't want to be wealthy? What if all you want is to be happy, healthy, and financially comfortable enough to give back to charities, or to friends in need? What if you don't actually want to dominate your career field, or maintain an athlete's body, or gain a million followers in social media? What if you haven't found your joy yet, simply because you were led to search for it in all the wrong places?

Encourage yourself to experiment; try new things, and be bold. You may be quite surprised at the person you find underneath all those emotional bruises and baggage once they've been cleared away.

Healing and moving forward

Forgiveness is an important part of your healing process. But you do not necessarily want to forgive your abuser. In fact, many victims of narcissistic abuse are too forgiving of narcissists, which is why they allowed the abuse to last as long as it did.

The person you need to forgive is yourself. First, acknowledge that the truth of your story has been obscured in your head for a long time; the narcissist was not a good person, and did not have your best interests at heart. It was all an act. They knew you were in pain, and instead of releasing you from it, they compounded it at every possible opportunity. You played into this because you wanted to see the best in them. You trusted and believed in them. You did nothing wrong to deserve this treatment. You deserve forgiveness.

But at the same time, on some level, you had to be aware that this relationship was unhealthy, and you allowed it to continue anyway. You put up with behaviors that you should have walked away from. You made excuses for your abuser and protected them from facing the consequences of their actions. This is where you begin to take personal responsibility for your healing, which is not to be confused with accepting blame for the abuse. Your goal here is not to make yourself feel bad, or convince yourself that you asked for this treatment; on the contrary, your goal is to try and understand why you allowed the abuse to happen, so that you can make better, healthier choices moving forward. There is no shame in this; usually, we accept abusive behaviors because they come alongside other things that we desperately desire, such as a sense of security, financial empowerment, or simply a feeling of significance. Many of us long to feel needed by someone, and it's that simple desire that leaves us vulnerable to narcissistic abuse. Recognizing your own points of vulnerability--the ones that continuously encouraged you to ignore the red flags and remain in a toxic relationship--is the best way to guard yourself against future threats of abuse.

Finally, you may feel stuck, paralyzed, or pulled in two different directions for quite some time after leaving a narcissistic abuser. Half of your soul will be drifting into the gravitational pull of the past, wanting to revisit memories and explore them, looking for answers. Meanwhile, the other half will be exhausted of this situation and eager to move forward, leaving the abuse behind like a snake shedding its skin. Understand that this dichotomy will tire you out quickly, so it may be best to set up designated timeframes to explore the past (therapy, meditation, or even just planned chats with trusted friends) and the future separately, allowing you to devote your full attention to each and live mindfully in the present.

Eventually, you will reach a point where you are able to meet new people, and you won't feel the need to explain what you've been through in order to justify your personality or behaviors. You may not be conscious of it, or see it happening, but when you get there, you will have officially freed yourself from the claws of narcissistic abuse. Don't forget your story, but recognize this as an opportunity to write a new ending, and change the entire narrative. And always remember that the abuse you've suffered through never made you weak--it only served to make you stronger, smarter, and more powerful in the end.

Chapter 9

Does genetics play a role?

This section first reviews the common phases of a narcissistic relationship – idealize, devalue and discard – touches on the common traits of victims and reasons individuals enter, willingly or unwillingly, into narcissistic relationships. Note: it's just as important to understand what drives people to these relationships as it is to understand what they've grown unwilling to accept.

Often, victims are so manipulated and accustomed to the abusive circumstances that recovery never comes. They experience years of abuse without fully realizing the severity of their situation. In the most severe cases, the victims believe, without question, that they're actually the problem and grow dependent on the possibility of their captor providing genuine and needed intimacy and bonding that never occurs. They're left confused and feeling powerless, constantly attempting to change their circumstances and left sorely disappointed.

Finally, this section culminates with tips to leave a narcissist, what to expect when one decides to move on, and ways to rebuild and renew.

Narcissists and relationships - the victim's false life

Living with someone that suffers from Narcissistic Personality Disorder is extremely confusing, disheartening, painful and downright debilitating. Victims are propelled to extreme highs, and equally extreme lows caught on a never-ending roller coaster of emotions without the means of getting off safely. They may feel as if they're stuck in a revolving doorway with no clear way to exit.

Sufferers go through a very specific set of relational stages, which, although more common than most expect, are actually very difficult for the victims themselves to recognize objectively and then manage to escape. These individuals are often caught completely off guard when the narcissist's mask comes off, having believed they were relating to someone who is immensely charming, charismatic and by all outward appearances 'perfect'.

Once the mask is removed, however, trust dissolves and the victims are affected deeply. They must learn to adjust their entire thought process, rethinking everything they knew to be true. Their lives are turned completely upside down and they are left reaching for nonexistent safety, a net no longer there, or that never really existed. There's a period of time, often prolonged, in which the victim feels lost—paralyzed as if they can no longer trust themselves or their judgment. And, since true narcissists are unable to feel empathy, it's only their victims who suffer once the red flags go up, leaving these individuals feeling even more lonely and desperate.

The narcissist is unable to believe that they've caused pain, and can't relate emotionally to their victim. They'll suggest their victim is crazy, thereby relieving themselves of any potential guilt. Extreme narcissists are typically unable to feel healthy emotions at all towards other people. They believe others, their entire network of family, friends, and acquaintances, are there simply to serve their needs. These people are not human beings; they're objects, there to provide narcissistic supply.

It's this inability to look inward that makes most narcissists unwilling to seek therapy. They're rarely the ones to seek out help with their relationships or initiate professional treatment. The victims are usually the seekers. What's most disheartening is that the victims often seek help for their own perceived mental imbalances, which the narcissist has convinced them they possess. It takes a highly intuitive therapist and one skilled in NPD to identify the true underlying issues, bring to light possible narcissistic abuse, and effectively help the victim cope and rebuild.

If the victim convinces their narcissistic spouse to seek couples counseling, danger to their well-being may actually increase.

An untrained counselor could fall victim to the narcissist's charm, leading to further disillusionment and self-esteem issues in the victim. The narcissist learns what triggers their victim to confide in others regarding her unhappiness and 'up their game', ensuring they work twice as hard the next time to keep their victim quiet.

It's difficult for therapists to identify narcissistic abuse and have the victim believe it's happened to them, for the victim to self-identify and for the therapist to secure their trust once their world falls apart. Well qualified therapists and successfully revived victims care are few and far between. A therapist needs to play detective and understand that the reason the victim believes they're seeking treatment may actually be an unhealthy consequence (i.e., anxiety, depression, stress, etc.) of a larger problem.

Therapists must be patient in working with potential abuse victims, not only getting them to accept that they've been abused and working with them on a plan to move forward but ultimately, within this process, helping them to better understand themselves and why they fell victim in the first place. In doing so, the cycle is less likely to repeat itself.

It's ultimately up to the victim to vocalize an understanding of what's occurred and gather the strength to move forward. Eventually, they may be willing to help other sufferers of narcissistic abuse, so that the condition is reduced nearly to the point of elimination. The cycle must be broken, and only those who have witnessed it have the power to help prevent it.

Supply and demand

The NPD relationship is a constant supply and demand struggle. Think simple economics. The narcissistic supply runs low as the demand for it increases within the narcissist and they need more attention. As the supply depletes, energy depletes in the victim, and the victim is unable to meet the demand. This causes the narcissist to explode. In the aftermath, the supply is refueled as control is reestablished and the victim is re-motivated to provide the needed reserves.

A narcissist shows no remorse for the terrible things they do. They never say sorry, but they'll hang out, still wanting desperately to be needed, or, at the very least, not discarded. If one summons the courage to leave and is successful, the narcissist will continue to insert themselves into the victim's life, hoovering to refuel their supply. They'll piece-meal the return of personal possessions if he still has access to them, and he may continue to do so for years to come, long after they're forgotten. As long as they're demanding attention and the victim is supplying it by allowing contact, this pattern will continue.

Chapter 10

----- ❧☙ -----

Freedom at last

In order to understand why you keep attracting toxic people in your life, you have to understand why you keep allowing that kind of treatment. Typically, this starts in childhood. Maybe you had a narcissistic mother who, no matter what you did, was simply never satisfied. Therefore, you developed a people-pleasing persona in order to fulfill what was lacking. There are two traits that are necessary in a person that manipulators look for—someone with a conscience as well as someone who has excessive deference.

People who have a conscience are less likely to hurt others, meaning that a narcissist will feel comfortable manipulating them since they will technically allow it to happen. If someone believes in love, they are less likely to remove themselves from a toxic situation since they may have been taught not to do that or that they can get through anything. In the same sense, someone who is a people pleaser will agree to a lot of what the narcissist wants or needs since they want to make them happy.

On one hand, there is a narcissist that looks for people who are vulnerable to be taken advantage of, and on the other hand, there are people who are wounded and try to please everyone to make themselves happy. Both make a very toxic situation.

So, how can this be avoided? In a sense, it is difficult to predict as it depends mostly on how educated people are about narcissists and empaths. If we see that someone's spouse is toxic and abusive, we may open up to them and tell them. The typical response may be a bunch of excuses to dismiss the behavior, or maybe the victim has already researched the behaviors but is still hopeful that their partner may change. Hope is the word that keeps many in situations where they do not belong.

In order to correct or stop yourself from being manipulated, you first have to understand how people might manipulate you. There are seven ways people manipulate, and they include:

- They place blame,
- They make you feel insecure,
- They use self-pity,
- They flatter you,
- They subtly intimidate you,
- They create a false discord, and

- They play dumb.

They place blame. This type is generally a silent form of manipulation. If someone is blamed over and over again, they will then take on that burden and apologize for everything. If your behavior is being judged, that is also another form of manipulation since they are trying to make you feel bad about who you are. If someone is telling you whether what you are doing is good or bad, that is a telltale sign of abuse.

They make you feel insecure. If you are insecure, then you can be easily manipulated since they will belittle you any chance they get. In this instance, they will also criticize you, which could leave you second-guessing your every move. They may also try to confuse you by turning little mistakes into really big mistakes.

They use self-pity. There are people on this planet that will pity themselves and will have sob stories about how terrible their life is. This is to get you hooked into helping them, and if they know you are a kind and caring person, they will try to manipulate that by using their pity parties.

They will flatter you. Flattery cannot always be believed since it could be used to get you to lower your guard to make you susceptible to manipulation. When someone does flatter you, they will earn your goodwill; however, this is not always with good intentions in mind. If you know yourself well, you will be more likely to combat this type of manipulation as you will be able to tell when someone is being fake.

They will subtly intimidate you. This is done in a subtle way, such as telling you that a certain behavior is dangerous. They will tell you that you should act a certain way in different situations. This is to imply that if you do not act a certain way, you will end up with a less-than-desirable outcome. This manipulation tactic is used to instill fear in you.

They create a false discord. If someone is always up in arms over little things, you are most likely being manipulated. This will keep you on edge, and you will wonder what you are doing wrong at any given moment. Manipulators do this to try to condition people to treat them a certain way or they will act out. This manipulation tactic is typically used to avoid any accountability, consequence, or punishment.

They will play dumb. People will play dumb to get out of doing work because someone else does it better. For instance, if a husband does not want to load the dishwasher, he will tell his wife that she is better at it. If someone pretends not to understand you, they are also trying to manipulate you by not taking accountability for an issue they are involved with.

All of these manipulation tactics will lead to toxic and dishonest relationships. If you recognize that someone is trying to manipulate you, it may be best to call them out on it so they may recognize the behavior. Chances are, if they truly are toxic, they will not own up to it anyway, which leaves you to run the other way.

Codependent or empath?

Codependent and empath are often used interchangeably; however, they are both different in the ways that they seek out validation, love, and understanding. Empaths can have codependent traits, but not all codependents can be empaths. Codependents are always looking to fix and help people, while empaths are spiritually in tune with how other people are feeling and absorb other people's energy. Both want to be loved, validated, and understood; however, they both react differently to narcissists.

Empath

An empath will typically bolt at any sign of a narcissist. The only way they will feel stuck in a place with a narcissist is if they were too young to understand the red flags or they were not educated on narcissists or empath relationships. When an empath is educated on the subject, or has been hurt by a narcissist and has done their own research, they are more likely to get out of toxic situations. Empaths have some of the following traits:

- They absorb others' emotions,

- They are highly sensitive and intuitive,

- They are able to see a point of view from all angles, and

- They deeply understand people, places, and things.

Narcissists do not have empathy, so they tend to latch onto empaths in order to feed off of them to fulfill that need. Empaths do have a lot to give; however, they get exhausted and drained very quickly. The good aspect of an empath is that they will recognize what is using their energy and decide to distance themselves from that source. So, if an empath has a narcissistic husband, there will be times when the empath has to pull away and isolate for a while in order to recharge. Empaths are very aware of themselves and their surroundings, and that will give them the upper hand as they will call out the narcissist's behavior.

Codependent

Codependents will waste their entire lives with a narcissist thinking that they can fix them or help them change. There may come a time when a codependent is fed up and wants out, but they are usually held in the relationship because of guilt from giving up on someone. Codependents have the following traits:

- They have low self-esteem,
- They look outside of themselves for validation,
- They are fixers and helpers,
- They attach to an alpha personality for identity,
- Their mood is dependent on the mood of the alpha, and
- They are looking for praise and have a desire to be liked.

A narcissist is not as afraid of a codependent as they are an empath, so codependents are the most sought after for a narcissist. Codependents have a poor sense of boundaries, so they may be easily taken advantage of, and once they try to enforce boundaries, they will notice severe resistance. It is difficult for a codependent to break free from a narcissist because they cannot see themselves separate from them.

The following chart will show the differences side by side, which may be easier to pinpoint exactly which one you might be:

Empath	Codependent
I can sit with your suffering	I want to and can fix you
I am comfortable with a variety of emotions	I have an emotional addiction and feed off people's emotions
I see why you believe, think, and feel the ways that you do	I want to believe, think, and feel the things that you do
I hold a space for your emotions	I want to take on your emotions like they are my own
My relationships are typically fulfilling	I tend to be taken advantage of and constantly feel drained from it

Let's picture the two in relationships. There is a narcissistic husband plus an empath wife and a narcissistic husband and a codependent wife. The empath wife, when she recognizes the signs of abuse, will be aware of her surroundings and will call out the behaviors since she will not put up with feeling drained from it. The codependent wife will recognize the signs but will think the problem is her, which will enable the husband to act as he does. Thus, the codependent will stay in the relationship and will continue to make excuses for why they are staying in a bad situation. An empath can have codependent traits, but unless the empath is drained beyond belief, they will have the strength and knowledge to step away from what is toxic to them.

How a trauma bond is formed

A trauma bond is formed over time, and it tends to keep victims in the relationships because they are hoping it will get back to the "good" phase. The main goal of an abuser is to continue to receive some sort of benefit from you. When you are completely drained and exhausted, they may become angry that you cannot fulfill the supply that they need at the time. You will then try to work harder to please your abuser and keep the relationship afloat. When someone says "it isn't always bad, there are good times too," they are typically living in this type of cycle in their relationship. There are signs that you have a trauma bond with your abuser, and here are the top five:

- You constantly feel tired.
- You feel like you can do nothing right for the narcissist.

- If you do try to leave, the angst of losing them pulls you back.

- You know they will cause you more pain, you are waiting for it, yet you allow it to occur.

- You put them as a priority. If they text you, you will drop everything to reply.

Trauma bonds are typically found in relationships that have an inconsistent reinforcement and they may even be referred to as the Stockholm Syndrome. Stockholm Syndrome is typically seen in prisoners of war or hostage situations. Over time, an abusive relationship will take the shape of Stockholm Syndrome, and the victims will actually protect, love, and depend on their abuser to survive. When the victim has completely disassociated (numbed) themselves from the pain of the situation, they start to feel helpless then fantasize about their abuser.

The type of environment needed to foster a trauma bond has "intensity, complexity, inconsistency, and a promise, [and] victims stay because they are holding on to that elusive 'promise' or hope" (Stines, 2015). When a relationship begins in a way that creates a good feeling or environment, the victim is always waiting for it to get back to that point. This is what will keep someone stagnant in a situation much longer than they should be because they keep hoping it will go back.

There are ways to recover from a toxic trauma bond. The primary six ways to recover include the following:

- Focus on making decisions that support your self-care,
- Learn how to grieve,
- Get used to understanding your emotions,
- Build healthy connections in your life,
- Make a list of behaviors that you will not accept, and
- Live one day at a time.

Focus on making decisions that support your self-care. In other words, do not make any decisions that are going to hurt you. You may be feeling weak from the trauma, and the last thing you should do is talk negatively to yourself or relive what you have just experienced. Be nice to yourself and allow your body and mind the time to process all that has happened.

Learn how to grieve. Losing a marriage or relationship that was different than you thought it initially was will be like losing a loved one. You need to allow yourself time to grieve the loss.

Get used to understanding your emotions. When someone is in a toxic trauma bond, they tend to think in the way they are manipulated into thinking. Thus, it will take time to detox from that mindset and think on your own. Allow yourself time to feel all of the emotions so you are able to process them and own them.

Build healthy connections in your life. The only way to create healthy connections is to eliminate unhealthy connections. Find who you have a strong bond with, without any drama, and invest in those relationships.

Make a list of behaviors that you will not accept. You have accepted immoral behavior for too long. Make a list of behaviors that you vow never to accept again and follow through with it. For example, I will manage my own finances or I will not argue with someone who calls me names.

Live one day at a time. There will be good days and bad days, so make sure to live each day like it is a fresh start. Do not focus on the bad days; focus on moving forward and getting your life back.

In order to detox from a trauma bond, it is important to be away from that person with no contact. It is not until then that the victim will see the devastation that they have endured for so long; once that is seen, the healing process will begin.

Coping-mechanisms for narcissistic abuse

Coping mechanisms can be used either when in an abusive relationship or when coping with the aftermath of the abuse. We will explore coping mechanisms for those that are still in the cycle of abuse to try to help them step out of it. Many of these can also apply to after the relationship has ended as well.

- Make yourself a priority and focus on improving your physical and mental health,
- Create and enforce boundaries,
- Understand that you cannot fix an abusive person,
- Do not blame yourself,
- Do not engage with an abusive person, and
- Work on creating an exit plan.

Make yourself a priority and focus on improving your physical and mental health. Instead of worrying about pleasing your abuser, focus on yourself. It may seem odd at first, or you may feel guilty, but you need to take care of yourself in order to function and stay healthy. Sleep is also very important as your body is most likely stressed all of the time and you need to be able to recover.

Create and enforce boundaries. Even if you did not have boundaries before, you need to create a list of boundaries for the abuser. Then, you need to enforce them. For instance, the abuser goes through your phone without permission. Add a passcode on your phone and let them know that it is not respectful to do that and if they need to see your phone, you can unlock it for them. That is just one example; another would be that they are not to insult you or call you names or else the conversation will end. Then, if they do not follow, walk away.

Understand that you cannot fix an abusive person. Abusive people are choosing to be abusive. The only way that they will change is if they choose to change. You will not be able to force them into changing or help them change. Do not change yourself to appease them into changing as it will never work.

Do not blame yourself. You may hear that everything is your fault, and you might even begin to think that it is, but remember, that is the manipulation. It is not your fault that someone else chooses to do something.

Do not engage with an abusive person. This is difficult...like, really, really difficult. When someone is hovering over you saying that you do things that you would never do, it is near impossible to not reply. However, whether in person or via text message, train your mind to focus on something else at the time. Maybe sing a little song in your head, count to ten, turn the phone off if they will not stop texting, text yourself the responses instead, write down how you would respond, or get up and walk away.

Work on creating an exit plan. We all picture what life would be like outside of the reigns of an abuser. Why not create that on paper and try to set up a way to make that happen? Yes, it is very scary, and you may not follow through with it, but sometimes all it takes is writing out what you wish to do. During this time, it would be best to meet with a domestic violence advocate or a counselor to assist with coming up with a proper plan.

You may also notice that you are developing unhealthy coping mechanisms in order to deal with your situation. Some might start drinking alcohol, eating fatty foods, stop exercising, start laying in bed a lot, begin drinking soda or pop, and/or not eating at all. There are plenty of other bad coping mechanisms, but either way, it is a way to take your mind off of the chaos around you to give you a sense of control as well as a bit of happiness as you indulge.

Recognizing signs of abuse is one thing, but what do you do if you are experiencing it? Well, if you find yourself in this situation and do not think you have a way out—which is very common—to ease your mind you can create a safety plan. A safety plan could include:

- Keeping a suitcase at a neighbor's house,
- Getting a folding ladder to keep in a room upstairs so you can escape,
- Parking in the driveway and not in the garage,
- Barricading yourself in a room with a heavy object, and
- Giving a trusted friend or family member a key or garage door opener to your home.

There are other ways to escape; however, if you are living in an abusive situation, but these are the first steps to take in order to safely get out of the home. When all other options fail, protect yourself and your children, if you have any.

Chapter 11

How to heal from narcissistic abuse

When you are attempting to heal from the narcissist after escaping, somewhere during the determination stage, you will need to find ways to take care of yourself. You need to heal all of the wounds that the narcissist's abuse left behind in order to become the person you are meant to be. Healing can be incredibly difficult if left to your own devices, and you may even feel tempted to move on without ever addressing the harm you endured. However, it is essential. You will never truly heal if you leave the wounds to fester and worsen. Your sense of self, your happiness, and you, yourself, will slowly wither away if you do not treat the wounds. Just as you know, you must treat a physical wound; you must care for your mental and emotional wounds as well. Take the time to really absorb the methods of healing from abuse, and really put effort into bettering yourself. You will feel so much relief after you have taken the time to heal.

Remember, running away or putting your head in the sand and pretending that you are fine is what the narcissist taught you to do. No matter how tempting it may be to try to grit your teeth and move on, you need to address your injuries. In moments of weakness, remind yourself that you only want to do what is familiar, but doing so will not help or benefit you. It is simply falling back to old ways that can lead to a further setback, and potentially send you spiraling back to the narcissist. Only by healing all of the wounds can you truly remove all of the chains the narcissist has installed and really free yourself.

Self-Care

One of the easiest ways, in theory, to help heal yourself is to engage in self-care. Self-care can be difficult for even those with healthy minds, who are happy with themselves and do not have some serious healing to do. It is easy to get caught up in the bustle of life and give up the self-care time in favor of doing something else, but it is important to engage in.

Self-care, at its core, is taking care of yourself. You are making your physical and mental wellbeing a priority for yourself, and you are not ashamed of doing so. Particularly for the victims of narcissistic abuse, who have internalized that their needs are met last, this can be difficult, but it is an important skill to learn. The easiest way to engage in self-care is to create a routine in which you have several things that you do regularly in order to create good habits. If you are unsure where to start with self-care, here are several ideas of ways to start your self-care routine.

- Good sleep hygiene: Make sure you are going to sleep at the same time every night and pay attention to things that could make sleeping difficult, such as having a television in your room that keeps you awake or using your phone in the dark in bed. Keep the bedroom just for sleep!
- Eat healthy food: Make it a point to nourish your body to keep it physically healthy. Your gut and your mind are believed to be linked, and if you can keep your gut healthy, you will likely find your mental health improvements as well.
- Exercise daily: Exercise is not just good for the body—the mind needs it as well. Make it a point to take at least thirty minutes a day to exercise, whether it is a fitness class, time at the gym, or even just a stroll through the park. Just make sure that stroll gets your heart rate up!
- Prioritize self-care: The easiest way to engage in self-care is to prioritize self-care. Make sure that you guard the times you set aside for caring for yourself and treat them as precious. You deserve that time for your own well-being.
- Take a trip: Sometimes, taking a weekend vacation away from the bustle of work, friends, and the city can be incredibly refreshing. This works even better

if you disconnect for a while and just let yourself enjoy your own presence. Keep your phone off, and enjoy your own company for a bit!

- Take breaks often: Mental health breaks are necessary to function effectively. Without them, you risk burning out and otherwise struggling to meet your responsibilities without being utterly miserable. Your breaks could even be simple five-minute breaks outside every couple of hours when working. Your sanity will definitely thank you for it.
- Caring for a pet: Pets bring an awful lot to our lives, even with the responsibilities that come with them. By having a pet, you encourage a relationship with something that is unconditional, lacking judgment, and can even lower your blood pressure. Dogs, in particular, are so good for self-care and healing that even PTSD sufferers have adapted them as service animals to help with mental health!
- Staying organized: If you are organized, you are less likely to stress out about forgetting something or how to fit everything in. Even something as simple as implementing a calendar or planner can benefit your mental health immensely.
- Cook at home: Along with eating healthily, cooking your own food can be surprisingly therapeutic.

There is just something about taking raw ingredients, preparing them, and creating something nourishing and delicious from them that is so satisfying! Cook at home often to reap the benefits.

- Read: Read often. Not only is it good for your brain, but there is also a world of knowledge out there. You could even read a book about learning self-care! Even if the books you read are fiction, you can still benefit from reading. It keeps your mind stimulated and will help keep you healthier.
- Learn a new skill: Learning something new can help you raise your own self-esteem. At finally learning to do something new, you are likely to feel proud of yourself, which is great! Try learning something new, especially if it is something that has always interested you.

Compassion

As there is even an entire stage in the healing process called compassion, it comes as no surprise that it plays a part in healing from your abuse. Remember to have the compassion for yourself to acknowledge that you did not deserve the abuse you endured, and to recognize that making mistakes is okay.

Oftentimes, victims of narcissistic abuse struggle to be compassionate or patient with themselves—they feel as though they are underserving of that compassion, even if they would tell anyone else in their shoes that it is okay and that compassion is necessary. Even little things can set off a victim of abuse, such as spilling a glass of milk. If you have endured abuse, you may tell yourself that you are stupid for making such a simple mistake, and you may even belittle yourself, calling yourself a klutz and worthless.

The problem is, those are not your words—they are the narcissists. Spilling a glass of milk is not a big deal in the grand scheme of things. In terms of a mistake, it is harmless. Even if the glass shattered, no one died. There was no irreparable damage to anything other than a glass, that most likely does not have some immense value anyway.

Remember to regard yourself with the same compassion you have always had for others. You deserve it just as much as the people you treat with that compassion and directing some of that inward does not take away from anyone else either. The compassion and willingness to forgive yourself will go a long way.

That compassion should also come with patience. Recognize that it will take a significant amount of time for yourself to heal from the narcissist's abuse, but that does not invalidate you.

That does not make you less valuable, and it does not say anything about your worth. It simply means that you are a human and you are likely to have roadblocks from time to time. Just because you trip and fall and make a mistake does not mean you should berate yourself or make yourself feel worse.

Allow Yourself Time to Grieve Properly

Grief is a natural part of living, in which people cope with loss. Typically, grief is reserved for people who have lost a close family member or friend, but as you go through the stages of separating yourself from an abusive relationship, you go through a similar process. This is because, particularly when involved with a narcissist, you have lost someone. You have lost the person you thought the narcissist was. Remember how the narcissist used a persona to draw you in—you fell in love with the narcissist's mask. You initially loved someone who turned out to be a figment of your abuser's imagination. However, the process of watching the narcissist morph from a perfect lover into a monster is devastating. It is not unlike watching someone fade away from a terminal illness, slowly losing him—but when you lose the narcissist's persona, you are left with a monster wearing your loved one's face as a constant reminder of what you lost.

When you met the narcissist for the first time, you saw someone charming, charismatic, friendly, and likely every single thing you have ever wanted. You essentially saw your soulmate standing in front of you, and over time, your soulmate faded away. First, the person you trusted with everything started to hurt you, a little at first, until the abuse was nearly constant. You were left, dismayed how someone you loved so deeply, who you thought loved you just as passionately, could suddenly shift into a monster, but he did. This is just as profound of a loss, even if you are losing the idea of a person. You still lost someone that you loved, and you should not minimize that. Grief comes in five stages: denial, anger, bargaining, depression, and acceptance.

Denial

When you get to denial, you want to deny that anything has happened. This was when you were ensnared by the narcissist, entirely convinced that the abuse was not as bad as it actually was. You denied that the person you loved was gone. After all, how could he be gone when you can see his face right there? You hold onto hope that the person you thought the narcissist was is still in there somewhere, and you make excuses. You may say that the narcissist was not so bad, or try to convince yourself that you are willing to stay behind because at least you get to see your loved one's face looking back at you through the abuse. You attempt to convince yourself that things will be okay. This is where you were before you reached the acknowledgment stage of healing. You refused to recognize the abuse for what it was.

Anger

Eventually, your denial gives in to anger. Your eyes are opened, and you finally want to break free. At this stage, you want to escape at all costs, telling yourself that you do not deserve this abuse. You feel angry at the narcissist for convincing you to stay with him, and for convincing you that the abuse is acceptable or normal. You feel angry that the person you loved is gone, or never existed in the first place. You feel betrayed and manipulated—because you were. The narcissist played a dirty trick on you, and you fell for it. More than anything, though, you feel angry at yourself for falling for it all. You tell yourself that you should have known better and you also push the blame onto yourself, even if you do not deserve it. You desperately want for the person you love to come back somehow, and you want the narcissist to pay for what he did to you. This is likely the stage in which you flee from the narcissist's abuse, no longer willing to put up with it anymore.

Bargaining

When you reach the bargaining stage, you are willing to give anything to return to the way things were before. You tell yourself that you will do whatever it takes to have the narcissist's persona back, whether it is putting up with the narcissist's abuse or anything else. At this stage, you are grappling with the permanence of the situation and are desperate for a sign that reality is not what it may seem. If you are religious, you may pray to your god to fix things, or that you will be more devout if your god can somehow give you a miracle and bring your loved one back to you without the narcissist. You promise to do anything that comes to mind, but of course, it does not work because your loved one was never a real, living person.

Depression

Soon after, you come to the realization of the permanence of the current situation. You see that you will never get your love back, and you fall into a depression. You are beside yourself that the person is gone and you are so miserable and unhappy with it that you stop feeling anything at all. You essentially turn off your feelings, instead of staying in self-pity. You recognize the futility of it all and wonder why you should even bother continuing with anything. Life feels hopeless, and you wonder if even the narcissist would be a better alternative than this hell alone. You miss the narcissist's persona so much it hurts, and the idea of never seeing that person you loved again is so overwhelming that you struggle to cope.

Acceptance

Eventually, you finally reach the stage of acceptance. Here, you finally see the light again. You recognize that the narcissist tricked you, but you also recognize that things will be okay. You still love the persona that you originally fell for, but you recognize that he was nothing but an attempt to manipulate you into falling for the narcissist. You see it for the weapon it was, and you accept letting it go. At this point, you seek to move forward, and you allow yourself to find enjoyment in other things and realize that what happened was not the end of the world and that you are open to the idea of finding real love again in the future.

Develop Support Networks

Recognizing that you cannot get through this process alone is probably one of the most indicative of whether you will be able to escape the narcissist's abuse. You need the support of other people to be there for you in moments of weakness, and when you feel like you can no longer go on without the narcissist. Having people, you can talk to and trust to help guide you makes you far more likely to make it through without going back to the narcissist for further abuse. Your support network can take many forms, but most of the time, it is built upon a foundation of four groups of people: Friends, family, support groups, and a therapist, if you have one.

Friends

Friends will be there for you through thick and thin, and even if the narcissist has managed to isolate you from many of them, if you were to send a message to some of your closest friends from before the abuse, you would likely be surprised about how many of them are relieved and thrilled to hear from you. They may share that they have been waiting for you to contact them for ages and that they were always so concerned for you. Your friends will likely make up the bulk of your support group. These are people who will meet up with you on a bad day to watch movies and binge eat cartons of ice cream, or will let you rant about just how betrayed you feel by the narcissist. They will gladly be there for you and simply enjoy being in your presence in general. If you do not have friends, you should try to make some. There are many different ways you can do so, such as going to classes to learn new skills or groups you can join with people who share your interests. Especially with the internet at your disposal, you can likely google any hobby of yours and the city you live in, and be surprised to find groups of like-minded individuals that would probably be thrilled to have you if you contacted them and asked to join.

Family

Your family will likely be there for you if you ask for more serious help, such as needing money, a place to stay, or general support while trying to escape. Especially if you are escaping with children, your own family is a fantastic place to start. Your family only wants what is best for you, and as your friends, you may be surprised to hear that many of your family members had suspected abuse for a long time. They will also likely be relieved at you leaving, and you can frequently find plenty of support from these people.

Support groups

Support groups are particularly useful when you need someone that understands what you are going through more so than just having a general idea of how you felt. You can typically find support groups for narcissistic abuse survivors by searching online, both in your own area and online. There are several different forums and boards of people who get together to discuss their abuse, and you will likely be able to find other people that have gone through almost exactly what you have. The people that will understand the intensity of the abuse, the way the narcissist so thoroughly manages to break people down, and how hard it is to leave are the ones who have gone through it before and know it out of the experience.

When you find a support group that clicks for you, you will be able to see people at all stages of healing. You will see people who have more or less fully recovered and are there, supporting other people through their journeys toward healing, and others who may have just left, or have been considering leaving that are trying to learn what to do. This can be particularly useful, as you can look at other people who are further along than you are for inspiration. You can ask for advice, talk to people who have been where you are, and even just enjoy a conversation with someone who knows what you have gone through. Ultimately, this can be an incredibly insightful experience, and you will almost always get something good out of browsing through these forums or meeting up with other survivors. What will be clear when you do this, however, is that you are not alone by any means. Many, many people have fallen victim to the narcissist, and unfortunately, many more will as well. At the very least, there are several safe spaces on the internet and in person where the survivors of narcissistic abuse can come together to support each other toward healing and bettering themselves.

Therapist

A therapist can be particularly useful in helping heal as well. While you will have a professional relationship with a therapist as opposed to a friendship, you will be able to talk to the therapist to help you deal with difficult feelings or to deal with things that you are struggling to handle. The therapist, though optional, is always a fantastic choice when recovering from abuse if you can make it happen.

Creating Healthy Outlets

When you have suffered through narcissistic abuse, you have probably developed some pretty toxic thoughts and feelings yourself. Many of these come from what is likely a tendency toward being empathetic, as that is one of the things the narcissist desires most, and you absorbed the narcissist's toxic feelings. Empaths are particularly prone to internalizing the feelings and tendencies of those around them, and the tendencies of the narcissist can be particularly toxic to the empath.

One of the best things to do when you have internalized all of that negativity is finding a creative, healthy outlet for it. You should seek out some sort of way to eliminate the toxicity from you, whether through art, music, learning, taking classes, or anything else that appeals to you. Exercising is a common tactic used, in which you literally sweat out the negativity. The important part here is that you manage to eliminate it in some way and that you feel better after you have finished whatever you have chosen to do. Over time, you will release all of the pent-up negativity, and you will begin to feel much better about yourself.

Therapy

Therapy can guide you toward healing as well. As briefly touched upon, a therapist is one of the greatest favors you can do for yourself. There are very few people in this world who would not benefit from therapy, and the likelihood of one of them being you is incredibly slim. The sooner you start it, the sooner you will start seeing results. There are several different kinds of therapy that could be useful for a victim of narcissistic abuse, and through therapy, you would be able to learn valuable skills, such as how to cope with the trauma left behind, understanding what made you vulnerable to the narcissist in the first place, and how to solve all of the problems that come with all of the emotions you feel whirling around within you.

If therapy is something that sounds like it would benefit you, try speaking to your primary care doctor for a referral, or seek out recommendations local to your area online. Even if the cost is an issue, there are plenty that will help you on a sliding scale, as well as online options that may be more affordable for you.

Conclusion

This book is not meant to prevent any harm from befalling you. Abuse is scary and the people behind it are unpredictable. It can be terrifying to try to deal with abusers head-on, and you are incredibly brave for doing so. If nothing else, appreciate yourself and your bravery already for being able to keep calm in the midst of a potentially dangerous relationship.

You are someone who can deal with anything if you can deal with an abuser or a toxic relationship. If you can look an abuser in the eye and know that someday, you'll be far away from them, that's more empowering than anything. The day I left my abuser was perhaps the scariest day I ever experienced throughout the entirety of the relationship. My blood ran cold, and I had no idea if they would find me and what they would do if they did. It's so empowering to be able to deal with the trials of abuse while still thinking about what you'll do after you make it out. Your abuser is cold and manipulative, and they will do anything they can to make it so that you never leave. This is their ultimate goal—keep their prey around for as long as possible until they've used up every ounce of spirit in their victim.

Despite this, you have many tools at your disposal to make use of your strengths when you do figure it out. After you address your weaknesses along with your strengths, you can figure out what to do from there based on what your particular situation calls for. That's also where this book comes in handy—there are countless different types of abuse and many different ways that abuse can manifest. Therefore, there are also countless different ways that you can react to that abuse properly and defend yourself against it.

This book is not only to determine how you're being abused and how you can keep yourself from falling for those tricks, but it's also to get you to consider where to go from there. Many books on abuse don't properly take into account the unpredictability of life immediately after a volatile relationship. Being able to look for different ways out, make notes of your abuser's behavior, and have different escape plans available can save you a trouble when you finally make your escape.

If you feel that this book has helped to empower you to grow past your abuse and take matters safely into your own hands, I'd be delighted if you would leave a review to let other people know your story and that they are not alone.

www.ingramcontent.com/pod-product-compliance
Lightning Source LLC
Chambersburg PA
CBHW071947070526
44583CB00015B/1095